Davidson
2000

CORNISH LITERATURE

CORNISH LITERATURE

Brian Murdoch

D. S. BREWER

First published 1993 by D. S. Brewer, Cambridge

D. S. Brewer is an imprint of Boydell & Brewer Ltd
PO Box 9, Woodbridge, Suffolk IP12 3DF, UK
and of Boydell & Brewer Inc.
PO Box 41026, Rochester, NY 14604, USA

ISBN 0 85991 364 3

British Library Cataloguing-in-Publication Data
A catalogue record for this book is available
from the British Library

Library of Congress Cataloging-in-Publication Data applied for

The paper used in this publication meets the minimum requirements
of American National Standard for Information Sciences –
Permanence of Paper for Printed Library Materials, ANSI Z39.48–1984

Printed in Great Britain by
St Edmundsbury Press Ltd, Bury St Edmunds, Suffolk

CONTENTS

To Peter Hutchinson

PREFACE

The aim of this book is to place the literature of Cornish into a broad literary context for the general reader, in particular for those with an interest in the middle ages, for it is from the later middle ages that the bulk of the surviving (anonymous) writings come. Those writings do not, as it happens, require special pleading in terms of literary merit, but even in specialist studies the emphasis has normally been on the language rather than on the works as literature, and this study is a literary one. Medieval literature does not exist in a vacuum, and although there has always been local interest in Cornish, its literature is not exclusively local, either in theme or in style. It is part of the literature of the British Isles, and part of a European tradition.

Of course, a specialist with primary interests in another culture could not tackle a project of this sort without help from those whose principal linguistic interests are in Cornish, and I am delighted to acknowledge the help, freely and generously given over many years, of scholars whose expertise can be gauged by the most cursory glance at the bibliography. Many of the scholars mentioned there have been most helpful, but I have to name first of all Oliver Padel, Myrna Combellack-Harris, Kenneth George, Andrew Breeze, Evelyn S. Newlyn, Lauran Toorians, Len Truran and James Whetter, as well as Jane Bakere, Andrew Hawke, Jon and Máire West, David Dumville, Gwenaël le Duc, and my colleagues in German, Linda Archibald, Robert Weihs, and especially Malcolm Read for much technical advice. As ever, I am grateful for the continued support of my wife, Ursula. Errors, of course, are my own. Some of the material developed in this book was given originally in lecture form at conferences in Galway, Oxford and Aberystwyth, and I am grateful for the comments of scholars present on those occasions. In particular, Oliver Padel was most encouraging when this book was first mooted, and I wish to recall here, too, the late David Greene, who first suggested that I look at some of the Cornish texts in detail when we worked together on religious poetry in Irish approaching twenty years ago.

Brian Murdoch   Stirling, July 1992

CONVENTIONS OF REFERENCE

Quotations from the Cornish texts are from the editions listed below (the plays by line-number), with verse renderings of my own (unless otherwise stated) based, of course, on existing translations. My versions are necessarily sometimes fairly free, but are designed to convey an impression of the original metre and rhyme-scheme. The choice of a text was determined in each case by availability, completeness and closeness to the earliest manuscript. The tailed *z* appears in some manuscripts (and printed texts) both for the voiced and unvoiced *th/dh* (the latter equivalent to Welsh *dd*), and sometimes also the sound *z* itself. Other manuscripts use *th* interchangeably, and I have where appropriate rendered the tailed *z* as *th* where it is used in print. Details of texts not listed here are given in footnotes. Full details of texts are given in the bibliography proper. The names by which the major Cornish works are known are sometimes rather different from those which appear in the editions or in the manuscripts, and my abbreviations are those most commonly found in other work on Cornish, even though some of them may seem not to relate immediately to the text in question.

BM:
Beunans Meriasek ("Life of St Meriasek," *The Camborne Play*; in the manuscript *Ordinale de vita sancti Meriadoci*; in Unified Cornish *Bewnans Meryasek*): Whitley Stokes, *The Life of St Meriasek* (London, 1872).

CW:
Gwreans an bys (in the manuscript, *The Creacion of the World;* in Unified Cornish *Gwryans an bys*): Paula Neuss, *The Creacion of the World* (New York and London, 1983)

CWBF:
Oliver J. Padel, *The Cornish Writings of the Boson Family* (Redruth, 1973)

MC:
Pascon agan Arluth, ("The Passion of Our Lord," untitled in the manuscript, formerly known as *Mount Calvary*; in Unified Cornish *Passyon agan Arluth*): Whitley Stokes, "The Passion, a Middle Cornish Poem," *Transactions of the Philological Society* (1860/1), 1-100.

OM, PC, RD:
Ordinalia (Origo Mundi, Passio Christi, Resurrectio Domini): Edwin Norris, *The Ancient Cornish Drama* (Oxford, 1859, repr. New York, 1968).

The following abbreviations are also used:

BBCS	*Bulletin of the Board of Celtic Studies*
CLB	Cornish Language Board/ Kesva an Tavas Kernewek
CMCS	*Cambridge Medieval Celtic Studies*
CS	*Cornish Studies*
EC	*Etudes Celtiques*
EETS	Early English Texts Society (Original, Extra and Special Series)
FOCS	Federation of Old Cornwall Societies
ICS	Institute of Cornish Studies
JRIC	*Journal of the Royal Institution of Cornwall* (Old and New Series)
OC	*Old Cornwall*
PL	J. P. Migne, *Patrologia...Latina* (Paris, 1844-64)
RC	*Revue Celtique*

Books of the Bible are cited according to the Vulgate (since the majority of the works studied are from the pre-Reformation period) using the conventional abbreviations.

CHAPTER ONE

WRITING IN CORNISH: FRAGMENTS AND LOSSES

When he revised William Camden's *Britannia* in 1695, Edmund Gibson commented in his additions to the section relating to Cornwall that

> three books in Cornish are all that can be found. One is written
> in an old court-hand on Velam, and in 1036 verses contains the
> History of the Passion of our Saviour...The other two are
> translated out of the Bodleian Library; one is translated, and
> the other is now a translating by Mr Keigwin, the only person
> perhaps that perfectly understands the tongue.[1]

The two works at that time in the hands of John Keigwin of Mousehole were also religious. One was a trilogy of medieval plays on the Creation, Passion and Resurrection, together making up a mystery cycle known collectively as the *Ordinalia*, and probably composed, as was the Passion-poem mentioned by Gibson, in the fourteenth century. The other was another dramatisation of the Creation, this time the first and only surviving play of a two-day cycle, composed probably towards the middle of the sixteenth century, even though the version from which Keigwin worked is a later and linguistically adapted copy.

Gibson was writing at a time when scholarly interest was beginning to develop into what must be called a rescue operation on the Cornish language and its literature, and the establishing of a canon of literary survivals had come at a time when Cornish was dying as a community language. Not too long before Gibson was writing, another seventeenth-century antiquary, the Vice-Warden of the Stannaries, William Scawen, who died in 1686, had thought that the Passion-poem, of which he had a copy, was the sole surviving "precious relict" of the literature. He seems not to have known of the plays. Unfortunately, as far as major works in Cornish are concerned, Gibson's reference to "three books" is not far wrong, even if one of them does contain an entire mystery-cycle. A further two-day drama-cycle was discovered in the 1860s dealing with the life of a saint with a cult in Cornwall, St Mereadoc, known in Cornish as Meriasek. Probably it was written towards the end of the fifteenth century. Finally, in the 1870s, an enigmatic fragment of what may be a play, and which is probably a little earlier than the other survivals, was

---

[1]   Edmund Gibson, *Camden's Britannia* (London, 1695, repr. Newton Abbot, 1971), col. 17. Scawen's comments are quoted in the preface to William Pryce's *Archaeologia Cornu-Britannica* (Sherborne, 1790, repr. Menston, 1972).

discovered on the back of a medieval charter. And that, essentially, is all that survives of early Cornish literature.

Even extending the term "literature" yields little more. Moving backwards into the earliest stage of written Cornish to include all the surviving monuments in the language adds only a number of glosses - individual words, that is, whose context depends upon another language - and one complete sentence. At the other end of the middle ages, all that the sixteenth century has to offer beside the Creation-play is a translation of some English sermons and a group of phrases, the point of which was pragmatic rather than literary. Finally, a number of smaller pieces - short verses, a song, a folktale - were written down in the seventeenth and eighteenth centuries in the attempt to save every scrap of what was by then failing fast as a community language. These survivals are in a number of manuscripts, and most of them have been reprinted. We are frequently in the realm of linguistic monuments rather than of literature, and the use of a single line of Cornish in a somewhat garbled form in a seventeenth century play in English called (of all things) *The Northern Lasse* has a symbolic finality about it. To be sure, the language (and also its literature) has in the present century undergone a revival, but the literature is not extensive and it often looks back, as does the restored language itself, to medieval traditions and styles.

Cornish is a Celtic language, its closest relatives being Welsh and Breton, with which languages it shares a common Brittonic source. From about the sixth century, the West Brittonic ancestor of Welsh separated itself from South-West Brittonic, the ancestor of Cornish and Breton. Welsh has preserved some sounds and combination of sounds that Cornish and Breton changed, and it adapted others that South-West Brittonic did not. From this period, too, groups of speakers of South-West Brittonic migrated to Brittany, but a clear distinction between Cornish and Breton seems not to have developed for some centuries. With several of the earliest documents of Cornish there is doubt as to whether the language is indeed Cornish or whether it is Breton. From the second half of the eleventh century to the middle of the twelfth, however, Cornish shows certain sound-changes that *do* distinguish it from Breton, one example of which is the shift from -*d* to -*z* at the end of words. Some Cornish placenames, notably those in eastern areas, where Cornish as a spoken language died out early, preserve (precisely because the spoken language *did* die out) the unshifted form of the word *bod*, "a dwelling", a word which has that form still in Breton (and incidentally also in Welsh). The best-known example is in the name *Bod*min. The word for a dwelling changed to *bos* in Cornish (using the spelling *s* for the voiced *z*), and placenames in areas where Cornish continued as a living language, primarily in the west, show this change, as in names like *Bos*castle, *Bos*coppa and others. In fact, the sound shifted again later on, moving to -*dz*, written as *j*, and in some placenames, this time in the far west, where the language survived longest as a spoken tongue, names occur like *Boj*ewyan, which appears in earlier documents as *Bos*yweyn.

By around 1200 Cornish was established as a distinct language, although still close to Breton, and it is at this linguistic stage, which is known as Middle Cornish, that the literature develops. It is in Middle Cornish that the Passion-poem and the *Ordinalia* plays were written. By the late sixteenth century, however, the language underwent some further changes, giving rise to the last stage of Cornish as a spoken community language, known as Late Cornish. To give a brief (consonantal) illustration once again, the sounds *n(n)* and *m(m)* developed to *dn* and *bm*, so that we find in the manuscript of the later Creation play (which was written down in 1611) forms like *pedn* "a head" instead of *pen*, and *cabm* "crooked" instead of *cam*. We may compare the placenames *Penzance* and *Toll Pedn,* too. The Cornish of the late and sometimes fragmentary survivals - short pieces written or collected by antiquaries - looks rather different in orthography from and is generally more phonetic than the larger survivals from the middle ages, so that a word like *pedn* might be written down as *peden* or *pedden* and so on. A separate problem is presented by the inclusion in Middle Cornish texts of an admixture of English. Sometimes whole phrases are used, even in the *Ordinalia*, and the number of English words increases in the later texts. In terms of literary evaluation, this has implications for source-study if whole phrases or indeed couplets are used, but the use of individual English words present a philological problem: it is not always easy to determine the status of borrowings, and occasionally an English word appears to have been adopted into Cornish by the revivalists; thus the word *snel*, clearly Germanic and common in Middle English for "swift," appears in modern dictionaries as a Cornish word, presumably on the strength of its appearance in the *Ordinalia*.

The customary view is that the Cornish language died out in the eighteenth century, but this is a confused concept. Socially, Cornish gave way gradually to the long-term pressure of the dominant English language, and from a relatively early period was pushed westwards, lasting longest in the far western areas of Cornwall. This was a process abetted by several factors, such as the absence of a tradition of printed material in Cornish, and also of an authorised liturgy. It is in any case more accurate to speak of Cornish having ceased to be used as a community language. The death of a language might, of course, imply the death of the last, or more reasonably the second-last monoglot speaker (since one person alone speaking a language is meaningless), or, rather differently, the death of the last person with the language as their principal mode of communication. Indeed, the death of Dorothy or Dolly Pentreath of Mousehole is still frequently taken to mark the death of the language itself, although Daines Barrington, the eighteenth century scholar who drew attention to Dolly Pentreath, later named other Cornish-speakers who outlived her. The principal alternative candidate is

William Bodener, a fisherman who died in 1789, later than Pentreath, although he tells us that he learned Cornish as a boy from older fishermen. Throughout the nineteenth century evidence was collected of people who knew some Cornish words or phrases. We do not really know the name of the "last" speaker of Cornish, whatever this is taken to mean, and the matter is, of course, academic. For all that, the demise of Dolly Pentreath (to whom a memorial was erected in 1860, claiming only that she was "said to have been the last person who conversed in the ancient Cornish language") retains a symbolic value. Cornish was probably restricted to the western part well before the start of the sixteenth century, and it had ceased to have a community function, even in the far west of Cornwall, by the end of the eighteenth. It was no longer, then, the normal language used every day inside and outside the home by people who had learned the language in the home from their parents, as a mother tongue, in fact. But in another sense it has never been a dead language in the way that, say, Etruscan is dead. At the time when it was falling out of everyday use, scholars and antiquaries were already beginning to take an interest, and preserved what scraps of it they could. The knowledge of the language never died out.[2]

In the early years of the twentieth century Cornish was revived, not primarily, as might have been possible, on the basis of Late Cornish and the subsequent development of Breton, but rather by applying a process of standardisation to *Middle* Cornish, because that stage of the language contained fewer English borrowings. A normalised spelling was developed between the wars by Robert Morton Nance, which was termed "Unified Cornish" and was used as the basis for teaching the language and for

---

[2]   The literature on the life and death of Cornish is large: see Charles Thomas, *Special Bibliography I. The Cornish Language* (Redruth, 1972). On the early history, see Kenneth Jackson, *Language and History in Early Britain* (Edinburgh, 1953, repr. 1971), pp. 3-30. Standard works such as Henry Jenner, *A Handbook of the Cornish Language* (London, 1904) contains much material, as do earlier studies such as Fred. W. Jago, *The Ancient Language and the Dialect of Cornwall* (Truro, 1882) and more recent ones such as those by P. Berresford Ellis, *The Cornish Language and its Literature* (London, 1974) and *The Story of the Cornish Language* (2nd ed., Penryn, 1990), or Martyn F. Wakelin, *Language and History in Cornwall* (Leicester, 1975). On the last stages of spoken Cornish the range is from Daines Barrington on Dolly Pentreath, "On the Expiration of the Cornish Language," *Archaeologia* 3 (1777), 278-84 down to P. A. S. Pool, *The Death of Cornish* (Penzance, 1975). There is a grammar of Middle Cornish by Henry Lewis, *Llawlyfr Cernyweg Canol* (Cardiff, 2nd ed., 1946, repr. 1980). Much has been published on placenames, most notably by O. J. Padel, *Cornish Place-Name Elements* (Nottingham, 1986). Linguistic analysis (some of it computer-aided) is still in progress; see for example Kenneth J. George, "A Computer Model of Sound Changes in Cornish," *ALLC Journal* 4 (1983), 39-48. Compare finally not only the parallel case of Manx, which survived in a similar manner into the present century, but the title of a recent book by Reg Hindley, *The Death of the Irish Language* (London, 1991). Irish is an official and national language, but is still in considerable difficulties.

publications, including translations and new literature, itself based frequently on the forms and themes of the medieval survivals. Attention has been drawn more recently to the flaws in this (it has to be said) artificial reconstruction of the language. These include beside phonological problems, too heavy a reliance on Welsh, rather than the more closely related Breton, to fill the inevitable lexical gaps. Other orthographic systems for revived Cornish (one based on Late Cornish) have recently been developed, not without some controversy and with resistance from the champions of Unified Cornish.

With the exception of some early essays and brief surveys, some of which are no longer readily accessible, most studies of Cornish have linked language and literature in such a way as to emphasise the former, and to group the surviving literary texts according to linguistic considerations, which has the effect, for example, of separating off the Creation play written down (but not composed) in 1611 and known as *Gwreans an bys* from the other plays. A literary study needs to take a somewhat different approach, so that the later Creation-play can be seen as a late medieval drama related to the *Ordinalia*. All the Cornish medieval literature has, indeed, been preserved in manuscripts later than the original composition of the work. The Passion-poem (referred to now as *Pascon agan Arluth*, "The Passion of Our Lord" and earlier as *Mount Calvary*) and the surviving plays form a group which can be related to one another in content, style, and perhaps even provenance, with strong pointers to a single literary centre. They constitute, indeed, almost a paradigmatic development of medieval religious writing, beginning with a poetic adaptation of the Gospels and moving then to the dramatisation of the divine plan of Creation, Fall and Redemption. The play of the life of St Meriasek (given the Cornish title *Beunans Meriasek*, since the Latin title in the manuscript is somewhat cumbersome) is unusual in Britain, where few dramatised saints' lives have survived in any language, although they are known throughout the middle ages elsewhere. In Cornwall, religious drama seems to have lasted beyond the Reformation and it is not surprising that in an area where the effects of the English Reformation were in any case somewhat delayed, the mid sixteenth-century should have produced another biblical cycle of which only the later, but dramatically more sophisticated Creation-play survives.[3]

The earlier stages of this development can be matched in English medieval literature, but there are no examples in English of a non-biblical saint's life

---

[3]   To the books by Jenner and Ellis add not only Thurstan C. Peter, *The Old Cornish Drama* (London, 1906), but the admirable summary by Crysten Fudge, *The Life of Cornish* (Redruth, 1982) and a discussion of the earliest works (*Charter Fragment* and *Pascon agan Arluth*) in Dutch by Lauran Toorians, "Passie, lief en leed; de oudste poëzie van het Keltische Cornwall," *Kruispunt* 129 (March, 1990), 3-55. Ellis' larger book (referred to here by the short-title "Cornish Language") is not always reliable, and should be used with caution.

in dramatised form. Continental parallels sometimes present themselves more readily, and Cornish might even have been influenced by Breton or French mystery cycles or hagiography. There is a Breton Creation-play, for example, which, although it was written down even later than 1611, contains features that seem to antedate *Gwreans an bys*, and Breton also has various dramatised saints' lives. On a purely comparative basis, late medieval drama in Italy and Spain, and even that of the German-speaking world can be interesting in terms of literary context. By coincidence, a two-day drama on the Creation and Flood (the theme of *Gwreans an bys*) was written at pretty well the same time as the Cornish play, but in Protestant Zurich by an adherent of the Reformer Zwingli. The two works compare well with each other.

That particular work (by a Swiss called Jacob Ruf) is barely known and has never been translated. With the central works of Cornish literature, however, there is no justification for ignorance of them in the English-speaking world, at least. Three published translations of the Passion-poem, three of the *Ordinalia* (and several partial translations), five of *Gwreans an bys* and five of *Beunans Meriasek* (one published only in part) make it surprising that they have not been examined more fully. Only in recent years have they been submitted to detailed literary scrutiny, but there has been some readiness to accept glib comments on an expected rusticity in the works. The volume devoted to Cornwall in the popular *Penguin Guides* informed its many readers that Cornish "had no literature worth serious attention," and even a partisan writer like Daphne du Maurier could claim that Cornish "never, even in olden times, produced a living culture," while Henry Jenner, the father of modern Cornish, saw the literature as of small value in his pioneering work on the language. The attitude is a well-established one: in 1910 (but in a work that was in print until 1970) the editor of the *Cambridge History of English Literature* dismissed *Beunans Meriasek* as "devoid of literary merit," while the *Penguin Companion to Literature* in 1971 described the plot of that work as showing us the Cornish saint's life "curiously mixed up with that Saint Sylvester." And yet the works need no special pleading: seen in their proper context, that of European religious literature and of drama in particular, the poem and the plays demand attention on the grounds of literary merit. On the other hand, comments about them that *are* based upon special pleading are not always very reliable. Thus a popular paperback published in 1980 with the title *The Spirit of Cornwall* includes a chapter on the drama in Cornish, but informs us with more enthusiasm than accuracy that "one of the earliest and most famous examples of purely Cornish drama was *Bewnans Meryasek*, sometimes known as the *Ordinalia*, a series of religious plays written in 1504 and widely performed at that time." It is an interesting coincidence that the chapter concerned opens with some remarks made by Richard Carew in 1600 on the supposed decay of Cornish drama. Carew's comments have frequently been taken as reliable, but the wisdom of doing so can be questioned when we find such confidently stated errors in a book printed nearly four hundred years later.[4]

As with most medieval vernacular literatures, it is likely that some Cornish has been lost, either because the manuscripts have not survived, or because the material was part of an oral rather than a written tradition. Circumstantial evidence points to a range of possible losses, the most tantalising of which is, perhaps, that there may have been Cornish material relating to the story of Tristan and Iseult. The location of the story in the major continental versions is Cornwall, and the early French version by Beroul has specific Cornish placenames. It is possible (though there are numerous counter-possibilities) to construct a case for the celebrated love-triangle having originated in Cornwall and having moved either to Wales or to Brittany, and thence into the mainstream of European literature. This has to remain a matter of speculation since we have no hard evidence of a Cornish literary saga, merely a location which becomes increasingly mythical. Gottfried von Strassburg, in what is arguably the finest retelling of all, in German in the early thirteenth century, tells us that the grotto shared by the lovers has been known to him for years. But he adds "and I have never been in Cornwall."

There is slightly firmer evidence of other lost writing in Cornish in the sphere of Arthurian literature proper. Geoffrey of Monmouth's Latin *History of the Kings of Britain*, completed between 1135 and 1140, makes frequent reference to Cornwall, especially in the context of Arthur himself, and there has even been speculation that the "very ancient book written in the British language" to which he refers in a dedicatory letter, might have been Cornish. Such speculations do not, of course, take us very far, but another writer, known to us as John of Cornwall, wrote in the middle of the twelfth century a series of verses with commentary in Latin called *Prophetia Merlini*, the "Prophecy of Merlin." This may have been based on the seventh book of Geoffrey of Monmouth's *History*, which consists itself of a series of prophecies of Merlin, translated "from the British tongue," or it may derive from an original either in Cornish or in Breton, or even in their common linguistic ancestor prior to differentiation. The manuscript of the work, which is dedicated to Bishop Robert Warelwast of Exeter (who established monasteries in Cornwall), contains in its commentary section a handful of what appear to be Cornish words and phrases - sometimes prefaced with the

---

[4]   J. W. Lambert, *Cornwall* (Harmondsworth, repr. 1947), p. 30; Daphne du Maurier, *Vanishing Cornwall* (Harmondsworth, 1972), p. 200; A. W. Ward and A. Waller, *The Cambridge History of English Literature, V: The Drama to 1642, Pt I.* (Cambridge, 1910, repr. 1970), p. 16; J. R. P[iette], "Cornish Literature" in: *The Penguin Companion to Literature I* (Harmondsworth, 1971), p. 119f. The final quotation is from Denys Val Baker, *The Spirit of Cornwall* (London, 1980), p. 87f. (where we move rapidly via the Padstow hobby-horse to modern "specifically Cornish" plays in English).

explanation *in nostra lingua*, "in our language." The words are neither extensive nor especially informative, and since the sole surviving manuscript was copied by someone ignorant of Cornish in the thirteenth century, some of the phrases actually beggar interpretation. The value of the remnants is linguistic, but while the text affords a fragment of evidence for lost Cornish writings, it is a dangerous foundation for judgements on lost material.[5]

Two further areas merit brief mention in the context of lost literature: religious writings and the drama. It is possible that religious texts other than those which have survived might have existed in Cornish, but once again there is little precise evidence. The Cornish saint for whom the twin parishes of St Columb Major and Minor is named is obscure, but early references relating to the parishes seem to imply a female *sancta Columba*, of whom little is known. Confusion with the famous male saint Columba (Colum Cille) of Iona or with the missionary saint Columbanus is inevitable, and the Cornish saint has indeed also been taken to be male. On August 7, 1607, however, Nicholas Roscarrock, the Catholic scholar and collector of the lives of British saints, commented in a letter (now in the British Library) to William Camden on this question, shortly before the appearance of the sixth edition of Camden's *Britannia*. Camden had derived the name of the parishes from the Scottish saint, "whereas in truthe yt taketh name of Columba, a woman St who was a vyrgine and martyre whose lyfe I have in my handes translated owt of Cornyshe, besydes the daye of her feaste differeth from the feast of St Columbanus or Columba..." The derivation was duly corrected in later editions, but the Cornish saint's life is lost, and we do not know if it was in prose or verse, nor its date, nor whether it was an original or a translation from Latin. Equally frustrating is a reference in a journal in 1727 to the translation of the Bible into "Cornish, or Cornubian Welsh," which could refer to a lost text, or to something that was never completed, or to the few

---

[5]   O. J. Padel, "The Cornish Background of the Tristan Stories," *CMCS* 1 (Summer, 1981), 55-81, referring back to Joseph Loth, "Le Cornwall et le Roman de Tristan," *RC* 33 (1912), 258-310 and 414-6. Padel questions the development outlined by, for example, Helen Newstead, "The Origin and Growth of the Tristan Legend," in: Roger S, Lewis, *Arthurian Literature in the Middle Ages* (Oxford, 1959), pp. 122-33. See the summary by W. Anne Trindade, "The Celtic Connexions of the Tristan Story," *Reading Medieval Studies* 12 (1986), 93-107 and 13 (1987), 71-80. The most recent study is that by W. J. McCann, "Tristan: the Celtic Material Re-examined," in: *Gottfried von Strassburg and the Medieval Tristan Legend*, ed. Adrian Stevens and Roy Wisbey (Cambridge, 1990), pp. 19-28. On Geoffrey of Monmouth: O. J. Padel, "Geoffrey of Monmouth and Cornwall," *CMCS* 8 (Winter, 1984), 1-28, with Geoffrey's text transl. Lewis Thorpe, *The History of the Kings of Britain* (Harmondsworth, 1966), pp. 170-6. On John of Cornwall, see P. Flobert, "La *Prophetia Merlini* de Jean de Cornwall," and L. Fleuriot, "Fragments du texte Brittonique de la *Prophetia Merlini*," *EC* 14 (1974-5), 31-41 and 43-56. See also Michael J. Curley, "A New Edition of John of Cornwall's *Prophetia Merlini*," *Speculum* 57 (1982), 217-49.

biblical fragments that were made in the seventeenth and eighteenth centuries. On the other hand, the claim on the title-page and in the preface of a booklet printed in the late sixteenth century that it was translated from "the Troyane or Cornyshe tounge" may be dismissed, in spite of the inclusion of a phrase of garbled Cornish in the text, as part of a deliberate comic fiction involving various other spurious personal names. The absence of religious lyrics from early Cornish and, indeed, the absence of much religious translation is striking, though there are a few liturgical pieces in late transcriptions. For the later period it has been suspected (on fairly thin evidence) that the shadowy John Tregear, who translated some homilies, may have translated other material. There is even a record (in Spanish) of a speech on Psalm xx: 5 having been made in Cornish before the Spanish king Philip III at the English College in Valladolid in August 1600 by a Cornish priest named Richard Pendrea or Pentrey; we have no version of the Cornish text, although there are records in Spanish and English of the occasion.[6]

In the drama, the major loss is of course the second day's play to follow the surviving *Gwreans an bys*. The far earlier *Charter Fragment* may also provide an indication of lost drama, although just what has been lost is hard to determine. There are references at the end of the medieval period, too, to the performance in Cornwall (as elsewhere) of what appear to be secular folk-plays, on themes such as that of Robin Hood, but we are not sure what language these plays were in. The plurality of references even in the Tudor period to performances of mystery plays makes us suspect that dramatisations of other parts of the Bible or of other saints' lives might have existed, matching comparable texts in English, French or Breton. Cornwall boasts an enormous number of saints with local cults, whose *vitae* must have offered possibilities. The writings of those seventeenth and eighteenth century antiquaries who devoted themselves to preserving what they could find of

---

[6]   The letter from Roscarrock to Camden is now in the British Library, fol. 77 of MS Cotton Julius C.V, not C.IV. as in Whitley Stokes, "Cornica III," *RC* 3 (1876-8), 86, and Ellis, *Cornish Language*, p. 218. On the Bible translation, see Fred. W. P. Jago, *An English-Cornish Dictionary* (London, 1887, repr. New York, 1984), p. xiii. Ellis attempts unconvincingly to use Roscarrock's letter to Camden (whom he promotes to Bishop on p. 69) to support the claim of the pamphlet (which is not, as he thinks, a play), entitled *A lyttle treatyse called the Image of Idlenesse*, which involves such names as 'Walter Wedlocke' and 'Bawdin Bacheler.' The pamphlet (containing stories in a pseudo-epistolary form), is listed in the British Library Catalogue under Wedlocke, as it is in the microfilm STC collection of early English published works (Ann Arbor: year 44, reel 1583). A glance at the preface should be sufficient to convince the reader of the fictionality. On St. Columb, see David H. Farmer, *The Oxford Dictionary of Saints* (Oxford, 1978), p. 87, who refers to Baring-Gould, who also took the saint to be male. On Richard Pendrea/Pentrey and his sermon, see Andrew Breeze, "Welsh and Cornish at Valladolid, 1591-1600," *BBCS* 37 (1990), 108-111. Ellis, *Cornish Language*, p. 63f. refers to earlier links between Spain and Cornish Catholics.

Cornish give an indication also of further losses. We learn, for example, that Richard Angwyn, who died in St Just-in-Penwith in 1675, could and did write in Cornish, but also that his manuscripts were not saved.

Our concern is with literature in the Cornish language, rather than with Anglo-Cornish (more properly Cornu-English) writing, but we may note in passing the part played by writers from Cornwall in the early development of English. The most important name is that of John Trevisa of St Mellion, in eastern Cornwall (where spoken English established itself very early on), who died in 1402 and who translated into still eminently readable English both the encylopaedic *De proprietatibus rerum* of Bartholomew the Englishman and the equally massive Latin history-book, the *Polychronicon* of Ranulph Higden. In his version of the latter, Trevisa makes an addition of his own in which he tells how two men with Cornish names, John Cornwall and Richard Pencrych, insisted upon teaching (Latin) grammar through the medium of English rather than French. It has been suspected, probably correctly, that Trevisa is being a trifle partisan in selecting these two as pedagogical innovators, but it is unlikely that any of them were Cornish speakers.[7]

The earliest writings in Cornish are glosses, single words and phrases written into manuscripts in Latin, and dependant upon that language, intended as aides-memoire for the understanding of the Latin. This situation is normal in the early stages in the writing of any western European vernacular, and the materials involved are not literary as such, even though it can be informative to note which Latin texts acquired glosses. With Cornish we have the added difficulty that the few early glosses may be, and indeed have been interpreted as Cornish or as Breton. This is the case with those to the Book of Tobit and others in a commentary on the much-used grammar of Donatus. A final and in fact earlier document contains Cornish names rather than glosses, and is of historical rather than literary interest. The so-called *Bodmin Manumission* gives details of the freeing of slaves, recorded in the late tenth and early eleventh centuries in a manuscript Gospel originally from the monastery of St Petroc at Padstow, but which had been moved to Bodmin after the sack of that monastery in the tenth century.

Clearly Cornish, however, and of great linguistic importance, is the so-called *Vocabularium Cornicum*, a kind of Latin glossary or thematically

---

[7]   Basil Cottle, *The Triumph of English, 1350-1400* (London, 1969), pp. 17-21 cites Trevisa, and Ellis *Cornish Language*, p. 47f. reports the views that Trevisa studied at Glasney, was one of the translators of the Wycliffe Bible, and contributed to *Piers Plowman*, all this based upon D. C. Fowler, "John Trevisa and the English Bible," *Modern Philology* 58 (1960-1), 81-98. Fowler's views have not found acceptance elsewhere and are based on slight evidence. Even the involvement with the Bible translation is "not proven": thus Anne Hudson, *The Premature Reformation* (Oxford, 1988), pp. 395-8. Fowler does not claim Trevisa as a Cornish speaker.

arranged word-list of approaching a thousand words, compiled by the Anglo-Saxon Ælfric, Abbot of Eynsham and a prolific homilist, translator and pedagogical writer, to attach to a grammar based once again on Donatus. This Latin word-list was provided with Cornish, rather than Saxon equivalents in around 1100 to give us a Latin-Cornish vocabulary - Latin remains the primary language. Some of the words have a second equivalent, this time in Welsh, although the implications are unclear beyond the fact that the glossator knew both languages. The manuscript (in which the seven pages of Cornish are described as Welsh) is in the British Library as part of the collection made by the antiquary Sir Robert Cotton in the seventeenth century, largely from dissolved monasteries, and bequeathed to the nation by his grandson.[8]

The beginnings of written literature proper are chronologically still some way off - some three centuries away from the *Vocabularium Cornicum* - and even then the earliest material is both fragmentary and problematic. Probably the first piece of recognisable literature is the so-called *Charter Fragment*, forty-one lines of Cornish verse written on the back of a charter dated 1340 and relating to St Stephen in Brannel. The lines themselves may belong to the latter part of the fourteenth century, although precise dating of the Cornish texts is never easy, and even the date of the hand is unclear. The fragment falls into two parts, the continuity of which is a matter of debate. The first twenty-six lines appear to be a speech in which someone is offering in marriage to a friend or companion (*coweth*) a girl who is praised highly and commended as a good housewife. She is, however, also described as a child, and the speaker assures the friend that she will do his bidding. There is in this section also a local reference, to the lack of distance "between here and the Tamar bridge."

The second part is linguistically more difficult. It seems likely that the lines are from a different speaker, and a woman is apparently being told how to control a man:

> lauar *the* sy by*th* ny venna
> lauar *thotho* gwra mar menny*th*...

---

[8]   Donatus-Glosses: A. de Jubainville, "Mots Bretons connus par un auteur Français du commencement du IXe siècle," *RC* 27 (1906), 151-4; Tobit-Glosses: Joseph Loth, *Vocabulaire vieux-Breton* (Paris, 1884), pp. 68f., 113 and 129; Bodmin Manumission: Max Förster, "Die Freilassungsurkunden des Bodmin-Evangeliars," in: *A Grammatical Miscellany Presented to Otto Jespersen* (Copenhagen, 1930), pp. 77-99; *Vocabularium Cornicum*: Eugene van Tassel Graves, *The Old Cornish Vocabulary* (Diss. PhD, Columbia, 1962: Ann Arbor, Mich., 1962 = microfilm). Illustrations of several of the manuscripts may be found in Ellis, *Cornish Language* and Fudge, *Life of Cornish*.

> tell yourself "I will not do it;"
> tell him "I will do your wishes..."

However, the woman is also assured that the man is of such gentility that he will not force her.

What are we to make of all this? It has been claimed with varying degrees of confidence that the fragment provides evidence of secular drama in the vernacular, or, going even further, that it shows us the role of a (female) matchmaker or even that of a bawd in such a play. In reality, every single one of the assumptions made about the fragment is questionable - that it is dramatic at all, that the whole passage is intended for a single speaker, that the speaker is a woman. Narrative verse containing dialogue is hardly uncommon, and there are historical arguments, too, against accepting this piece as (secular) drama without reflection. Such a survival would be unusual. A fragment from a religious work would be more likely, for all that it is hard to think of a plausible context; one possible exception might be the apocryphal betrothal scenes of Joseph with the Virgin that we find in the English N-Town plays, but even so the lines we have are hard to fit. The reference to the Tamar bridge might, on the other hand, not indicate a local setting, but could be some kind of proverbial circumlocution, just as *in oll kernow*, "in all Cornwall" is used with a generally distributive meaning in the *Ordinalia,* even though the setting is biblical. Some critics have indeed wondered whether the passage might come from one of the secular portions of a religious play, and there are certainly passages in the *Ordinalia*, such as conversations between soldiers, which would not be recognisable as belonging to a religious work if they were taken out of context. One such passage in the *Origo Mundi* has a butler offering to get a girl for one of his mates (*coweth*) and the passage contains the same rhymes (*powes/ mowes*) that we find here in the *Charter Fragment* ("rest" and "girl", OM 2071-2). The offer seems to be a formulaic one, and it is encountered elsewhere in Cornish, sometimes ironically. The use of *coweth* and the whole tone of the first part makes it very unlikely that a woman is speaking, although it is easier to hear the second part as spoken by a woman. The fragment may be divided into strophic units which are not unlike (though not exactly parallel to) those found in the major works of medieval Cornish. An initial strophe (based on sense-division) has 12 lines, varying between four and six syllables, rhyming *aabbbbccdccd*. A quatrain rhymed *abab* follows, and the first part is concluded with a ten-line strophe in rhymed couplets, nine of the lines having seven syllables (the most common metric line in Middle Cornish). The variety of strophes is itself striking.

The second part need not have followed the first in the original, and it seems at least to have a different speaker, as indicated, perhaps a woman. There is at least one line which seems not to fit, the meaning of which is unclear, and the tense of which is not in accord with the rest of the work, although it does contain the interjection *re'n Offeren*, "by the Mass." The speech is addressed not to a friend, but to another woman, who may be the much-praised lady of the first part. If this is the case, there is a clear contrast between the original assertion that "she will not refuse you" and the attitude that she is told to adopt here. The second part is also harder to divide into strophes. Four lines rhyming *abab* seem to form an individual quatrain, and six lines in rhymed couplets follow which are rather longer than those used thus far. The hyperrhythmic line noted above comes next, and we then have a further *abab* quatrain.

However varied the metrical patterns, the real problem is that of interpretation: what kind of text is this, is the transmission coherent, and what was the purpose of writing it down? We may be dealing with acting parts, although if the speakers are different this is less likely. Until convincing outside parallels are established or more of the text is found the questions will simply not be answerable, and meanwhile it is dangerous to make assertions about the fragment in support of any hypotheses about one type of drama or about attitudes to women.[9]

The place where the fragment was actually written is unknown. The other medieval Cornish works group, however, around a single literary centre, albeit one that has now disappeared. There were various monastic centres in early Cornwall, such as St Germans, Padstow and Bodmin - the first-named being the diocesan centre until the see was moved to Crediton in 1042 and then later to Exeter, a Cornish see being re-established at Truro only in the nineteenth century. In 1265, however, the Bishop of Exeter, Walter Bronescombe, established a college of secular canons with a constitution that

---

[9]   W[hitley] S[tokes], "Cornica IV: The Fragments of a Drama in Add. Ch. 19,491, Mus. Brit.," *RC* 4 (1879-80), 258-62, also in Ellis, *Cornish Language*, p. 42f. (with errors); Henry Jenner, "The Fourteenth-Century Charter Endorsement," *JRIC* 20 (1915-20), 41-8; R. Morton Nance, "The Charter Endorsement in Cornish," *OC* 2/iv (1932), 34-6 and: "New Light on Cornish," *OC* 4 (1943-51), 214-6. The most recently published texts with commentary are those by Enrico Campanile, "Un frammento scenico medio-cornico," *Studi e saggi linguistici* 3 (1963), 60-80, and by Lauran Toorians, *The Middle Cornish Charter Endorsement. The Making of a Marriage in Medieval Cornwall* (Innsbruck, 1991). He discusses the text in his "Passie, lief en leed," pp. 8-11. I cite Toorians' version, and his edition has a description of the MS by J. P. M. Jansen. The manuscript uses the tailed *z*, here resolved as *th*. Richard Axton, *European Drama of the Middle Ages* (London, 1974), p. 21 sees the work as secular, and Evelyn S. Newlyn considers the words to be spoken by a stereotype female matchmaker in her paper "Between the Pit and the Pedestal: Images of Eve and Mary in Medieval Cornish Drama," in: *New Images of Medieval Women*, ed. Edelgard DuBruck (Lampeter, 1989), pp. 121-64, esp. p. 142f. Further work by Dr Newlyn on the fragment is, however, in progress. Toorians' goes against previous editions in reading and interpreting the first word of the "by the Mass" line as *cas* rather than *ras*, "hate" rather than "grace." This may serve as an indication of the difficulties of the text.

was based on the chapter of Exeter cathedral, near Penryn (itself now overshadowed by Falmouth) in the woods of Glasney. The college and its collegiate church (or more strictly its chapel, since St Gluvias is actually the parish church) was to be dedicated to St Thomas Becket, and it was consecrated to St Thomas and to the Virgin on March 26, 1267, the day after the Feast of the Annunciation. It was well endowed, with thirteen canons (one as proctor, later provost), with thirteen priest-vicars to support them. Major celebrations were to be that of the church's *dedicatio* on March 26, which would have overlapped with the Annunciation, and in view of the joint dedication doubtless the other Marian feasts would have been emphasised, as well as the patronals (December 29, and the translation of St Thomas on July 7) and the obit of the founder on St James' Eve, June 24. The college was dissolved in 1545.

The cartulary of the collegiate church, a manuscript of the fifteenth century, records amongst the various charters of church appropriation the Latin legend of the foundation of the college as a result of a dream had by Walter Bronescombe (who is here, as elsewhere, named as "Walter Goode") during a serious illness, in which St Thomas himself directed the bishop to Glasney, "of which there was an ancient prophecy in the Cornish language: *in Polsethow ywhylvr anethow.*" Reference to the antiquity of the prophecy takes us back even beyond the late thirteenth century for the supposed age of this Cornish sentence; it is unclear how old the words actually are, and foundations legends are usually vigorously backdated, but the rhyme has a literary ring. The words mean "in Polsethow/ shall wonders show," but as the Latin goes on to point out, the noun *anethow* might also mean "dwellings." The name Polsethow is itself interpreted in the cartulary as meaning a place where animals wounded by arrows (*sethow*) come to die, and it was applied to a marshy area in the Glasney region.

Glasney was not the only secular college in Cornwall. Similar establishments were known at various times throughout the Middle Ages at Crantock, Launceton, Probus, St Buryan, St Columb Major, St Endellion, St Michael Penkevil and St Teath, as well as for a time at St Germans. There are strong links, though, between the major works of Cornish literature and the college at Penryn. The place-names in the *Ordinalia* make its provenance in the Penryn area quite clear, as scholars such as David Fowler and Jane Bakere have shown, and the close thematic links between the *Ordinalia* and the earlier Passion-poem might indicate a common source. There are actual quotations from the *Origo Mundi* play in the later Creation-drama. It may even be significant that the Glasney appropriations included by 1355 the church of St Just-in-Penwith, near one of the surviving rounds or playing-places, where the dramas might have been performed. *Beunans Meriasek* is associated firmly with Camborne, the centre of the saint's cult, but the probable time of composition (not too many years earlier than the manuscript,

14

which is dated 1504) coincides with the move of Master John Nans from the provostship of Glasney to Meriasek's church at Camborne. Nans, also a prebendary of Exeter cathedral, who died in 1508, might at least have encouraged the copying of the work. The strong Marian elements in the play might also be relevant. The dissolution of the college came at about the time that the last major work in Cornish, *Gwreans an bys*, was composed, and the juxtaposition is not coincidental. The English Reformation brought an end not only to Glasney College, but also to the medieval religious drama. The last of the Cornish rebellions - the so-called Prayer-Book Rebellion, in support not of *Cornish*, but rather of the retention of the familiar *Latin* prayer-book set aside by the Act of Uniformity in 1549 - was crushed in spite of Cornish Catholic support, and the Act made no provision for a Cornish liturgy anyway. The Reformation contributed in various ways (including the hindering of relations with Catholic Brittany) to the demise of Cornish as a community language, and although *Gwreans an bys* was copied as late as the early seventeenth century, the Reformation effectively marks the end of pre-revival Cornish literature.[10]

The bulk of surviving Cornish literature is composed in strophic verse. Although the stanzas used in the different works vary, and the linguistic texture of the individual writings depends only to an extent upon the forms adopted, some introductory comments about Cornish verse may be useful. While it is possible to make comparisons (which need not, of course, imply influence) on specific similarities, it is difficult to find sustained links between the prosody of Cornish and that of medieval English, French or Breton. Even weaker are the links with Welsh, in which a system of strict rules (according to the system known as *cynghanedd*) embraces regular inner rhymes, assonances and consonances, and which, as Henry Jenner commented, Welsh-speaking Welshmen "no doubt really can [appreciate], though it is not as easily understood by the rest of the world." There are, as Jenner goes on to point out, sometimes internal rhymes and echoes in Cornish lines, but this is textural and individual rather than systematic.

The line in medieval Cornish is short, and as in Breton or French, is essentially syllabic. Where medieval French plays, such as the *Mystère*

---

[10]   There is a translation and synopsis of the Glasney material by J. A. C. Vincent, "The Glasney Cartulary," *JRIC* 6 (1878-81), 213-59. See G. R. C. Davis, *Medieval Cartularies of Great Britain* (London, 1958), p. 85 on the date. On medieval secular colleges, see David Knowles and R. Neville Hadcock, *Medieval Religious Houses, England and Wales* (London, 1953), pp. 325-46, and specifically Thurstan Peter, *The History of Glasney Collegiate Church* (Camborne, 1903), James Whetter, *The History of Glasney College* (Padstow, 1988), J. M. Adams, "The Medieval Chapels of Cornwall," *JRIC* NS 3 (1957), 52 and Nicholas Orme, *Education in the West of England 1066-1548* (Exeter, 1976), p. 167f. Orme's *The Minor Clergy of Exeter Cathedral 1300-1548* (Exeter, 1980), p. 13 lists a John de Glasneye as a vicar choral in 1309.

d'Adam, the *Mistére du Viel Testament* and many others use octosyllabic lines (varied with some that are shorter or longer), and much early Breton poetry also uses lines of eight syllables, in Cornish the most common line has seven syllables, which Jenner saw as trochaic, but really with an irregular rhythm. Four-syllable lines are also used, but any deviation from the pattern of seven or four syllables is so rare as to arouse suspicion of unrecognised elision or of a corrupt reading, even in *Gwreans an bys*, where a larger number of lines show apparent irregularity. The poem *Pascon agan Arluth* is the most regular of all, composed in strophes of eight heptasyllables rhyming *abab.abab*, although in the manuscript it is laid out as quatrains of long-lines. The plays contain a wide variety of strophic forms, ranging from heptasyllabic couplets to the relatively common strophe of six seven-syllable lines rhyming *aabaab* or *aabccb* (with parallel versions using four-syllable lines), to longer strophes of up to twelve lines. Combinations also occur of four- and seven-syllable lines. The texture of the work can be affected by variations of line and of strophe, as indeed it can by the use of individual devices within the strophes, such as repeated phrases or anaphora. All the plays demonstrate a range of linguistic registers indicative of mood and character, again interlinked with the choice of form.

The rhyme-schemes vary somewhat, but rhymes are regular and repetitive; the relative brevity of the syllabic line makes for frequent recurrence of a given rhyme, and chevilles occur. Jenner also makes clear the emphasis on eye-rhyme, which sometimes involves grammatical adaptation, although this is hardly restricted to Cornish. There are some similarities to the evolving *rime croisée* found in medieval French works, but even more with the six-line strophes, primarily of octosyllables, and with a regular *aabccb* rhyme found in Breton in poems such as the *Buhez mab den* ("The Life of Man"). The same pattern is found elsewhere in Breton in a Passion-play and in some hagiographic plays, although the long lines in rhyming couplets of the *Creation ar bet* ("Creation of the World") distinguish it very markedly from its Cornish counterpart, *Gwreans an bys*. The Breton six-liners, however, typically have a complex and often striking pattern of inner rhymes, at least down to the seventeenth century, which is closer to *cynghanedd* than to Cornish. For purposes of illustration, in fact, the strophes of the Cornish drama can be matched by examples from some of the English plays, although clear differences remain. The following (from the N-Town play of the Adoration) do, however, offer reasonably close equivalents to common Cornish forms, and the Chester or Towneley plays might have furnished examples as well, even if heptasyllabic lines are not particularly common in

the more rhythmic English plays, where the eight-syllable line is standard
much of the time:

> Such hevynese haue vs cawght,
> I must drynk with yow a drawght,
> To slepe a lytyll whyle
> I am hevy heed and footte,
> I xulde stumbyll at resch and root
> And I xuld goo a myle.

and

> I sawghe a syght,
> Myn hert is lyght
> To wendyn home.
> God, ful of myght,
> Hath us dyght
> Fro develys dome.

The strophe which follows the second example rhymes *aabccb*, a form not
uncommon in the N-Town plays. It has to be borne in mind that, quite apart
from the rhythmic regularity and more than occasional alliteration, the English
plays use overall a great variety of strophe lengths and other patterns. There
are no Cornish equivalents for the long-lines and rhyme-scheme of the Digby
St Paul any more than there are for the Breton couplets in the Creation-play.
It is impossible to link the existing Cornish strophic forms exclusively and
conclusively with those in literatures which are culturally close, although the
use of English phrases and sometimes whole lines within Cornish does bring
the English plays necessarily a little closer. But the Cornish forms are
individual, and within the constraints of a distinctive structuring based upon
rhymed strophes with seven- or four-syllable lines, the Cornish works are
quite able to provide literary variation and to sustain interest, at its most
sophisticated level, perhaps, in *Beunans Meriasek*. As Jenner notes, some of
the Late Cornish writings (which are sometimes artificial - he uses the word
himself of Lhuyd's elegy on William of Orange) employ different verse
forms, and it is pointless to speculate on the putative forms of lost materials.
But it is of interest, too, that precisely the earlier patterns, relatively rigid in
line-length, and with an increasing freedom in strophic form and speech-
register, have been readopted in imitative works in the period of revived
Cornish beside the more clearly English forms used for composition in
Cornish by the eighteenth-century antiquarians and by some of the more recent

revivalist writers (who do, nevertheless, occasionally maintain more typically Celtic vowel-patterns), the English forms adopted ranging, however, from the limerick to the Shakespearean sonnet.[11]

[11]   See Jenner, *Handbook*, pp. 178-88 and Joseph Loth, "La métrique cornique," in: H. d'Arbois de Jubainville, *Cours de littérature Celtique* (Paris, 1883-902), XI, 204-16. On Welsh and Breton see Toorians, "Passie, lief en leed," pp. 42-6, and on the complexities of *cynghanedd* see for example J. E. Caerwyn Williams, *The Poets of the Welsh Princes* (Cardiff, 1978), pp. 53-62. As examples (with metrical notes) see for French Barbara M. Craig's edition of *La Creacion...of the Mistére du Viel Testament* (Lawrence, n.d.), pp. 33-7 and Paul Studer's of *Le Mystère d'Adam* (Manchester, 1918, repr. 1949), pp. li-lv. For Breton, see the *Trois poèmes en Moyen-Breton*, ed. Roparz Hemon (Dublin, 1962), pp. x-xii and the text of *Buhez mab den*, pp. 76-101. The English texts are cited from the EETS *N-Town Play*, ed. S. Spector (London, 1991), I, 178-80 (vv. 285-90 and 323-8).

CHAPTER TWO

"AN ANTIENT MANUSCRIPT..." THE POEM OF THE PASSION

The earliest full Cornish text to have survived - and one that was thought for a time to be the only surviving example of early Cornish literature - is a poem in 259 stanzas describing in detail the Passion of Christ, based primarily, but not exclusively upon the Gospel narrative. The work is untitled in the earliest manuscript, but it was given the name *Mount Calvary* (see stanza 162) when it appeared in print in an inadequate edition with translation in 1826, the first of the early Cornish texts to be printed. This name is retained for the abbreviation of the work, although it is now known by an *ad hoc* Cornish title, *Pascon agan Arluth*, "The Passion of Our Lord." It was edited more acceptably, again with an English translation, at the end of the nineteenth century, and more recently in a version in Unified Cornish by Robert Morton Nance (as *Passyon agan Arluth*), also with a translation. There is an edition of the original text with Nance's version and a translation into Breton.[1]

At first glance there appears to be an extensive manuscript tradition, but this is misleading, since the dozen or so copies all derive from one fifteenth-century manuscript, BL Harleian 1782, presumably that owned by William Scawen in the late seventeenth century, and described by him as "an antient manuscript...written upon a rough old vellum;...and by the rude pictures set out therewith, it may seem to be before the art of painting became better amongst us." Scawen arranged for the text to be translated by John Keigwin (and others). The Harley manuscript (associated in one of the copies with the church at Sancreed) is probably a copy of an earlier version, and the illustrations, ten line-drawings with coloured wash, are indeed crude. They are, however, the only illustrations in a Cornish manuscript apart from stage-

---

[1]   The text is cited from the edition by Whitley Stokes, "The Passion, a Middle Cornish Poem," *Transactions of the Philological Society* 1860/1 (also as an independent publication, and sometimes with added pages of corrigenda). The first edition of the work was by Davies Gilbert, *Mount Calvary* (London, 1826). Nance first published his edition in the journal *Kernow* 1-14 (1934-6), and the most recent version is that edited by E. G. R. Hooper, *Passyon agan Arluth. Cornish Poem of the Passion...by R. M. Nance and A. S. D. Smith* (St Ives, 1972). The Cornish text only was printed in *An Lef Kernewek* 81-103 (1963-8) by Hooper, and various extracts have also been printed. The Breton edition is that by Goulven Pennaod, *Passyon agan Arluth. Passion hon Aotrou, barzhoneg kernevek eus ar 15. kantved* (= the journal *Preder*, 232-4, 1978). See my bibliography: *The Medieval Cornish Poem of the Passion* (Redruth, 1979). I have discussed the content in: "*Pascon agan Arluth*: the Literary Position of the Cornish Poem of the Passion," *Studi medievali* 22 (1981), 821-36 and there is a lucid and sensitive commentary on it in Toorians, "Passie, lief en leed," pp. 12-41.

diagrams. Andrew Hawke enumerates twelve manuscripts beside Harley 1782 (with the possibility of another), all of them with the Cornish text and English translation, although only three have both parts complete, dating from the late seventeenth to the late nineteenth century, one with an interlinear and literal Welsh version of fifteen stanzas. While the copies are of linguistic interest, and bear witness to a continued interest in the poem, their literary importance is limited. Some of them give the work the title by which it was known originally in English, namely "Mount Calvary."[2]

The provenance of the original is unknown, although there is a clear connexion with the *Ordinalia*, the Passion-play of which uses a few passages from the poem. Other motifs in the work crop up in the plays, although these are often religious commonplaces. But it is possible that there was a copy of the poem at Glasney. The work seems to have originated in the earlier part of the fourteenth century, and it is composed in regular eight-line stanzas of seven syllables, rhyming (usually in a fairly pure form) *abababab*, set out in the manuscript in groups of four lines. Only one stanza (208) adds an extra long line.

The poem is certainly older than the *Ordinalia,* although the chronological priority of the plays has been asserted, a judgement perhaps influenced subconsciously, at least, by the supposedly greater literary importance of the latter. Six stanzas of the poem have exact metrical equivalents in the *Passio Christi* section of the *Ordinalia*, and there are three further cases where stanzas from the poem have been adapted in the play, but have either been expanded or contracted. Additions in the play are either repetitions or chevilles ("the Scripture is true indeed"). Elsewhere the dramatist of the *Passio Christi* omits the *inquit*-formulas of the poem, and in one of the closer parallels - stanza 12 of the poem, part of the description of Christ's temptation in the wilderness - an exegetical explanation of the words of Christ is placed somewhat uncomfortably into an actual speech, which necessitates in the play

<hr>

[2]   The list of manuscripts in my bibliography was corrected by Andrew Hawke, "The Manuscripts of the Cornish Passion Poem," *CS* 9 (1981), 23-8 with valuable additional detail (although I hope it is not ungracious if I point out that some of the "additions" *are* in my original, such as the reference to Jenner's reproduction of some of the MS, and that sometimes my comments have been misunderstood, as the reference to the Bodleian library in the 1777 text of Scawen's *Observations*.) On Scawen's ownership of MS BL Harl. 1782, see Andrew Hawke, "A Lost MS of the Cornish *Ordinalia*?" *CS* 7 (1979), 50. Edward Lhuyd apparently began a rhyme dictionary based on the poem: see Henry Jenner, "Descriptions of Cornish Manuscripts I," *JRIC* 19 (1913), 163. On the illustrations of the Harleian MS see my bibliography, p. 22. They are reproduced and discussed, however, in an unpublished dissertation by Mark Herniman, "*Pascon agan Arluth*: A Critical Study of the Cornish Passion Poem" (Diss. MA, typescript, Exeter, 1984; see his Appendix B).

the presence of the disciples as an audience.[3] The common source is the Gospels, but extra-biblical motifs are found both in the poem and the play.

Pascon agan Arluth is not a versified Gospel as such - of which there are many medieval examples[4] - but rather a treatment of the Passion as the central incident in the divine economy of fall and redemption. There is no nativity, and the work begins with the temptation in the desert. It sums up aspects of the ministry, before dealing with the Passion in detail, covering the liturgical Gospel readings from Quadragesima Sunday to Passion Week, although only some of the Lenten pericopes are selected. In addition there are other biblical passages, and also several non-biblical motifs, either expanding the narrative or interpreting the events in a doctrinal or devotional manner. The purpose of the poem is to describe the events of the Passion in a vivid form (evoking the affective piety of Bernard of Clairvaux, frequently given the designation "Gothic"), and to explain it at the same time in plain terms as the point of salvation for fallen man.

The poet claims to be a man of modest learning (*Kyn na goff den skentyll pur.* "Even though my skill is slight," MC 8),[5] but he puts forward his theme in programmatic form, stating at the same time his motivation for writing a devotional poem:

> Suel a vy*nn*o bos sylwys.
> golsowens ow lauarow
> A ih*e*su del ve helheys.
> war an bys avel carow
> Ragon menough rebe*ki*s.
> ha dys*pres*ijs yn harow
> yn growys gans kentrow fast*i*s.
> peynys bys pa*n* ve marow (MC 2)

---

[3]   See Murdoch, "Literary Position," and Bakere, *Ordinalia*. The counter-view was put by David C. Fowler, "The Date of the Cornish *Ordinalia*," *Medieval Studies* 23 (1961), 91-125. The precedence of the poem is now accepted.

[4]   For a survey of relevant texts (including major Latin works such as Ludolf of Saxony's *Vita Christi* and others) see K. Whinnom, "The Supposed Sources of Inspiration of Spanish Fifteenth-Century Narrative Religious Verse," *Symposium* 17 (1963), 268-91

[5]   In text-citations I have resolved the tailed *z* as *th* as appropriate. Stokes discusses, p. 3, the use of the tailed *z*, which sometimes appears, presumably in error, for *s* or *z*. Phonetic distinctions are not always clear, and it is not in accord with the other MSS to adopt Unified Cornish *dh* or Welsh *dd*. In citations, italicised *th* always represents the tailed *z*; other resolutions are by Stokes. The text is laid out as eight-line stanzas for convenience, and full points separate half-lines in the manuscript. It is not possible to imitate the internal additional rhymes in translation (see the echoes on *-ow-* in stanza 2, below), nor indeed to recreate the effect of foreign words like *dyspresijs*.

> Anyone who would find grace,
> let him come, my words to hear:
> Jesus was hunted in the chase
> here in the world like a deer.
> For our sake rebuke he faced,
> much despisèd, and in fear,
> then on a cross with nails placed,
> put to death by torture there.

That stanza sets the tone for the whole; the presentation of the Passion expands the Gospel narrative by the use of a system of biblical cross-referencing which derives from typological exegesis. Christ as the deer hunted down and killed, for example, echoes the prophetic Psalm xxi, with the image of the speaker hunted by dogs and torn to pieces, and related in medieval thought and art to the Crucifixion.[6]

An introductory group of nine stanzas sets out the aim of the work, which is the presentation of the Passion as a means of man's redemption through Christ, foreseen in the divine wisdom and demonstrated in the temptation in the desert, the pericope for the first Sunday in Lent, interpreted as Christ resisting the temptations to which Adam fell victim. The presentation and elucidation of the pericope takes up thirteen stanzas, after which the poem moves to the ministry. The healing miracles and the hostility of the Jews echo the Gospel readings for the third Sunday and other masses in Lent (Luke xi: 14-28 etc., John viii: 21-9), and take up stanzas 23-6, after which four are devoted to Palm Sunday, with a further indication of the anger of the wicked. Stanzas 32-4 present the pericope of the woman taken in adultery (John viii: 3-11), and the next seven stanzas are concerned with Judas and the ointment, and then his betrayal of Christ. Liturgically this takes us to Maundy Thursday, and the bulk of the work deals with the actual events of the Passion: the Last Supper (42-4), the washing of the feet (45-6), Christ to Judas (48), Peter's assertion (49) and Christ to the disciples before and on the Mount of Olives (50-61). The last section adds details of Christ's humanity. The taking of Christ, together with the severing of Malchus' ear follows (62-75), and the Gospel narrative is followed with the trial of Christ before Annas and then Caiaphas, a section interlinked with the denial by Peter (76-97). The presentation of Christ to Pilate (98-107) is interrupted (103-6) with an expansion of the biblical despair of Judas in Matt. xxvii: 3-5, telling how, after he had hanged himself, his soul could not leave through the mouth that

---

6   See F. P. Pickering, "The Gothic Image of Christ," in his: *Essays on Medieval German Literature and Iconography* (Cambridge, 1980), pp. 3-30, esp. p. 9, and James H. Marrow, *Passion Iconography in Northern European Art of the Late Middle Ages and Renaissance* (Kortrijk, 1979), esp. pp. 33-9

had kissed Christ. Christ is sent to Herod (108-12), and his sufferings are enumerated, after which he is returned to Pilate (113-21), who admires him in spite of the condemnation by Caiaphas, Two stanzas (122-3) are then devoted to a modified version of the incident with Pilate's wife mentioned briefly in Matt. xxvi: 19f. and expanded considerably in medieval drama. Pilate's reiteration of Christ's innocence follows, then the scene with Barabbas, and Christ's assertion of his divinity (124-9). Ten stanzas describe the details of the Passion in graphic terms (130-9), including such non-biblical details as the piercing of the brain by the crown of thorns, a motif found in Cornish and elsewhere. The final encounter with Pilate and the latter's washing of his hands (140-8) leads to an acceptance of the blood of Christ by the Jews (Matt. xxvii: 25) in stanza 149. The crucifixion as such occupies a major portion of the work (150-211), with a number of additional motifs, the most striking being the legend found also in the *Ordinalia*, in which the hands of the smith who has refused to make the nails miraculously appear to be leprous. Christ is stretched and jolted upon the cross,[7] and the sorrows of the Virgin at the event are described, although there is only brief mention (177) of St Veronica, whose legend and its links with the fate of Pontius Pilate is exploited in the *Ordinalia*. There are pointers towards meditation from time to time (as stanza 182), but in the main the narrative follows the biblical Passion closely.

Immediately after the Crucifixion comes a version of the harrowing of hell in very general terms and with no clear source (212-3), and the narrative continues with the taking of the body by Joseph of Arimathea after the deposition, and then the entombment (214-37). In this passage, however, further extra-biblical motifs appear: the healing of blind Longinus, another well-known and widespread legend used also in the plays; the details of the sorrows of the Virgin; the 5,475 wounds of Christ and the prayers associated with them. The final stanzas of the poem (238-59) follow the Gospels more closely, presenting in rapid sequence the Maries at the tomb, and the report of the soldiers to Pilate, who tells them to say that robbers took the body. Christ's appearance at Galilee and a concluding prayer close the poem (MC 258-9). The prayer, which is linguistically impressive, with a complexity of rhyme-echoes and some anaphora, links with the crucifixion and with the good thief, but makes clear - and this is of great importance - the significance of the narrative for the listener:

---

[7]   See Pickering, "Gothic Image," pp. 6-8. On the Pseudo-Anselmian *Dialogue* (PL 159, 271-90), see p. 6 of Pickering's paper. Pickering refers to the *Northern Passion* as a vernacular example of the *jacente cruce* crucifixion.

Del sevys mab du ay veth.
yn erna *then* tressa dyth
yn della ol ny a seff.
deth brues drok ha da yn weth
obereth dremas a dyff.
yn erna rych ef a vyth
drok *th*en yn gythna goef.
the gryst y fyth anbarth cleth (259)

As God's son rose from the grave
at that time on the third day,
so, good or bad, we shall have
risen up again on Doomsday.
Good works shall the good man save,
at that time he'll have rich pay.
But woe to the wicked knave -
on Christ's left hand shall he stay.

The poem frequently combines narrative with commentary to explain the significance of what is being presented. Many of the legend additions may be found in standard works such as the *Historia scholastica* or the *Legenda aurea*, for example. The French biblical scholar, Peter Comestor, wrote the former, an expanded biblical history, in the later twelfth century and it was widely known and translated; James of Vorazzo (Jacobus a Voragine), Bishop of Genoa in the later thirteenth century, compiled the collection of saints' lives and legends known as the *Golden Legend*, and it was equally widely used as a source-book throughout the middle ages. Apocryphal narratives linked with Old and New Testament characters also expand upon the lives of Adam and Eve, or of Pilate or Judas, and these, too, were widespread. Actual *Quellenforschung* is always difficult, but Cornish literature, in drawing on these materials, is very clearly part of a European tradition.

The reason for the Passion is the salvation of mankind, and the poet draws attention to the relationship between Christ as the son of God (*mab du*) and mankind (referred to as *mab den,* literally, "son of man," but implying Adam's progeny) in the programmatic opening section. The redemption of man through the incarnation is brought about by the Trinity (presented in terms of the Trinity-formula associated with the school of Abelard, and consisting of *potentia, sapientia* and *benignitas*)[8] in direct response to the

---

[8]   The formula, here as *vertu, skyans* and *thadder*, derived from Abelard, is put succinctly in the *Sententiae Florianenses*, for example, ed. H. Ostlender (Bonn, 1929), p. 4. The scholastic variation on the Augustinian triad (to which I refer in error in my bibliography

lamentations of men who have lost the homeland that was intended for them, their *patria paradisi*:

> An dus vas a *th*eserya.
> *theth*e gulas nef of kyllys
> gans aga garm hag olua.
> ih*es*us *cr*ist a ve mevijs (MC 4, 1-2)

> The good folk wanted to gain
> the land of heaven they lost,
> and by their weeping and pain
> Jesus Christ was moved at last...

The notion is Adamic; man was expelled from Paradise and desires to return, but is prevented from doing so by the devil. The defeat of the devil is the point of the incarnation, and this is the central motif in far earlier Gospel adaptations in the vernacular, such as the early Germanic *Evangelienbuch* of Otfrid or the Old Saxon *Heliand*. The link with Adam is made explicit in the sixth and seventh stanzas, and the poet's aim is to show us Paradise regained. The relationship between fall and redemption leads into the first part of the narrative, the pericope of the temptation, taken from Matthew iv: 1-11. The interpretation in the context of Adam's fall is a medieval commonplace, and even though the specific link with Adam is not made in this version, it remains implicit, and provides (as in many comparable works) a suitable starting point for a narrative of the significance of the Passion based on its necessity for the salvation of man. In the exegesis of the Matthew version (Luke reverses the order of the last two temptations, and Mark is very brief) the devil tempts Christ with gluttony, to make the stones into bread, vainglory by showing Christ the possibility of being saved by angels if he were to cast himself from the temple, and avarice or covetousness in offering Christ power over the world. Adam, runs the interpretation, had fallen prey to all three sins resisted by Christ (greed in eating the fruit, covetousness of knowledge, and the vainglorious desire to be like God). That two of the sins named appear in English form (*gloteny,* MC 13, 1 and *covatys,* MC 15, 1, rather than Latin *gula* and *avaritia*) might indicate an English source, possibly a sermon for the opening of Lent. The Chester Plays also refer in this context to *glotanye* and *covetose of highnes.*[9]

---

of the poem, p. 17) of *memoria, intelligentia, voluntas* was widespread after the time of the Schoolmen. The first illustration in the Harley MS is of the Trinity.

[9]   See my book *The Recapitulated Fall* (Amsterdam, 1974), for the theology of recapitulation based on this passage. I analysed German and English vocabulary in: "Zu einer quellenbestimmten Lexikologie des Altdeutschen," *Forschungsberichte zur Germanistik/*

Christ's humanity is indicated first of all when the poet mentions his hunger after the long fast, and when Christ refuses to turn the stones into bread, the poet comments:

> dre w*orth*yp *c*rist yn vrna.
> le*mm*yn ny a yll gwelas
> lauar du maga del wra.
> neb a vy*nn*o y glewas (MC 12, 3-4)

> By the answer that Christ made,
> all of us may see it clear
> that the word of God is bread
> to whomsoever would hear.

This is the passage of commentary that Christ is made to address to the disciples in the *Ordinalia* (PC 69-72). As in the Bible, the disciples are not present in the poem at this point. The temptations continue according to Matthew, adapted to local circumstances - the pinnacle of the temple is that of a "fine church" (*eglos tek*) - but at the end of the section the poet makes first a general and then a tropological comment. Having been defeated three times, the devil has lost heart, and this point is important as the first indication of the defeat of the devil as master of the world. The sins of Adam have been compensated by Christ, and Paradise can now be regained. The dramatist of the *Ordinalia* makes this even more clear, by giving the devil a speech in which he complains of having lost his former power over men (PC 145-50).

Four stanzas are devoted, however, to a tropological interpretation of the whole: if the devil tried to tempt Christ, how much more vigilant should man be against the wiles of the devil, who stalks us like a lion his prey. Nevertheless, man should not be disheartened, because the Scriptures provide evidence of comfort, that man *is* able to rise after the devil has cast him down. None of this is in the *Ordinalia*, although there might be an echo of the ideas contained in these stanzas in the somewhat oddly placed initial comments of the devil, who in the *Passio Christi* actually states that he will

---

Doitsubungaku Ronko/Osaka, 13 (1971), 43-63, and have augmented the list of analogues to Milton's *Paradise Regained* given in my own work and in Watson Kirkconnell's *Awake the Courteous Echo* (Toronto and Buffalo, 1973) in "Thematic Analogues of Paradise Regained," *Etudes Anglaises* 31 (1978), 203-7. The Harley MS contains an illustration of Adam and Eve set against the first temptation of Christ: see Mark Herniman, "*Pascon agan Arluth*: A Critical Study of the Cornish Passion Poem," (Diss. MA Exeter, 1984), pp. 161f.

not be able to tempt Christ (PC 53-8).[10] The homiletic tone of the stanzas is patent, however, especially in the shift from warning to comfort. The reference to the devil as a lion alludes to Psalm ix: 30 and more specifically to I Peter v: 8-10, which the Cornish poem echoes, and it is perhaps not accidental that this passage should be followed by a reference to Christ preaching, itself accompanied by a tropological stanza. The descriptions of the healing miracles are contained in a single stanza, and the hostility of the Jews, the entry on Palm Sunday into Jerusalem and the cleansing of the temple are all relatively briefly treated. The incident in which the disciples are sent to find an ass and a colt (in fulfilment of the prophecy of Zacharias ix: 9) is more fully treated in the play, which contains - unlike our poem - the welcome by the *pueri ebreorum*, but in contrast to the Cornish (though not most of the English) plays, the poet does include the so-called *adultera* pericope, again a Gospel reading towards the end of Lent, though before Palm Sunday. It is part of a sequence of incidents to show Christ in opposition to those trying to trap him, and it is followed by the story of Judas and the ointment as told in Mark xiv: 3-7, used as a lead-in to the treachery of Judas, on whose villainy the poet lays great emphasis:

> Eff [o] harlot tebel was.
> woteweth lad*er* vye
> *then* e*the*won y ponyas.
> crist y arluth rag gwer*the* (MC 38, 3-4)

> He was a foul, wicked man
> and a thief he came to be,
> to the Jews he quickly ran
> to sell Christ, his lord, for fee.

This takes us to the events of Maundy Thursday and to the Last Supper and the washing of the disciples' feet, but additional comment is made once again about Judas, pointing out (in blunt and somewhat homely terms) that Christ was aware of his nature:

> bos Iudas ef a wo*thy*e.
> p*ur* hag*er* ha molo*thek*
> an ioul ynno re drecse.
> may *tho* gweth ag*is* cronek (MC 47, 3-4)

---

[10] See Murdoch, *Recapitulated Fall*, pp. 133-6 on this somewhat odd motif; the relevant lines of the play are probably based on the last part of MC 7.

> For Judas, as he well knew,
> was ugly and was accursed.
> the devil dwelt in him, too;
> than any toad he was worse

All the concentration is on the central figure of Christ, and the narrator draws attention to the pain suffered undeservedly by Christ at the outset, from Christ's prayer on Olivet (MC 54), reiterating it in several of the following stanzas. An essentially narrative but non-dramatic motif (it is not in the play) introduced at this point and developed in an additional stanza is the notion that Christ sweated water and blood, found in Luke xxii:44, and here linked not only with the Crucifixion, but with the importance of that event for man:

> dowr ha goys yn kemesk*is*.
> weys *c*rist rag *the* gere*n*se (MC 58, 4)

> Blood and water mingled there
> did Christ sweat for love of you.

The main point is one that will be encountered in the play of Meriasek, where elementary doctrines of Christianity are explained to unbelievers: Christ needed to become flesh because as the Godhead he would not have been able to experience suffering. The homiletic tone is once again clear, particularly in formulas like *Lemmyn ny a yl gwelas. hag ervyre fest yn ta* (MC 60, 1), "Now we may all see and we may consider very well."

In the narrative of the taking of Christ the poet is at pains to make the loyalties clear throughout; thus Jesus attracts the adjective *caradow*, "dear", while those who come for him are simply *ethewon*, "the Jews," sometimes with adjectival comment such as *goky*, "foolish." The vilification of Judas continues, however, to a greater extent than in the drama. Even Christ condemns him in a non-biblical statement:

> moll[o]*th* den ha go*ur* ha gwrek.
> a *the* pora*n* er*t*hebyn
> peynys ad wra more*t*hek.
> yn affarn down pub *t*er*m*yn (MC 66, 3-4)

> The curse of men and women too
> will be upon you for sure,
> and vile pains will torment you
> deep in hell for evermore.

The humanity of Christ, which enhances the suffering, is clear in the stanzas which depict the events leading up to the crucifixion. Thus when Christ is bound (as in John xviii: 12), the bonds are so tight that the blood springs out, a motif that occurs more frequently later on, but here is part of the emphasis on the torture. Christ is brought before Annas as midnight,[11] and this is linked with the crucial statement (based on John xviii:20) that Christ himself preached *pur apert hag yn golow* (MC 79, 1), "openly and in the light." The denial by Peter is retold dramatically, though relatively briefly, and resembles the *Ordinalia* in Peter's extensive remorse (expanding Matthew xxvi: 75); in the play, of course, Peter can lament what he has done. In the poem, we are told that he weeps, but also that he refuses to eat.

The Passion-narrative proper follows in the main the Matthew text, but for the trial before Pilate uses the Johannine version. Authorial insertions are rare, and of the kind seen already: small additions descriptive of Christ as *an kveff colon*, "the kindly heart" (MC 101, 1), and of those who attack Christ as kindred of the devil (MC 111). Of special interest is the death of Judas. That he hangs himself is biblical, and that he mispriced Christ by taking only thirty pieces of silver is found elsewhere, as is the motif that when he hanged himself his soul could not leave from the mouth that had kissed Christ. The ideas are present in the *Golden Legend*, in the *Historia scholastica*, and in other vernacular passions, as well as the *Ordinalia*.[12]

A larger addition is the development of Pilate's wife's dream, mentioned briefly in Matthew xxvii: 19. This is expanded in a composite apocryphon, the *Gospel of Nicodemus*, which is combined with the *Acts of Pilate*. In Greek, Latin and vernacular versions the Jews, when told of the dream had by Pilate's wife, claim that Christ himself sent it, because he is a sorcerer. Here, the devil is concerned about the harrowing of hell, and attempts to forestall this by sending the dream. The motif is expanded in the *Ordinalia*, in which a diabolical council (of the sort convened in hell to arrange for the temptation of Adam and Eve, and also of Christ in the wilderness) makes a

---

[11] Other vernacular metrical versions have Christ bound (*sore and faste* in the Cambridge version of the *Northern Passion*, for example: *The Northern Passion (Supplement)*, ed. Wilhelm Heuser and Frances A. Foster, London, 1930 = EETS/OS 183, p. 14, l. 523). The same text has Christ complain that he has been taken by night, which does echo the Gospels.

[12] See my "Literary Position," p. 829 with details of analogues. On the first point, see L. Kretzenbacher, "Verkauft um dreissig Silberlinge," *Schweizerisches Archiv für Volkskunde* 57 (1961), 1-17. The second motif is found in the *Northern Passion* and its French source, as well as in works like the *Cursor mundi* and shorter poems, such as that in BL MS Harley 2277, the *Vita Iude cariote*, edited by Frederick J, Furnivall, "Early English Poems and Lives of Saints," *Transactions of the Philological Society*, 1862, p. 111. See Frances A. Foster, *The Northern Passion* (London, 1913-16 = EETS/OS 145 and 147), II, 677 with reference to other sources (the Comestor is in PL 198, 1650).

last attempt, by trying to persuade Pilate's wife that vengeance will come upon her husband if Christ is killed. The point is, of course, that if Christ is spared, then man will not be redeemed, even though any suspense depends upon Pilate's *rejection* of the idea. Once again the poet's source might be the *Golden Legend* or a similar standard work. The motif also appears, for example, in the early fifteenth-century poem of the *Parlamentum of Feendis*, in which the devil comments on how " Pilatis wijf y bad bisily geue tent/ Þat ihesu were not doon on Þe crois."[13] The Cornish poem adds more detail:

> Own boys *c*rist mab du a*n* neff.
> an tebel el an geve
> rag hen*n*a scon y *th*eth ef.
> *th*e wrek pylat may *th*ese
> han tebel el hag*er* bref.
> yn y holon a worre
> wa*r* y mes*ter* venions cref.
> y to Ih*es*us m*ar* la*th*e (MC 122)

> Fear that Christ was God's own son
> seized the evil angel then,
> and therefore he hurried on
> and to Pilate's wife he came;
> the serpent, the evil one
> her heart with the thought inflamed
> that on her lord venegance strong
> would fall, if Jesus were slain.

Pilate attempts to save Christ, but it is not entirely clear why he does so.[14] This point is far clearer in the play, where he decides to try and save Christ immediately after the messenger has brought word. At all events, the Jews demand the release of Barabbas *dre bur envy*, "out of pure envy" (MC 126, 1). Pilate's attitude is defended throughout, and he is aware that the Jews are envious. He is, of course, unable to save Christ, and the description of the torments (ten stanzas) includes details of the two scourges and their form (based on the single word *flagellum* in the Gospels) and the intensity of the crown of thorns, the spines of which pierce Christ to the brain. Every part of Christ is wounded. In this extended section the poet adds authorial comments from time to time, either in assertion of source (the Bible is invoked, and the sharpness of the thorns is attributed to a *den scyntyll*, a "learned man"), or

13   In *Hymns to the Virgin and Christ*, ed. F. J. Furnivall (London, 1868 = EETS/OS 24), p. 48, vv. 215f.
14   On Pilate and his wife, see Toorians, "Passie, lief en leed," pp. 21-4.

more fully, in a stanza which has a formulaic feel about it, to underline the pathos, whilst stressing the point of meditation on the Passion and its implications:

> Colon den a yll crakye.
> a vynha p*r*est p*r*edery
> an paynys bras an geve.
> han dyspyth heb y dylly
> hag ol rag *the* gerense.
> ih*e*sus c*r*ist as go*the*vy
> lymmyn gorqvyth y gare.
> ha gweyth dene*tar* na vy (MC 139)

> The heart of a man might break
> if he fully considered
> all the pains Christ bore, and great
> despising, all undeserved.
> For your love, and for your sake
> Jesus Christ all things endured.
> So give him all your love; make
> sure that you are not deterred.

The effect of the crown of thorns is found in Cornish not only in the *Ordinalia*, but also in the play of Meriasek, and although only the Towneley plays have the point in English, it is there in French drama, and in texts like the Middle English *Cursor mundi* and the *Stanzaic Life of Christ*, where it is ascribed to St Bernard, as it is in the *Golden Legend*. It may be found, indeed, in most of the European vernaculars, including Breton.[15] Other writers (such as Peter Comestor) stress the number and sharpness of the thorns, and the origin of the motif might be the typological parallel found in such medieval handbooks as the *Pictor in carmine* between Samson's blinding and the treatment of Christ.[16] There is clearly a typological basis for the

---

[15] See Murdoch, "Literary Position," p. 835. In Breton the motif is found in the *Grand mystère de Jesus*, ed. H. de Villemarqué (Paris, 1865), pp. 109 and 111, and in a range of other texts, including Passions from Vannes (Dublin, Institute of Advanced Studies MS 13, fol. 42v), Rennes (Town Library MS 17 816, f. 76r), Landévennec and elsewhere. See also the Dublin MSS in the Institute of Advanced Studies 6, f. 46v and 7, f. 64r. Most of these are from the eighteenth and ninteenth centuries, but somewhat earlier is a Christmas Hymn from Vannes which contains a graphic presentation of the sufferings: Roparz Hemon, *Christmas Hymns in the Vannes Dialect of Breton* (Dublin, 1956), p. 88. I am indebted to Gwenaël le Duc for a number of these references in Breton religious writings.

[16]   M. R. James, "Pictor in Carmine," *Archaeologia* 94 (1951), 141-66: see p. 161, section xcviii.

concept expressed in stanza 135 that Christ's wounds extended over the whole body, since this is again a regular feature of medieval vernacular Passions, deriving from Isaiah i: 6, which refers to wounds from head to feet; it is in the *Legenda aurea*, Welsh, Breton and most vernaculars.[17]

The second debate with Pilate exonerates him more fully than the Gospels justify or, indeed, than is the case in the *Ordinalia*. Here Pilate is actually contrasted with *an debel dus* (MC 143), "the evil people", and his famous self-exculpation in Matthew xxvii: 24 is extended to anticipate the comments on the Jews accepting the possibility of vengeance, as in the next verse of the Gospel:

> glan off a wos an dremas.
> rag ay woys venions a the (MC 149, 2)

> I am clean of the saint's blood;
> from his blood vengeance will come

This return to the Matthew narrative comes after a section in which the Johannine Gospel has been the source, something found in other Passion-narratives.[18]

The Holy Rood is very briefly introduced. We are told simply that a Jew knew where there was some suitable wood, and that it was from the tree by which Adam had sinned. This is a highly condensed version of the extensive and very widely known legend of the cross, which is treated in detail in the *Ordinalia*, and the stanzas (MC 152f.) in which the motif occurs is closer to the liturgical juxtaposition of the first and second Adam in hymns like Venantius Fortunatus' *Pange, lingua, gloriosi...* The *Legenda aurea* develop the parallelism at length, but here Christ is the fruit on the tree of the cross that redeems the sin of Adam, which was caused by the fruit of a different tree. The Holy Rood legends realise the liturgical typology of the *deuteros Adam* by having the rood-tree grow from seeds of the tree of life placed in the mouth of the dead Adam. The wood is eventually hidden at Bethesda. The very brevity of this passage assumes an awareness on the part of the audience of the whole background, and the same assumption has to be made for

---

[17]   H. de la Villemarqué, "Ancien noëls bretons," *RC* 10 (1889), 291f. (=IX, 137); Hemon, *Christmas Hymns*, p. 88f. The Vannetais hymn printed by Hemon (which is admittedly considerably later than our poem) also refers to the tightness of Christ's bonds at the time of the flagellation. For Welsh examples, see D. Simon Evans, *Medieval Religious Literature* (Cardiff, 1986), pp. 42-4.

[18]   See G. Jones, *A Study of Three Welsh Religious Plays* (Aberystwyth, 1939), p. 71. The Welsh material is different in many respects, but Jones' introduction contains details of other vernacular parallels.

medieval iconography in particular. Thus for example a miniature by
Berthold Furtmeyer in the fifteenth-century *Salzburg Missal* shows the tree of
life bearing fruit, but also host wafers and a small crucifix with the body of
Christ upon it, while Adam sleeps below the tree. The Virgin administers
host wafers to the faithful on one side of the picture, whilst Eve gives the fruit
to sinful man on the other.[19] The theology of MC 153 is similarly concise:

> En prynner a ve kerhys.
> en grows scon dy*thg*tis [l. dyghtis?] may fe
> hag y*n*ny bonas gorys.
> ragon ny cryst a vy*n*ne
> ha war an pren frut deg*is*.
> may fe sur *th*agan sawye
> may teth frut may fen kellys.
> rag adam *the* attamye

> The timbers were quickly brought,
> so the cross could soon be made,
> and it was for us Christ sought
> upon that cross to be laid,
> so that it would bear a fruit
> that would us all surely save,
> although our fall it once wrought,
> when Adam the first bite gave.

Both the French *Passion des Jongleurs* and the English *Northern Passion*
follow the narrative of the Rood (which covers around 800 lines in one of the
Northern Passion texts) with the legend of the forging of the nails, a narrative
expanded further in the *Passio Christi*. The legend is of interest as a reversal
of the divine curing of leprosy, since here the smith's hands appear by a
miracle to be leprous so that he cannot make the nails, and his wife agrees to
make them instead.[20] Various other motifs are also introduced, notably the
restoral of what is presumably the seamless robe, here described as having
been made by the Virgin as Christ was growing up, an unusual motif with no
parallel in the drama. Mary is frequently depicted as weaving or sewing at the
time of the Annunciation, however.

As with the English Passions and indeed the *Ordinalia*, the poem now

---

[19]   The miniature, one of the most concise expressions of medieval typology, is the
frontispiece and ill. 44 in Roger Cook in *The Tree of Life* (London, 1974).

[20]   The textual history of the somewhat misleadingly named *Northern Passion* is
complex: see Foster's and Heuser's edition (notes 11 and 12 above). The parallel *Southern
Passion*, ed. Beatrice Daw Brown (London, 1927 = EETS/OS 169) is less close.

presents the meeting of Mary with her son on the way to Calvary, and adds his words to the women as in Luke xxiii: 27. In the poem, this passage stresses not only the physical sufferings of Christ once again, but also those of the Virgin. The narrative emphasis of the work lies in human detail, rather than in more complex theological explanation, directed at the pity of the (presumably) lay audience, although some points are taken for granted, of course, that might nowadays require explanation. Thus in stanza 177 there is a possible reference to Veronica, who is not named, and who covers the whole of Christ against the cold, rather than just his face. The image of Christ is not mentioned.

Simon of Cyrene (identified in the Cornish play with Simon the Leper) willingly carries the cross in the play, and prophesies vengeance on the Jews; but a different approach is found in the poem. Simon refuses, and is forced to carry the cross for fear of his life. Matthew xxvii: 22 speaks of the Cyrene stranger being forced to carry the cross, and this is found in the *Northern Passion*. The Cornish poet adds a comment to the audience admonishing them to act justly, and not to take service with the wicked. Whether this is an implicit rebuke against Simon (who has no choice in the matter) is unclear, but the passage is also linguistically difficult to interpret. The Gilbert version is pretty well incomprehensible, but the Nance-Smith-Hooper reading is far clearer than that by Stokes. They take the final word *soth* as Cornish, meaning "service", rather than the English word "sooth," which Stokes considered):

> pub er t[h]e *then* gura lewte.
> beva de*n* yonk bo de*n* coth
> or*th*aff ma*r* my*nn*yth cole.
> neffre gans an fals na soth (MC 175, 3-4)

> O man, at all times be just,
> whether young or in old age,
> and if my words you would trust,
> do not give false men your aid.

Christ reaches Golgatha, and that the removal of the clothes causes more bloodshed is another commonplace of medieval Passion poems, as is the stretching of Christ to fit the cross and the jolting received when the cross is raised. These latter points are part of the *jacente cruce* (rather than the *erecto cruce* alternative) tradition deriving ultimately perhaps from the Pseudo-Anselmian *Dialogue* (PL 159, 282f.)[21] Again both ideas are found in the *Northern Passion* and similar works. The stretching of Christ is developed in

---

[21]   See Pickering, "Gothic Image," p. 7f. and 14-18 and Foster, *Northern Passion*, II, 66.

fulfilment of the words of Psalm xxi, as is the idea voiced in stanza 183 that it was possible to count all Christ's bones. The addition of a formula like *scrifys yw in suredy* (MC 183,1), "for it is surely written" indicates awareness of the typological background, but the poet also introduces a generally devotional note into the whole section once again, urging meditation upon the pains of Christ to ensure right behaviour:

> lemmyn me ag*is* pys oll.
> a baynis c*ri*st p*r*edery
> ha na vo gesys *the* goll.
> ab lahys a rug *thy*nny (MC 182, 3-4)

> now I pray that you all must
> think well upon Christ's great pain,
> and that the laws he gave us
> should never be lost again.

Unlike the *Ordinalia*, the poem does not name the robbers crucified with Christ, although the words to the penitent thief are present. So indeed is the inscription over the cross (not always included as one of the symbols of the Passion), the division of the garments and the mockery of Christ by the Jews, including spitting at him on the cross. Some of these motifs are in fulfilment of prophecies and hence are usually present. One small additional point is the idea that the cross was erected at the side of the road, and thus the inscription is more visible (a general point made in other Passion-narratives, including the *Northern Passion* again).

The last moments of Christ are dealt with in less detail. Christ's commendation of John to the Virgin (John xx: 26) is there, as is the earthquake and the darkness. Christ's final words are not elaborated, as they are in texts such as the *Southern Passion*, and the vinegar and gall are interpreted as a further example of torture. The interesting motif that Christ was able to find no rest the cross is linked with Luke ix: 58 and the comment that Christ had nowhere to lay his head. The idea is again essentially a narrative point, and it occurs in the *Golden Legend*, as well as in its many vernacular offshoots, in an expanded version of the *Northern Passion* and also in the *Southern Passion*.

The composition of this part of the work is slightly problematic and it looks either as if the poet has ceased to follow a source directly or that the transmission is corrupt. Stanza 207 describes the death of Christ, but 208 stands out first of all for the fact that it adds a long-line, making it unique within the strophic pattern. The extra line does form part of the rhyme-scheme. The stanza contains the words of the Centurion (here as elsewhere named "Sentury") when he sees Christ, and this version seems slightly closer to the Luke than to Matthew in that Centurion only speaks, and he does so through awe, rather than fear (as Matthew xxvii: 54). In Luke xxiii: 48, however, just after the centurion has spoken, there is a reference to other witnesses, which may lie behind the last line, which otherwise looks like an afterthought, although it does have biblical authority. The stanza refers to the miracles at the time of Christ's last moments, and these have been mentioned already in stanza 200. That earlier stanza, however, has a weaker final line referring, after the earthquake and the darkness, to "other wonders." After the passage about "Sentury", the poet picks up the earthquake and the darkness, adding this time the rending of the veil of the temple, and he goes on in 210 to mention the breaking of the graves and the departure of their inhabitants to the city, clearly following Matthew xxvii: 53. This passage of the Gospels is frequently expanded in medieval vernacular writings, primarily narratives, of course, because in drama they would have to be reported.

The familiar harrowing of hell is followed rapidly by the binding of Lucifer and the release of Adam and Eve. In this instance, the *Northern Passion* is quite close (with Satan instead of Lucifer):

> Sathanas he bonde ful fast
> wyth stronge bondys þat wolden laste
> for he schulde be bounden Ay
> Tyl it were domys daye
> he vnbonde Adam & Eue
> And other mo that were hy*m* leue
> A non he ledde hem out of helle
> how many he lefte þer I can not telle

Citing this text (written in the southern midlands, probably in the fifteenth century), does not, of course, imply a direct relationship, which is unlikely, but the whole is a condensation once again of a well-known narrative, the immediate source of which cannot be pinpointed, but which goes back to the *Gospel of Nicodemus*.[22] Similar comments may be made of the next legend, that of Longinus, which will need to be dealt with at greater length in the context of the *Ordinalia*; here, however, the soldier (whose name is given as *Longis* - it varies, and "Longius" is common), is exonerated. He is blind, a familiar feature of the very legend, and acts apparently without being aware of what he is doing, a point made more clearly in the *Passio Christi*. Here the water and the blood restore his sight when he rubs his eyes, and his words underline the allegorical point of the legend:

---

[22]   Foster, *Northern Passion*, I, 212-4. The passage cited is from the manuscript in Cambridge University Library, Dd 1. 1, lines 1817-24. Other texts are somewhat different at this point.

Eddrek m*ur* an ke*m*eras.
rag an ob*er* re wresse
*th*y ben dowlyn y co*th*as.
arluth gevyans yn me*the*
dall en ny welyn yn fas.
ow bos m*ar* veyll ow pewe
Ih*es*us *thoth*o a avas.
pan welas y edrege (MC 220)

By great sorrow he was seized,
seeing the work he had done.
He fell down upon his knees
"O Lord," he said, "your pardon -
I was blind and could not see
how vile a race I had run!"
Jesus from sin set him free
when he saw his contrition.

Particularly striking in the poem, however, is the presentation of the sorrows of the Virgin, a passage which might have occasioned Scawen's comment about a work which contains "some inoffensive and harmless traditions, and a word may be let slip of the Virgin Mary." The reaction of the Virgin at the cross occupies six stanzas, and refers not only to her tears, but to the motif of an arrow striking her heart, causing her to weep tears of blood, something she does also in a number of other medieval works, part of the extensive tradition of the sorrows of the Virgin.[23] In the poem there is a careful parallelism between the piercing of Christ's side, which directly precedes this passage, and the piercing of the Virgin by an arrow of sorrow, which causes her to weep blood. The concluding stanza in this section (MC 226) stresses the role of the Virgin as *mygternas...yn nef*, "Queen of heaven" and stresses how the Son worships her. The entire section is echoed a little later (MC 231) when Mary assists at the deposition, giving us a visual pietà. The primary passage is followed by a further expressly devotional section, which affords a clue to the purpose of the work. The poet relates how

---

[23]   See Murdoch, "Literary Position," p. 835, and the studies on the topic by Andrew Breeze, with special reference to the Celtic literatures: "The Virgin's Tears of Blood," *Celtica* 20 (1988), 110-22; "The Blessed Virgin's Joys and Sorrows," *CMCS* 19 (Summer 1990), 41-54 and "The Virgin Mary, Daughter of her Son," *EC* 27 (1991), 1-17. There may be an echo of Luke ii: 35 (the *Nunc dimittis*; see also the use of the idea in the *Stabat mater* and elsewhere in the Marian tradition). Andrew Breeze has informed me in a letter of iconographical representations of the Virgin's tears, and her heart breaks in three places in the *ABC Poem on the Passion of Christ* in BL MS Harley 3954 edited by Frederick J. Furnivall, *Political, Religious and Love Poems* (London, 1866 = EETS/OS 15), p. 275.

Christ's body had 5,475 wounds, and then notes that the saying of fifteen Paternosters a day for a year will imitate this. Again the point is not unknown in the later Middle Ages,[24] though a specific source cannot be identified.

The story of the entombment follows John, but the poet returns to Matthew for the vigil of Mary Magdalene, here mentioned only, and for the incident in which the Jews demand a guard on the tomb (Matthew xxvii: 61-6). The actual narrative of the Resurrection also follows Matthew, although the details are not precisely as in the Gospel. The Cornish poet, unlike the Evangelist, permits us to see Christ rise from the dead, although the reference to the shining light in MC 243, 3b possibly echoes the description of the angel in Matthew xxviii: 3. Of particular interest here, however, is a further link with the *Ordinalia*. MC 243 contains the lines:

> ha Ihesus a *thetho*ras
> hag eth yn le may fynne
>
> and Jesus rose up again
> and went wherever he would.

This corresponds with a Latin stage direction in the *Resurrectio Domini* :

> Tunc surrexit Ihesus a mortuis et iet ubicunque uoluerit

The match is close, but a common liturgical source seems most likely, since there is no other verbal evidence of a close relationship with the third *Ordinalia* play. Indeed, an adaptation for dramatic purposes of Wipo's *Victimae paschali* (which is still used in the Roman rite just before the reading of Mark xvi on Easter Day and elsewhere) might even suggest itself, although it is not used in the Sarum missal at this point. In the *Ordinalia* it is the soldiers who wish to guard the tomb, but they do not propose flight when Christ is gone, nor is there evidence in the poem of the liturgical element which follows in the play, namely the singing by the angels of the *Christus resurgens* (Rom. vi: 9) as in the Sarum Easter liturgy and still used at other

---

[24]   Murdoch, "Literary Position," p. 830f. has a reference to a German example of the same point (ascribed in the sixteenth century to St Bernard). It is discussed in full by Andrew Breeze, "The Number of Christ's Wounds," *BBCS* 32 (1985), 84-91, with an addition in his "Postscripta," *BBCS* 35 (1988), 50f. Evans, *Medieval Religious Literature,* p. 43, speaks of 4,566 wounds.

points in the year.[25] A further dramatic insertion in the poem which matches the *Ordinalia*, albeit not precisely, is found in the reaction of the soldiers at finding the tomb empty. That they go eventually to the magistrates and tell them what has happened is biblical (Matthew xxviii: 11), but the preliminary debate about what to do is not. This expansion, however, is found regularly, and the same pattern (sleep, fear, consideration of flight, Pilate's bribe) is found in the various texts of the *Northern Passion*.

The visit of the Maries to the tomb is not entirely clear in the Gospels - whether it is just the Magdalene (as in John), or whether she is accompanied by one or more women, and indeed, who they are. The Cornish poem clearly follows Mark xvi, however, rather than John, since the Magdalene is not alone and it is already daylight (in John xx: 1 it is dark), and Mark provides support for the reading of the Cornish *tyr marea* as "three Maries", in spite of Keigwin and Stokes. The poem is in line with most dramatisations, including the third play of the *Ordinalia* and others; the York *Carpenters' Play* has *tres Marie*, and both the *Ordinalia* and the N-Town plays of the Resurrection name them as the Magdalene, Maria Jacobi and Maria Salome, as does the *Cursor mundi*, though other poems in English, such as the *Southern Passion*, speak of the Magdalene and *hure ffelawes tweye*.[26] The finding at the tomb of a young person dressed in white is from Mark, as is the injunction to find Peter and the meeting at Galilee.

This is, however, the end of the poem. The doubt of Thomas and the vision on the road to Emmaeus are absent, and the conclusion is more in line with the last verses of Matthew, although the narrative in objective terms is turned into something more homiletic, with an injunction to do good in the penultimate stanza, and then, in a stanza cited already, a final reference to Christ's resurrection as a pattern for man's resurrection at the last judgement. The opening of the poem, and especially the second stanza, which stresses the need to hear the Passion story for man's own salvation, is thus reiterated at the end, stressing the devotional point of the whole.

Pascon agan Arluth is not the same kind of work as the *Ordinalia*, although the source is naturally the same, and there is clearly some overlap not only in the verbal correspondences, but also in the use of individual extra-biblical motifs and in one case with the stage directions of the third play. The poem, though, is a narrative, with explanatory comments and additions, though all of the latter are intrinsic to the biblical structure. There are, of course, no

---

[25]   Stage direction at RD 423, Norris, II, 34. On the liturgical point, see R. Longsworth, *Ordinalia*, p. 106f., and Bakere, *Ordinalia*, p. 73. On the *Victimae paschali* and drama, see Adrian Fortescue, *The Mass* (London, 1955), p. 276f.

[26]   Keigwin/Gilbert and the main Stokes text seem to take *tyr* as an adjective meaning "beautiful" rather than the older form of the feminine of *try*: see Lewis, *Llawlyfr*, p. 24 (= 21.3). The citation is from Daw Brown, *Southern Passion*, p. 66, l. 1811.

torturers, messengers or other developed characters. It is simple work in narrative style - there are few source-comments, and those are vague. By and large, the text follows the Bible, though it adapts and selects, placing great emphasis on the suffering of Christ and indeed on that of the Virgin. Meditation on their sufferings is intended, but the work is one that implies hope for a lay audience in the ultimate stress on the necessity and purpose of such meditation for individual salvation. The Harley version of the *Northern Passion* in fact promises 100 days pardon for reading the text, and if our poem is less specific, the purpose of the work is the same.

CHAPTER THREE

SEEING AND BELIEVING: THE CORNISH *ORDINALIA*

The three plays known as the *Ordinalia* are the high point of medieval
Cornish literature, the point at which Cornish merges most fully into the
literature of medieval Europe. It is impossible to do justice to the three days
of play in a single chapter, and the best that can be hoped for is an indication
of their breadth and value in the context of other comparable medieval
dramas. Here, however, some preliminary statements need to be made. First,
the Cornish trilogy differs from the English cycles in several respects, and
although these, too, are now recognised as displaying more unity than was at
one time thought, the Cornish plays have a much clearer unifying factor in a
thoroughgoing christology that is unusually but extensively based, moreover,
on the apocryphal legend of the Holy Rood. Nor, secondly, is this the only
unusual theme. The Cornish trilogy develops incidents which do not appear
in the English cycles at all, or are rare, though they do have continental
parallels on some occasions: striking examples are in the presentation of the
adultery of David with Bathsheba, and later the death of Pilate and the story
of St Veronica.

There is only one manuscript of the *Ordinalia* (although there are several
later copies): MS Bodley 791, and presents the plays with Latin stage
directions in a hand of the fifteenth century.[1] The date of composition is
probably in the latter part of the fourteenth century, later than that of the
poem *Pascon agan Arluth*, which was known to our dramatist, since parts of
it are used in the second play. The play was composed, we may assume, in
the vicinity of Penryn: the researches of David Fowler and Jane Bakere have
demonstrated the association of the place-names mentioned with the area, and
although the few names in the Passion-play are *not* linked with Penryn, there
are sound reasons for this - in three cases they are formulaic and in the last
necessary for a rhyme.[2] The names in the other plays are all of land-grants

---

[1]   The number of copies of the Bodley MS 791 made at a later date has been
questioned. A. Hawke, "A Lost Manuscript of the Cornish *Ordinalia*," *CS* 7 (1979), 45-60,
describes copies with or without a translation by John Keigwin in the Bodleian (Bodley MSS
28556 and 28557, now Corn e 2 and 3) and in the National Library of Wales (Peniarth 428
and Llanstephan 91, both datable to around 1700; and NLW 21001). He considers unlikely
the possibility, expressed by Phyllis Harris in her Washington PhD thesis edition of the *Origo
Mundi*, of a further lost MS.

[2]   See Fowler, "Date," and Bakere, *Ordinalia*, pp. 12-49. On the names in the second
play, see my paper "The Place-names in the Cornish *Ordinalia*," *BBCS* 37 (1990), 116-8.

given to various characters, are frequently found in rhyme position, and have, in fact, no bearing on the substance of the plays. They serve to localise the work as a literary product (though not, of course, to set it anywhere but in Palestine or Rome) in Glasney/Penryn, and may help with the dating, although this is less sure.[3] As already noted, the central play of the trilogy, that of the Passion, owes a little to the slightly earlier poem, and as an illustration of continuity, a couple of hundred lines from the first play, the *Origo Mundi*, reappear in the later fragmentary drama *Gwreans an bys*.

The language, of course, is the principal difference from the English cycles. The Cornish of the *Ordinalia*, however, contains a certain amount of loan-words, and sometimes whole lines in English (as well as French and Latin), the most striking being the song of the three Maries at the tomb, which is an English couplet. In spite of attempts to discern a system in the use of English or anglicized Cornish, however, no such pattern seems to exist. The work is metrically more varied than the Passion-poem, with a preponderance of the eight or six-line strophe of seven-syllable lines, with (usually) two or three rhymes per strophe. There are also four-syllable lines. The six-line strophe rhyming *aabccb* predominates.[4]

A third difference between (all) the Cornish plays and their English equivalents lies in their production in an open-air amphitheatre (perhaps adapted from earlier earthworks), known as a round, in Cornish *plen-an-gwary*, of which two survive, one at St Just-in-Penwith and the other - Perran or Piran Round - near Perranporth. There is evidence for others. The illustration of Piran Round in William Borlase's *Natural History of Cornwall* in 1758 shows raised earth banks for spectators, openings, a central *platea* and a trench and pit, possibly for entrances. The surviving rounds are between 120 and 140 feet in diameter.

The manuscripts of the *Ordinalia* and of *Beunans Meriasek* include sketches of the layout for each day, as a circle with names around the periphery. There appear to have been platforms or raised scaffolding (stage directions refer to *sedes, pulpiti, tenti* and even *domus*) around the circle, linked with specific characters. The action presumably took place on different levels, and characters are referred to as "descending" into the main area. Other scenery is conjectural, though there is a chapel in the centre for the first day of *Meriasek*. The action must have shifted around the *platea* from the various platforms, especially when the plays have sharply contrasting episodes. All of the Cornish plays have complex and informative stage directions, those of the

---

[3]   Bakere, *Ordinalia*, p. 44 refers to the Carminow family (and their links to the Arundells), whose estates are mentioned, and who were prominent for a variety of reasons in the fourteenth century.

[4]   See on the distribution of stanzaic forms T. D. Crawford, "The Composition of the Cornish Ordinalia," *OC* 9 (1980), 146f.

Ordinalia in Latin, and we are given indication of action and props. All the Cornish plays have been performed in modern times, but as far as early performances go, speculation must be tempered with caution. As already noted, Richard Carew included in his 1602 *Survey of Cornwall* a much reprinted description of a play in which an unskilled actor repeats literally everything the prompter says. The joke is old, and need not even be taken at face value; certainly it need not be used as general evidence. The fact that the plays lasted several days, with the audience invited to drink or dance at the end of some of the individual days indicates, finally, that they must have had considerable significance as public events.[5]

The *Ordinalia* plays all have Latin titles and each of them is around three thousand lines in length, the central play being the longest: *Ordinale de origine mundi*, 2846 lines, *Passio Domini nostri Jhesu Christi*, 3242 lines and *Ordinale de resurrexione Domini nostri Jhesu Christi*, 2646.[6] Within the

---

[5]   A list of rounds is given in Evelyn S. Newlyn, *Cornish Drama of the Middle Ages* (Redruth, 1987), pp. 8-10 and Bakere, *Ordinalia* has a survey, pp. 26-30. Borlase's illustration is in R. Morton Nance, "The Plen an Gwary or Cornish Playing-Place," *JRIC* 24 (1935), 190-211 and Bakere, *Ordinalia*, p. 25. Richard Southern's *The Medieval Theatre in the Round* (London, 1957), argues for a wider use of rounds beyond (West) Cornwall, but ignores Piran Round on the dubious basis of Treve Holman, "Cornish Plays and Playing Places," *Theatre Notebook* 4 (1949/50), 52-4; see Natalie C. Schmitt, "Was There a Medieval theatre in the Round?" in: *Medieval English Drama*, ed. Jerome Taylor and Alan H. Nelson (Chicago and London, 1972), pp. 292-309. On techniques, see Neville Denny, "Arena Staging and Dramatic Quality in the Cornish Passion Play," in his *Medieval Drama* (London, 1973), pp. 124-54, and also the *Souvenir Programme* of the performance at Perran or Piran Round (July, 1969) with articles by Charles Thomas and by Denny. For interesting notes on Penryn, see P. R. Long, "New Light on the Mystery Play of Cornwall," *OC* 77/x (1972), 458f. Bakere, *Ordinalia*, p. 12f. cites Carew with a warning, as does George E. Wellwarth, "Methods of Production in the Medieval Cornish Drama," *Speech Monographs* 24 (1957), 212-28. Carew's comments are reprinted as an appendix in Paula Neuss' edition of *Gwreans an Bys*: CW, p. 239.

[6]   The edition cited is that of Edwin Norris, *The Ancient Cornish Drama* (Oxford, 1859, reprinted New York, 1968, with play-abbreviation and line-number. The edition of the *Origo Mundi* by Phyllis Harris is a dissertation, difficult to obtain and is of one play only. Note, however, that the modern Unified Cornish version, with translations, by R. M. Nance and A. S. D. Smith, revised by Graham Sandercock, has been published by the Cornish Language Board in attractive paperback volumes, and the Board had already reprinted several extracts originally published by the Federation of Old Cornwall Societies (Abraham and Isaac, David and Uriah, The Three Maries). A full prose translation was published by Markham Harris, *The Cornish Ordinalia* (Washington D.C., 1969). Interestingly, F. E. Halliday published a translation into English free verse of a shortened version of the central thematic element, *The Legend of the Rood* (London, 1955), adding the scene with the Three Maries and also the Death of Pilate. The latter episode is also included in a verse adaptation (from Norris), which owes little to the Cornish original and seems to omit lines at will, in John Gassner, *Medieval and Tudor Drama* (New York, 1963), pp. 188-203, though it is there in a more acceptable form in A. C. Cawley, *Everyman and Medieval Miracle Plays* (London, 1956), pp. 234-63.

individual plays, however, subheadings occur, and the Latin stage directions vary in force, ranging from the opening of the Abraham section, which is indicated simply by the presentation of a new character: *hic pompabit Abraham* (SD, OM 1259), meaning little more than "enter Abraham," to a thematic statement like *Hic incipit de noe et nave* (SD, OM 917), which might mean "the beginning of the Noah episode." In the last play there is, finally, what looks like a firmer division into three, when, after an opening *Hic incipit ordinale de resurrexione...* the first section ends *et sic finitur resurreccio domini*, followed closely by: *et incipit morte pilati* (SD at RD 1588). The last part closes the *Mors Pilati* in the same way, following it with *et incipit ascencio...* And yet even in these cases we are not faced with separate plays which have been thrown together. The sections interact and balance each other, as they also echo parts in the other plays. In the same way, the three plays of the *Ordinalia* as a whole balance one another in the move from the fall of man to the triumphal return of Christ, the new Adam, the legend of the Rood linking the whole trilogy. There is a danger in the evaluation of medieval plays of stressing the disparity of individual elements, but the notion of dramatists "eking out" their work by the gratuitous inclusion of extraneous interludes has been applied to the *Ordinalia* (as also to *Beunans Meriasek*) in the past, and it stems in part from a failure to recognise connexions which might be liturgical or typological rather than simply narrative. Indeed, attempts have been made to separate out sections of the plays on poetic grounds, as when Nance attempted to extrapolate a "far shorter religious poem" from the Passion by taking the lamentations of the Virgin and reassembling them outside the work. Ruth Harvey reminded us in 1980 precisely in the context of medieval drama, that "evocations of the Bible story...were not designed to arouse the passions or induce self-identification except in certain very limited areas such as the lament of the Virgin over the body of her son in the passion plays..." All that may be taken from Nance's idea is that the plays contain striking lyrical passages.[7]

The plays are sometimes referred to as "the Cornish Corpus Christi plays," and the (summertime) feast of Corpus Christi, which became popular in the fourteenth century, has been associated with the emergence of popular drama. Alternatives performance times include the minor Rogation days before the feast of the Ascension, but there are strong arguments for the association with Corpus Christi, even if the two factors of liturgical appropriateness and fine

---

[7]   R. M. Nance, "A Cornish Poem Restored," *OC* 4 (1943-51), 368-70. Harvey's comments were made in a lecture given to the Sir Robert Taylor Society in Oxford just before her death and published as a memorial: *Studying Medieval Literature Today* (n.d., n.p. [1980]), p. 10. See also C. Fudge, "Aspects of Form in the Cornish *Ordinalia*," *OC* 8 (1973-9), 457-64 and 491-8.

weather for an outdoor performance that would not interfere with agricultural activity make either alternative possible.

The theme of the cycle is the divine economy of history, the *felix culpa* of a fall by means of a tree which was redeemed by the tree of the cross. The major source is, of course, the Bible, while the selection of a particular motif or the emphasis placed upon it might also echo the liturgy. Next comes the legend cycle of the Rood, but a single text is difficult to identify. The dramatisation of the Holy Rood legends is unique in England; none of the English drama cycles has it, although it is used in continental drama (not, admittedly as a large-scale structuring element) such as the *Mistére du Viel Testament* in French, and in the Paradise play of Arnold Immessen and slightly earlier in the *Redentiner Passion*, both in Low German.[8] The Middle Ages knew a range of apocrypha quite unfamiliar to us, which expand and develop material from the Old and New Testaments. Thus a whole series of incidents relating to Adam and Eve after the fall exist in an amorphous collection in a variety of languages, but known in Latin from the fourth century under the title of the *Vita Adae et Evae*. At the death of Adam, Eve and Seth visit Paradise and are given the twigs that will grow into the Holy Rood. Although this precise legend was not known to the writer of the *Ordinalia*, he clearly knew well a related, but later, twelfth-century sequence of legends which trace the Holy Rood from Adam to Christ. These also begin with Adam, and Latin versions are sometimes known by the opening words *Post peccatum Adae*. Seth goes alone to Paradise this time, and receives the seeds of the cross; the history is then traced through Moses, David, Solomon and so on. A rather different sequence of cross-legends involving the history from Moses to St Helena is known as well, as are legends associated with its defence and preservation. A single source (even if there was one specific text) is unlikely to present itself, but we may refer to a basic form of the *Post peccatum* Sethite story which appears in Latin and many Western European vernaculars, and was referred to as the *Legende* by its principal editor, Wilhelm Meyer. For a variety of reasons, however, it seems likely that the dramatist knew the legend in English, rather than Latin (or for that matter Welsh or French); English terms are used for specific points (oil of mercy,

---

[8]   The importance of this ramified tradition should not be underestimated. See Esther C. Quinn, *The Quest of Seth for the Oil of Life* (Chicago, 1962), with the standard edition still that of Wilhelm Meyer, "Die Geschichte des Kreuzholzes vor Christus," *Abhandlungen der Bayerischen Akademie der Wissenschaften*, phil. Kl. 16/ii (1882), 101-66. See for insular material J. R. Mozley, "A New Text of the Story of the Cross," *Journal of Theological Studies* 31 (1930), 113-27 and Betty Hill, "The Fifteenth-Century Prose Legend of the Cross Before Christ," *Medium Aevum* 34 (1965), 203-22. English texts are in Richard Morris, *Legends of the Holy Rood* (London, 1881 = EETS/OS 46) and Arthur S. Napier, *History of the Holy Rood Tree* (London, 1894 = EETS/OS 103). See also Hans-Martin von Erffa, *Ikonologie der Genesis I* (Stuttgart, 1989), pp. 400-413.

Mount Tabor and others), and the same is true, in fact, of other legends used by the dramatist later on, including that of Pilate's death.

A second apocryphal text that requires mention here is the so-called *Gospel of Nicodemus*, also known as the *Acts of Pilate*, once again a text with no definite version. The work combines the story of the Passion with the harrowing of hell, and it exists in a variety of Latin and other versions. The harrowing of hell portion contains a variation of Seth's journey, but not the later history of the Rood. The *Ordinalia* contains elements from this work as well, and it is followed in some detail in the first part of the final play, as it is in works in English, Anglo-Norman and French. A further legend known in the Middle Ages is that of the death of Pilate, which exists as a separate work in various forms, though M. R. James claimed that it "hardly ranks as an apocryphal book." Even more circumscribed, finally, is the story of the smith and the nails, a pious legend again found independently. Many of these tales appear in the standard handbooks of the middle ages, such as the *Golden Legend*, or in the *Historia Scholastica* of Peter Comestor. Actual source study is rarely possible, and often the best that can be done is to indicate the widespread nature of a motif. On the other hand, there are incidents that cannot be identified, such as the crying out of the earth when Adam begins to cut the soil, and his bargaining over land after the expulsion. A few extra-biblical motifs familiar in all kinds of medieval works, including dramas, are, however, *not* present, such as the fall of the angels, although there is an indication that it may have been there earlier: an otherwise ineffective stage-direction refers to an apparent entrance by Lucifer shortly after God's creation of the world. But it is by no means necessary to assume that this was the reason. The devil gives an explanation for his jealousy of Adam and Eve later.

The first play, the *Origo Mundi* is dominated by two things: the fall and subsequent sinfulness of man, and the early history of the cross, which incorporates the promise of salvation. The world is created by God as *trinitas creator*, a familiar motif for the creation of the world as a whole and for both Adam and Eve (where it is reiterated).[9] God the Father's opening speech, in ten strophes of eight lines, concludes with a four-liner containing the prohibition regarding the Tree of Life. In accordance with the first chapter of Genesis, Eve is created just before the creation and naming of the beasts, which are then placed in the charge of the protoplasts. The dramatist takes into the narrative of Genesis i at this point a few elements of the alternative version of the creation of Eve in Genesis ii. The trinitarian creation of Adam is attached as usual to the first version of the creation of man, and only the notions of Eve being made from one of the ribs of Adam, her name, and the

---

9   The idea is there is *Pascon agan Arluth*. See F. P. Pickering, "*Trinitas Creator*: Word and Image," *Reading Medieval Studies* 2 (1976), 77-90.

naming the animals have been taken from Gen. ii. It is here stressed that Eve, too, shares the image of God. The position of the creation of Eve and the fact that Adam has not only beasts and birds, but also fish to name, derive from Gen i: 28. Unlike the version in the second chapter of Genesis, Adam is given command of the animal world, which he affirms in Cornish (OM 137).[10] The actual naming of (a few domestic) beasts is unusual in such an early play, although it is found *in extenso* in at least one later continental version.[11]

The fall of man is dealt with relatively quickly. Motifs which are developed elsewhere are here passed over without comment, such as the role of the devil as serpent. A stage-direction tells us simply that *diabolus tanquam serpens loquitur ad euam*, and he is designated first *serpens sive demon* and then just *demon* in the indications of speakers. No indication is given, as it is in later works such as *Gwreans an bys,* that he is anything but serpentine in appearance. He does, however, speak wickedly (*male*) to Eve, and his blandishments to the woman are well done. He assures her (with some irony) that he comes from heaven (OM 165) - after the deed she refers to him as an angel - and he does not mention the fruit at once. Instead he teases her with the promise of information that would delight her, leading her to declare that, whatever it is, she will not be angry with him when she hears it. This has the effect of putting her in the wrong when she *does* hear - and initially reject - his proposal. By a mixture of cajolery and attack, and with hints that God is preserving knowledge selfishly, the devil causes Eve to sway, and then suddenly - as in the French *Mystère d'Adam*[12] -hurries her:

> torr'e yn ow feryl vy
> heb hokye fast haue ydo
> hag inweth gvra the'th worty
> may tebro ef annotho (OM 197-200)

> You can put the blame on me,
> but be quick! Without ado,
> go to your husband, and he
> can then eat some of it, too.

---

[10]   There is no reason to assume, as Newlyn, "Pit and Pedestal", p. 130 does, that this description of the creation places Eve under Adam's control. In fact she is Adam's equal, a point made by God (OM 101), and she states herself that she too has the image of the triune God (OM 405-10). There is in fact more emphasis on Eve's equality than is found in either biblical chapter.

[11]   See my "Jacob Ruf's *Adam und Heva,*" *Modern Language Review* 86 (1991), 109-25, with a briefer note in "The Breton *Creation Ar Bet,*" *Zeitschrift für celtische Philologie* 36 (1977), 167. See also v. Erffa, *Ikonologie*, pp. 139-45

[12]   See Erich Auerbach's famous analysis, *Mimesis*, trans. Willard Trask (New York, 1957), pp. 124-51

Where in the French play the devil actually gives her the fruit, here Eve asks the devil to bend the branch towards her, and thus there is a gradual movement towards complicity with the devil on Eve's part. We have to assume that the stage direction *accipiet pomum* means that she eats the fruit, but this is not clear; at all events, on the prompting of the devil, she urges Adam to eat, giving him a version of events which does not correspond to what has actually happened:

> My pan esen ov quandre
> clewys a'n nyl tenewen
> vn el ov talleth cane
> a vghaf war an wethen (OM 213-6)

> Just now I was wandering,
> and there the sound came to me:
> an angel began to sing
> up above me, on the tree.

Eve claims that the supposed angel (a motif that occurs also in the N-Town play of the Fall) told her that they would be like God (although OM 219 has been amended to read "like gods", in accordance with the Bible). Adam refuses to eat, even when Eve reiterates her assurance that it was an angel. This forces Eve's hand, so that suddenly she has to threaten Adam with the loss of her love - a motif found elsewhere - if he continues to refuse; she augments this by saying that Adam will never see her again, and he at once capitulates, realising immediately what he has done.[13] The punishment of the protoplasts again closely follows the Bible, although Eve's request that God kill the serpent is neither canonical nor known in the various apocryphal versions. The most interesting variation, however, is the curse on the serpent, whose identity with the devil is stressed by the fact that although God ostensibly addresses the snake, the devil is present: a stage direction tells us

---

[13]   The devil in angelic disguise is not uncommon. He adopts this guise in the second temptation of Eve (after the expulsion) in the Adambooks, and there is a hint of it at the time of the fall itself in the Greek analogue to the *Vita Adae*. In the N-Town play, the serpent is described by Eve to Adam as a "ffayr Aungell, and in the judgement scene Eve refers to "A werm with An Aungelys face:" see Rosemary Woolf, "The Fall of Man in *Genesis B* and the *Mystère d'Adam*," *Festschrift for Arthur G. Brodeur* (Eugene, Oreg., 1963), p. 198f., with reference to our play. But it is not true, as Woolf seems to imply, that the devil here "disguises himself as an angel of light;" Eve merely *says* he did, and not even in those terms. There is no evidence that the *Vita Adae* was known to the dramatist in any case, and the matter is handled rather differently in *Gwreans an bys*. On the "chivalric Adam," see J. M. Evans, *"Paradise Lost" and the Genesis Tradition* (Oxford, 1968), p. 203f. and Newlyn, "Pit," p. 134f., who notes the difference in motivation of the protoplasts in eating the fruit.

hic demon sit presens. It is the devil who answers, even though the curse is the biblical one upon the serpent. The devil, however, explains his deed, which requires a certain amount of background knowledge, since the play does not contain a detailed fall of the angels:

> My a leuer thy's an cas
> rag bos thethe ioy mar vras
> ha my pup vr ow lesky
> rag henna my a's temptyas
> the behe may fe ellas
> aga han kepar ha my. (OM 305-10)

> I'll tell you why - it is this:
> because they enjoyed such bliss
> while I must burn for all time.
> So I tempted them forthwith
> to sin. Now "alas, alas"
> is their song, as it is mine.

The protoplasts are expelled from paradise, but although Adam has heard the judgement of damnation for a thousand generations to come (and it is interesting that God specifically precludes Adam from blaming the whole thing on his wife), he asks nevertheless for the oil of mercy. This is the first indication of the legend of the Rood and the quest of Seth for the oil of mercy, instead of which he receives a promise of salvation and the seeds. It is not unusual in Paradise plays for Adam to be given a promise of the redemption even at the time of the fall: this is entirely in accord with the customary exegesis of Gen. iii: 15, the so-called *protevangelium*. The reference to the oil of mercy is in English, which may be a source indication. Similar references are made in the same place in the Middle English verse *Cursor mundi*, the use of the Rood legends in which is similar to our play.[14] In the *Ordinalia* God does indeed promise the oil of mercy at the end of the world both to Adam and also specifically to Eve: the equality of the two is stressed.

The immediate effect of the expulsion is of considerable interest within the context of the drama of Adam and Eve. The protoplasts leave paradise to delve and spin, but at Adam's first attempt at tilling the soil, the earth itself

---

[14]   See the edition by Richard Morris of the widespread Northern work of the early fourteenth century, *Cursor Mundi* (London, 1874-93 = EETS/OS 57-68), I, 63f. (vv. 955) and I, 78-91 (vv 1237-1432) for the Sethite story. The *Cursor* also stresses tithing (I, 64f., v. 976) and includes a *locus amoenus* description of Paradise rather longer than Seth's in our play (I, 66-9, vv. 999-1044).

cries out and will not allow him to dig until God commands it. The origins of this motif are unclear. In the *Vita Adae* tradition, the archangel Michael is sent to show Adam the rudiments of agriculture, but an active role for the earth is known otherwise only when it cries out at the death of Abel (the verb *clamat* is used in the Vulgate, as in the Cornish stage-direction). This hardly provides a close parallel to the motif here, however, which may be simply a concretisation of God's promise of the difficulties Adam will have to face. The motif-complex is continued with another new motif, namely Adam's bargain with God about the amount of earth he can till. He is given first of all a spade's length, then two, arguing that he will need more land to nourish his putative family. Adam's pleading with God is both cunning and comical, and eventually God gives in and tells him to take all he needs. In other vernacular Genesis-adaptations the goodness of God in giving Adam the whole world for his use is stressed, but that Adam bargains for it is unusual. One wonders if there is a hint here of the variant (and large) Cornish acre?[15]

The third significant element in this section of the work continues throughout the Noah section as well: the need for tithing and sacrifice. Prior to the Cain story, God demands of Adam a tithe and a sacrifice, and this links not only with the ensuing story of the fratricide, but also with the end of the story of Noah, when the altar of sacrifice is again invoked. God declares:

> Adam a ol the drevas
> an degves ran thy'mmo gas
> wheth in atal the kesky
> ha gans colen tha hep sor
> gorre the'n meneth tabor
> yn gorthyans thy'm th'y lesky (OM 425-30)

> Adam, of your harvesting,
> one-tenth for me you should bring.
> That I do require of you.
> With good heart and mind, therefore,
> burn it upon Mount Tabor.
> This honour to me is due.

The reference to Tabor is unbiblical. Later in the work, however, Moses plants the rods or twigs that will grow into the cross on Mount Tabor in accordance with the Holy Rood tradition, and presumably this gave the idea of Tabor (here in rhyme position following the formula *hep sor*, "without ill-

---

[15]   Sometimes as large as 64 midland acres: Frank Barlow, *The Feudal Kingdom of England 1042-1216*, 3. ed. (London and New York, 1972), p. 22, and see F. W. Maitland, *Domesday Book and Beyond* (Cambridge, 1907), pp. 362-99.

will") as a place of sacrifice. The *Golden Legend* notes that Adam taught his sons about sacrifice, although it does not mention the place.[16]   What is crucial here, of course, is simply the fact of the tithe and the insistence on sacrifice as due to God.

The movement into the Cain and Abel narrative is thus smoothly effected, and here, too, the dramatist expands upon the biblical text. Most effective is the request by Abel for his parents' blessing, and the refusal of Cain to do likewise. Cain, however, is in essence a rationalist, unable to see the point of the offering at all. This makes a theological point in contrasting Abel, who accepts the will of God as including the demand for such works, with Cain, who rejects the sacrifice. Abel reiterates the notion of the tithe (*dege*) on several occasions. Cain decides to offer only a part of the full tithe (*cayn offerat partem decimarum*, SD at OM 499), claiming it to be the full amount in his invocation to "God the Father, full of pity" (*a das dew luen a byte*, OM 502), but he adds, presumably for his own benefit:

> hay dew myr orth ov offryn
> ha ressef thy's ov dege
> rag mar ny wreth my a vyn
> y thon genef arte dre.   (OM 505-8)

> Now God, see my offering,
>   and take your tithe of it then!
> If you don't, well, then I'll bring
>   it all home with me again!

God accepts only Abel's true tithe. The moral and social implications (possibly with respect to the support of Glasney College itself)[17] for the audience are clear in all of this. Cain becomes angry with Abel and kills him, by striking him on the jaw (possibly an echo of the notion that Cain kills Abel *with* a jawbone). The stage directions call for Abel to be struck simply on the

---

[16]   Longsworth, *Ordinalia*, p. 38 comments on the mention of Tabor, but does not make the connexion with the Holy Rood. OM 427 is obscure and no claims are made for the version offered. Markham Harris, in the notes to his translation, p. 252, is also worried about the real location of Mount Tabor, which occurs several times later in the play and is located in Arabia. But for the dramatist it is merely a name, and the source is clearly the Holy Rood legends. It is referred to once, furthermore, as *Mount Tabor*, indicating perhaps an English-language source.

[17]   On tithing (and on the objections to it), see for example Morris Bishop, *The Penguin Book of the Middle Ages* (Harmondsworth, 1971), 203f., and G. G. Coulton, *Ten Medieval Studies* (Cambridge, 1906). Whetter, *Glasney College*, pp. 81-92 is extremely informative on the economic implications of various types of tithe for Glasney College.

head, and the weapon varies in medieval writing.[18]   Abel is then taken off
to hell by Lucifer and his associates, the first appearance of the devils.

God questions Cain, and in a curious addition, the substance of God's
image in Gen. iv: 10, that the blood of Abel is crying out, is made real in the
stage direction.   Cain despairs, and if this is developed considerably in
Gwreans an bys, here, too, he declares that his sin is too great for mercy, and
falls into the sin of *desperatio*. Cain is marked (we do not know what the
mark is), and left to face Adam, who curses him and his own fate, declaring
that he will never lie with Eve again, a motif once again from the Holy Rood
legends Eve, too, weeps tears of blood,[19] but an angel persuades Adam to
return to Eve, and Seth is born.

This leads into the Holy Rood story proper.   Seth is sent to Paradise,
following the withered footprints which burned the earth as the protoplasts left
in shame - an idea found not only in the Holy Rood legends, but as an
independent motif[20] - and he sees on the instigation of the guardian cherub
not only the fountains of paradise, but a tree that is dry in the upper part. The
roots reach down to hell, and there is a serpent in the tree. Looking for a
third time, Seth sees a child in the upper part, which the cherub tells him is
the Son of God, who is also the oil of mercy promised to Adam and Eve. He
is then given three seeds to place under the tongue of the dead Adam, which
will grow into the Rood. On Adam's death, Seth carries out the demands of
the angel, but again an interpolated passage shows us the devils dragging
Adam's soul to hell to join that of Abel.

The story of Noah is not in the Holy Rood legend, and is here told
noticeably briefly, with only minor non-biblical additions (the ark is covered
with cloth, presumably reflecting the stage practice, and the children of Noah
take food on board). No indication is given of the increasing wickedness of
man - this is simply stated by God. Nor, in contrast with some of the English
plays, is much made of Noah's wife, who agrees to do all Noah wishes. The
raven and the dove incident is included (with the exegetical commonplace that
the raven stays because it feeds upon corpses). More striking than the flood
is the extended sacrifice at the end. Biblically an altar is set up where the ark
lands, at Ararat (in the Old Latin version in Armenia), but here it is at
Calvary. This is connected with the legend, part of the Rood cycle, that

[18]   See M. D. Anderson, *Drama and Imagery in British Churches* (Cambridge, 1963),
p. 144f. and J. K. Bonnell, "Cain's Jaw Bone," *PMLA* 39 (1924), 140-6.
[19]   See Breeze, "Tears of Blood;" both Eve and the Virgin weep tears of blood, but a
typological parallelism of Abel and Christ which might link the two women is not present,
though.
[20]   Kari Sajavaara, "The Withered Footprints on the Green Street of Paradise,"
Neuphilologische Mitteilungen 76 (1975), 34-8, and in Welsh, see J. Jenkins, "Medieval
Welsh Scriptures, Religious Legends and Midrash," *Transactions of the Honourable Society
of Cymmrodorion* 1919/20, p. 130f.

Adam's grave was on Golgatha, the skull implied in the Hebrew name being his. In apocrypha writings, Adam's body is sometimes taken onto the ark, and depictions of the crucifixion often show a skull beneath the cross, sometimes with the blood of Christ flowing into the mouth in symbolism of the eucharist. Stress is laid here, however, on the matter of tithing once again, and specific offerings are made.

The story of Abraham and Isaac (also absent from the Holy Rood legend) is included here as a typological parallel to the crucifixion (the sacrifice of the son, who carries the wood on which he will be sacrificed to a hilltop), again a medieval commonplace, and familiar in the liturgy.[21] The text follows the biblical narrative closely, but two points may be mentioned. First, Abraham submits to the divine will in what is for the play a new verse-form, a four-syllable, ten-line strophe (arranged in the manuscript as six lines):

> dynythys of . the'th volungeth
> arluth porth cof . yn deyth dyweth
>   am enef vy
> lauar thy'mmo . pandra wrama
> y'n guraf ytho . scon yn tor-ma
>   yn pur deffry   (OM 1271-6)

> I come as called . thy will be done.
> Remember, Lord . when time is gone,
>   my own soul's rest.
> What I must do . you need but say.
> I'll do it true, without delay
>   in earnestness.

A second non-biblical addition (which is in accord with the typological implications), is that Isaac accepts his role in the sacrifice, just as in, for example, the Brome *Abraham and Isaac*. In our play, Isaac asks to be bound firmly so that he will not flinch from martyrdom, but the sorrow of Abraham is not developed as it is in the Brome play, nor is the pathos of Isaac as striking as in the Chester plays, where he asks for his eyes to be bound. The angel of Genesis is here interpreted, again with typological implications, as Gabriel. The passage concludes with the actual sacrifice of the ram, with both Isaac and Abraham using the short-line verse form.

---

[21]   See Longsworth, *Ordinalia*, p. 41f. and Bakere, *Ordinalia*, p. 54f. On the dramatisations, see John R. Elliott, "The Sacrifice of Isaac as Comedy and Tragedy," in: *Medieval English Drama*, ed. J. Taylor and A. H. Nelson (Chicago, 1972), pp. 157-76. The Brome play is in the EETS edition of *The Non-Cycle Mystery Plays and Fragments*, ed. N. Davis (London, 1970).

The entry of Moses returns us to the Holy Rood legend, but we are also shown earlier incidents in his life: the burning bush, the rod and the serpent and his ultimate submission to the will of God in confronting Pharaoh. Pharoah is drawn in lively fashion as he dismisses Aaron, and the sound-patterns are noteworthy:

> out warnas harlot pen cok
> scon yn mes quyk a'm golok
>   na tryk y'm cur
> mar a'th caffaf re iovyn
> y'th lathaf kyns ys vyttyn
> a'm dew luef sur (OM 1529-34)

> Out, you whoreson fool, I say!
> Out of my sight straight away,
>   leave me alone!
> By Jupiter! If you still
> remain by morning, I'll kill
>   you on my own!

Aaron and Moses recognise that words will not sway him, and what ensues is a very contracted version of the plagues, which cause Pharaoh to expel the Jews. After they leave, he pursues them, and once again it is Gabriel who instructs Moses how to cross the Red Sea. How the drowning of Pharaoh's army was presented - there is more detail here than in, say, the York version - is unclear. Details of the death of Pharaoh *are* found in the Holy Rood legends, however, and then Moses finds on a mountain (usually it is in Hebron, where Adam was buried) the three rods which have grown from the seeds given to Seth. He notes their savour and blesses them as an expression of the Trinity. All this is in the *Legende*, as is the soteriological point of the sick kissing them and being healed. Prose versions normally refer to their efficacy is healing venomous bites (one of the trees involved is cedar, which traditionally repels snakes), and here we are shown incidents illustrating the point. Just before he dies, Moses plants the rods on Mount Tabor.

In the *Legende* the next scene is the discovery of the rods by David. In the play, however, we have first of all an unusual and comic scene between David and his butler, with the latter using a line of French when he brings David the wine the king had asked for. David sleeps, and Gabriel brings a dream of the rods, spelling out (again following the Holy Rood material) that they will eventually become the instrument of salvation. He finds them, rejoices, and uses them at once to heal the blind, the lame and the deaf, encircling them eventually with a silver fence. This and the healing miracles, which clearly prefigure the acts of Christ, are in the source. The dramatist now moves from the Holy Rood legends to make an addition in which David places the butler and a companion on guard over the rods. The latter again has a comic speech, assuring his companion that he will keep watch effectively, and adding that he would be able to provide a woman for his companion if he wants one. The passage has formulaic elements found elsewhere in Cornish drama, echoing even the *Charter Fragment*, and although it looks at first glance like simple comic relief with a touch of bawdry, it introduces the story of David and Bathsheba. This relatively rare episode is treated in none of the English cycles, for all its dramatic promise, probably on account of moral difficulties.[22] In the Holy Rood story it is mentioned in passing as David's "great sin" (*peccatum grave* in the Latin texts), which causes him to write the penitential Psalm lvi, *Miserere mei, Deus*. In contrast with another medieval version, that of the *Mistére du Viel Testament*, which follows the Bible closely, there are some striking departures here from the narrative of Reg. xi and xii. The Bible incident contains a number of key points: David's lust at the woman bathing; the immediate conception of a child; the attempt to cover the offence when Uriah returns; the strategy of using the Hittite to carry his own death-warrant; Bathsheba's mourning for Uriah; and the condemnation by Nathan. Some of the adaptation is clearly for economic reasons: thus Joab is omitted to save a character. But the replacement of Nathan by Gabriel in condemning the king is in line with the role played by Gabriel throughout, and makes the message to David from God the clearer. The irony of the letter was perhaps too complex to make clear in a play like the *Origo Mundi*, and accordingly it is omitted. Instead, David himself urges Uriah to be brave and fight in the forefront of battle, which makes the king's treachery seem worse.

Bathsheba is developed, however, although it needs to be stressed that she only has four speeches, two to David and two to her husband, a total of under thirty lines. First of all she is seen washing garments rather than herself, doubtless for performance reasons. Her compliance with David's invitation, however, is intensified by being put into words, and if there is no mention here of her pregnancy, she is clearly made into a negative character by her explicit rejection of her husband, and by the fact that she puts into David's head the idea that Uriah might be killed. David agrees to this, and Bathsheba reinforces the point with an abrupt

ov arluth whek ol lathe (OM 2131)

My lord and sweet love, kill him.

---

22   See Inga-Stina Ewbank, "The House of David in Renaissance Drama," *Renaissance Drama* 8 (1965), 3-40. Peele's *David and Bethsabe* is too late to be of special relevance to our play, even in comparative terms. See on the characterisation Newlyn, "Pit and Pedestal" p. 126f. and Nance's introduction to the separate edition, which he called "Davyd hag Urry."

When Uriah actually leaves, however, having asked for a blessing from David (which is hypocritically given), Bathsheba has two further speeches. She expresses her sadness at the departure of her husband (who calls her his 'faithful spouse') in an eight-line strophe which betrays none of her guilt, and he asks her to pray for him. The passage in which she agrees to do so is, however, somewhat difficult. In a six-line strophe which she speaks after she has left her husband (thus the stage directions), she first of all complains at the loss of her sweet lord (*arluth whek*, the term she has used for David), but then she says that she will pray that Uriah never returns.[23] The motivation for this gratuitous malice is unclear. It is not biblical - there Bathsheba mourns the death of the Hittite - and she has no further part in the play. Instead, Gabriel comes to David and puts to him the parable of the rich man and the poor man that Nathan tells in the Bible. David's judgement on the hypothetical thief (which is, of course, himself), is expressed here in a different verse form, and when the point becomes clear he sits beneath the Tree of Knowledge (thus the stage directions), and composes the Psalter. The Holy Rood legends mention only Psalm lvi at this point, but the stage directions refer to the *psalterium* and cite the first Psalm, *Beatus vir*.The *Legende* does go on to say that David composed the whole Psalter, but the link between David (who is also a type of Christ), the cross (and the tree of paradise) and Psalm i is found elsewhere.[24] In spite of the fact that the Psalm does not match the legends, David does after this incident ask his counsellor (who represents Nathan, perhaps), to teach him a penitential hymn, although instead he is given the task of building the temple. The incident with Bathsheba is used here, as elsewhere, to make the point that even the righteous are prey to sin. We may note, finally, that the lascivious butler, whom we saw promising a girl to his companion, is reported to have fallen with Uriah.

David initiates the building of the temple (rewarding the builders with land-grants naming manors near Penryn, whose great tithes, as Jane Bakere has pointed out, belonged to Glasney). The play follows the Holy Rood material in having God indicate to David that for his sins it is his son, Solomon, who will complete the temple, although neither play nor legend mention that Solomon is the son of Bathsheba. Solomon and his workmen (who include

---

[23]   The text is not clear. Norris translated it to read as if she would pray for his return (there is confusion between "ever" and "never"). However, even the verbal parallel he cites seems to mean "never," and other translators have taken the passage to mean that Bathsheba prays that he will *not* come back. This makes her earlier speech thoroughly hypocritical as well, of course.

[24]   On David as Christ, see H. Steger, *David rex et propheta* (Nuremberg, 1961). On the links between David, Christ and the cross, see also Jennifer O'Reilly, *Studies in the Iconography of the Virtues and Vices in the Middle Ages* (New York and London, 1988), esp. p. 345.

what Markham Harris calls a "stock...bibulous Welshman" named Griffin) continue the work, and Solomon, too, rewards the masons and carpenters with (the great tithes from) land in Cornwall, on one occasion an entire parish, Budock (*plu vuthek*, OM 2463).[25] The workmen eventually cut the Rood as the last beam, only to discover that it will fit nowhere, and seems to change its dimensions, until it is placed in the temple.

Solomon consecrates a bishop to look after the temple, and this is his last substantive act in the play, apart from his pronouncement of the epilogue to the first day's action, and the whole first play concludes with another striking element - almost the last - from the Holy Rood legend, the episode of Maximilla (her name varies a little). Here as in the legend, she enters the temple and sits on the wood, causing her clothes to burst into flames, at which she calls on the name of Christ, for which she is martyred as a blasphemer. The stage directions echo the Latin version to an extent, although there are English overtones as well.[26] What matters, of course, is Maximilla's prophecy, recalling the original comments on the rods as a symbol of the Trinity; David's act of joining them so that they grow together underlines this. The stanza is added later in the Bodley manuscript, though this is unlikely to be significant:

> onan yw an tas a neff
> arall crist y vn vaaw eff
> a vyth a wyrghas genys
> ha'n sperys sans yw tressa
> try hag onan ow trega
> yn vn dewsys me a grys (OM 2661-6)

> Our Father above is one;
> another is Christ, His son,
> who will be born of a maid.
> The Holy Ghost makes one more,
> three in one, of that I'm sure,
> dwelling in the one Godhead.

Condemned for blasphemy, on the grounds that there is no-one called Christ in the law of Moses, Maximilla gives occasion for the first appearance of a

---

[25]   See Bakere, *Ordinalia*, p. 37f. for an interesting discussion of the meaning of *Carrek Ruan*.

[26]   *Concremantur*, "they are set on fire" echoes the Latin versions, but *stuppa*, which can mean "stove" (as Norris translates) but also -- as *stupa* -- flax, hemp, tow, is used in the Latin as an image. Maximilla sits on the wood (*super lignum*) and begins to burn like tow (*ut stupe*). The OM stage direction is confused.

group of torturers or executioners in surviving Cornish drama. Urged on by the bishop (who on one occasion has a line of French) and his crozier-bearer, the torturers take enormous and sadistic delight in telling the audience what they are about to do to Maximilla. The language is distinctive (in one stanza the rhyme-words are English, for example, OM 2685-90) and vulgar: one torturer claims that he doesn't give a fart for the power of her God. The luckless Maximilla, who continues to call upon Christ (and thus becomes, as the *Legende* notes, the first martyr, and not an anachronistic one, of course, since the three persons of the Trinity co-exist in each other from the beginning; the world, we recall, was created here by the Triune deity), is mocked and eventually killed, with one of the torturers continuing to stone her body even after she has died. Some versions of the legends - the Middle English *Canticum de Creatione*, for example - specify that she is stoned to death.[27] The parallels with the Passion are quite clear. The bishop rewards the executioners with land, and the wood of the future cross, which has caused the whole incident, is removed, as in the *Legende*, to Bethsaida. The Latin and English Holy Rood versions refer at this point to the *piscina probatica*, which is located at Bethsaida/Bethesda in John v: 4. The waters of the pool then acquire healing powers, and the wood is removed to Cedron, where it is used as a bridge. The legends conclude with the narrative of how the Queen of the South, Sybilla, refuses to walk on the bridge, but this is omitted from the play. One can only speculate on the precise version that the dramatist knew, but the outline *Legende* is followed quite closely, with occasional divergences, although the last part is missing. The story does not resume until the Passion play, however, for now Solomon speaks out of his role to summon the people for the next day to see the Passion, and to ask the minstrels to play.

The second play is more clearly biblical, although as has been noted, a few passages from the poem *Pascon agan Arluth* have been used directly, if not always very effectively, in the work. There are, however, general similarities between the accounts of the Passion in the two works that might lead us to suspect a more general influence of the poem or a common source other than the Bible. As in the poem, additional material has been introduced - the explanation of the dream of Pilate's wife, and the miracle of the smith; these are also found in the poem. The play develops, too, the well-known legend of Longinus. All the additional material is traditional, however, and although

---

27   Ed. Carl Horstmann, *"Canticum de creatione* aus Ms. Trin. coll. Oxf. 57," *Anglia* I (1878), 329

attempts have been made to establish various of the French *mystères* as direct sources, none provides close enough parallels for this to be conclusive.[28]

Like *Pascon agan Arluth*, the second play begins not with the nativity, but with the temptation in the desert. The English cycles include the birth of Christ, and most of them also have the temptation scene. The presence of the disciples at this point in our play is not biblical, but Christ needs an audience for his comments, which are effectively an exegesis according to the *sensus tropologicus* of the temptation-pericope. Of greater interest is the attitude of the devil, who makes it clear from the start that he will not be able to tempt Christ:

> sur awos ol ow gallos
> byth ny allaf yn ow ros
> the wul pegh vyth y cachye
> den yw the pup the weles
> saw y ober ha'y thyskes
> pup ol a wra tremene (PC 53-8)

> I have great powers, and yet
> surely I shall never net
> Him, or catch Him at some crime!
> He shall atone for all things.
> But for his work and teaching,
> men would be doomed for all time.[29]

The exegesis of the reading for Quadragesima Sunday (the Matthew temptation rather than the Lucan, which has the temptations in a different order), indicates that the devil is defeated, but the devil's own resignation is interesting.

The next scene is that of Palm Sunday; Longsworth and Bakere, building on comments made far earlier by Jenner, have both stressed the probable links between the greeting of Christ by seven Hebrew boys and the ceremonies of, and particularly an antiphon for Palm Sunday in the *Sarum Missal* which also specifies - uniquely - the number seven.[30] The cleansing of the temple, which

[28] See Longsworth, *Ordinalia*, p. 66, rightly rejecting the suggestions of J. G. Wright, *A Study of the Themes of the Resurrection in the Medieval French Drama* (Bryn Mawr, 1935) linking the *Passion d'Arras* with our play.

[29] The translation is free, but the verb in line 56 is presumably linked with *dewelyans*, used for atonement in various places, rather than with the verb *gweles* 'to see', which is how Norris interpreted it. For a survey of the dramas in which the episode occurs, see Murdoch, *Recapitulated Fall*, pp. 119-47 (with bibliography of further studies).

[30] Longsworth, *Ordinalia*, p. 109; Bakere, *Ordinalia*, p. 60f.

follows, is relatively unusual (it is present in English, for example, only in the Chester plays), but it provides occasion here for Pilate and Caiaphas to question the prophecy of Christ (in the Johannine account, another Lenten pericope) that he will raise the temple again after three days. The explanation given in John ii: 21 is not provided, nor, of course, is Pilate present in the biblical version. A few elements have been adopted from the synoptic parallel in the reference to the *spelunca latronum* of Matthew xxi: 13 (*fowys the laddron plos*, PC 336 "caves of wicked thieves"). The introduction of Pilate here is of dramatic interest, as he will be developed as a contrastive and negative figure throughout. The healing miracles which follow are interspersed with further discussion between Pilate and Caiaphas, in which the former asks the latter to try and catch Jesus out, a brief exchange which is worthy of special interest, however, since Pilate echoes the devil's remarks that all men are following Christ; only when Caiaphas talks him round does he agree that he will try to catch Jesus. The same verb was used by the devil. The next incident is that of Simon the Leper, the Magdalene and the ointment, with the roles as in the Johannine version, rather than the Matthew-pericope. The episode was seen as a condemnation of Judas for undervaluing Jesus in *Pascon agan Arluth*, but such an objective interpretation would be unlikely here. The Matthew-narrative continues, however, when Judas negotiates with Caiaphas and Annas (who swear, incidentally, as standard medieval pagans, but in English, by Mahomet - *wolcom by mahommys blout*, PC 575), and insists on thirty pieces of silver. After a lengthy set-piece scene of the Last Supper which is, however, the eucharistic pivot, with the distribution of the host, and then the laving scene, the whole concludes with Peter and the swords. Judas leads the soldiers to Gethsemane, and the submission of Christ to the will of the father is expressed in three stanzas, developing Matt. xxvi: 42, though without the image of the chalice; the central expression reads:

> ow tas ma ny yl bones
> may treylyo mernens the ves
> > sav y wothaf thy'm a reys
> the volnegeth re bo gures
> rak an scryptor bynyges
> > reys yv y vos guyr porrys   (PC 1069-4)

> Father, if it may not be
> that death turn away from me,
> > but I must take it freely,
> then let what must happen be!
> Fulfil of necessity
> > the Scripture's prophecy.

The betrayal itself (the meeting with Judas, the kiss and the arrest) is marked by a different verse-form, a four-syllable pattern similar, in fact, to the *quem quæritis* section of the third play. Within the biblical structure (including the incident of Malchus' ear, for example), the torturers once again have a large role, tormenting and mocking Christ. These scenes are interspersed with those of Peter's denial, and the torturers strike Christ in the face during his interrogation by Caiaphas, during which witness is brought against him that he talked about rebuilding the temple in three days. As with the Passion-poem, the apparently excessive insistence on the efforts of the torturers (addressed by Caiaphas as *tormentours cardowyon*, "my dear torturers," PC 1357) is developed beyond the graphic but brief accounts in the Gospels in fulfilment of the Old Testament prophecies about the Messiah in Isaiah 1: 6-9 and similar passages, which make up a complex system of symbols of the passion.

There are, however, some notable expansions. Peter's contrition, which in Matt. xxvi: 75 is expressed simply as *flevit amare*, "he wept bitterly," becomes a striking speech of five six-line strophes. Another addition is the legend found also in the Passion-poem that Judas' soul could not leave through his mouth, since he had kissed Christ. Judas repeats *me re peghes marthys trus*, ("I have sinned very greatly" PC 1505 and 1518, varied in 1519), stressing that his sin is greater than God's mercy, and thus falling into *desperatio*. But it is Satan who tells him that his soul cannot emerge from his mouth, and he is taken to hell.[31]

The presentation of Pilate is complex in most of the medieval mystery plays, and he can be vilified or exonerated.[32] The biblical narrative is followed here in the first instance, Pilate finding no guilt in Christ and referring him to Herod, which gives occasion for a debate before Herod in which the *doctores* consider the possibility of Christ being what he says he is. Christ, biblically, says nothing. The burden of the debate is whether (and how) Christ can be both God and man, and it is of interest that one of the doctors uses the idea of the mermaid to express the possibility of dual nature in a person:

> y gorthyby me a wra
> ef a alse bos yn ta
> hanter den ha hanter dev
> den yv hanter morvoron
> benen a'n pen the'n colon
> yn della yw an ihesu (PC 1739-44)

---

[31]   Peter, *Cornish Drama*, p. 25f. refers to an early German analogue to explain how this might have been performed.

[32]   See Arnold Williams, *The Characterisation of Pilate in the Towneley Plays* (East Lansing, 1950). The episode of the death of Pilate complicates the matter, however.

I shall answer, if you will:
it is clearly possible
   to be half god and half man.
Mermaids are human in part,
woman from head down to heart.
and therefore this Jesus can.

Where the dramatist has the point is unclear, though the figure of the mermaid on bench-ends is not unknown in Cornwall. Probably the image is deliberately far-fetched, because the sceptics remain unconvinced, and Christ's silence is contrasted with the somewhat absurd image. More important is the reiterated reference to the rebuilding of the temple in three days, a recurrent typological prefiguration of the resurrection.

Like Pilate, Herod finds no cause to condemn Christ, although this is not in the Luke narrative which is being followed here. Pilate is given a more negative image, however, when he decides to put Christ into prison (a recurrent theme in the rest of the cycle) as a kind of protective custody for the moment. Claiming that Christ can "rest," Pilate commends him to the jailer and his assistant (who is named *whyp an tyn* "whip-arse"), suggesting that a woman might be provided for him. The *powes-mowes* rhyme in this context crops up in the *Charter Fragment*, in the *Origo Mundi*, and later, and seems therefore just to be formulaic, without special significance.

An incident is now developed, however, which rests upon very small biblical evidence, though it is found in expanded form in apocryphal writings, most notably in the *Acts of Pilate/Gospel of Nicodemus*. The reference in Matthew xxvii: 19 to Pilate's wife having dreamed that she suffered on account of Christ, who was innocent, is interpreted in the *Gospel of Nicodemus* by the Jews, who claim that Christ is a sorcerer and has sent the dream himself, but the play - like the Passion-poem - sees it as having been sent by the devil in an attempt to avert the harrowing of hell. The motif is widespread, as Jane Bakere has shown, and there are analogues in English poems and French drama, with the *Historia scholastica* as "an important point for the dissemination of the tradition."[33] The scene is not included in all the English cycles, but it is dealt with *in extenso* in some of the French plays, most notably in the Passion-play of Jean Michel, in the *Passion de l'Auvergne* and in the St Geneviève Passion. The tradition is complex, Pilate's wife is often named (Procula), and she is sometimes accompanied by her children.[34]

---

[33]   Bakere, *Ordinalia*, p. 91

[34]   In spite of a possible corruption which led Norris to include a named daughter at PC 1967, with an unconvincing justification from the N-Town plays, Pilate's children are simply mentioned here as part of the threat. On analogous texts, see (for Michel) *Mystère de la Passion (Angers 1486)*, ed. Omer Jodogne (Genbloux, 1959), p. 375; *La Passion d'Auvergne*,

The English *Devils' Parliament* shows a *parlamentum offeendis* debating with increasing agitation how they can stop Christ from harrowing hell. They advise Herod on the massacre of the innocents, essay the temptation in the desert, and also send the dream to Pilate's wife. In the Cornish play the devil has already admitted defeat after failing to tempt Christ in the wilderness, and in the present scene Beëlzebub (Belsebuc) is sent by a despairing Lucifer and Satan to announce to Pilate's (here unnamed) wife that if Jesus is condemned, she and her children will suffer. There is a nice irony in all this, that the devils, for the wrong reasons, should be trying to save Christ, who is indeed innocent, but who *has* to die in fulfilment of the Scriptures. Pilate's wife sends off her messenger in the name of "St Jove" (PC 1962), reminding us that she is still an unbeliever. The scene does add dramatic variety (it was played in a different part of the *plen-an-gwary*, perhaps) to the debates and details of the Passion, whilst reminding us of the purpose of the sacrifice, the ultimate defeat of the now seriously worried forces of evil.

Pilate's interrogation of Jesus is biblical, and the flagellation scene again gives the torturers scope for much action, as they vie with each other in sadism. Even the crown of thorns placed upon his head pierces the brain, as in *Pascon agan Arluth*. The point is emphasised when the torturers force the crown onto Christ's head, a motif found in iconography and linked, perhaps, with the wine-press imagery.[35] Pilate still insists that Christ is innocent, and at this point the messenger brings Pilate news of his wife's dream, which is ascribed to an angel:

> el a'n leuerys dethy
> haneth ha hy yn guyly
> pur thyfun myns re geusys (PC 2202-4)

> By an angel this was said
> last night; she lay in her bed
> awake; he told her all this.

Eve also took the devil's message for the words of an angel. Pilate, however, agrees that Christ should not be killed, and there is irony again in the fact that

---

ed. Graham Runnals (Geneva, 1982), p. 13 and *A Critical Edition of La Passion Nostre Seigneur from...Saint Geneviève* (Chapel Hill, 1976), pp. 47-9. *The Devil's Parliament* is in *Hymns*, ed. Furnivall, pp. 41-57. See also C. W. Marx, "The Problem of the Doctrine of Redemption," *Medium Aevum* 54 (1985), 20-32.

[35]   See Marrow, *Passion Iconography*, pp. 58-63 and 83-94. There are parallels with Samson (Jud. xvi: 21) and in Breton see the *Grand Mystère de Jésus*, ed. H de la Villemarqué (Paris, 1865), pp. 109-11. The motif of the thorns is widespread. See Honorius Augustodunensis in PL 172, 787.

he does so not out of pure justice, but because he is afraid on behalf of his wife. He calls for Christ and some thieves to be brought to him for judgement. There follows a lengthy (delaying) scene between the jailer and his servant which is really an interpolated knockabout, ending in a brawl which Pilate breaks up. Christ, the thieves Dysmas and Jesmas (the traditional names for those crucified with him) and Barabbas are brought to Pilate, where there is again a debate between the *doctores* (invoking the mermaid argument, and referring again to the restoring of the temple), resolving this time into a direct argument between one who wants Christ condemned and another who asserts that Christ is the son of God. The people cry out for crucifixion, and Christ is condemned, Pilate washing his hands as in the Gospels, before handing Christ and the thieves over to the torturers again. At this point the legends of the Rood are reintroduced, since no cross can be found for Christ. As in the *Legende*, the wood is retrieved from Cedron and made into a cross for Christ to carry. As he does so he encounters the Virgin, who voices a poetically distinctive *planctus* with a repeated anaphoric *ellas*, "alas," and variations in the line-length. The distinctive nature of this passage led Nance to extract it as a separate poem, but it adds greatly to the effect at this point of high pathos. Her words are echoed shortly afterwards by Mary the Mother of James and Mary Salome.

The legend of the smith, whose hands appear diseased by a miracle when he does not want to make the nails for the crucifixion, is introduced at this point. That the smithy is situated in the play in Market Jew (*marghes yow*, PC 2668) is of no special significance, but just provides a handy rhyme for *kentrow* "nails."[36] The outlines of the story are as in the Passion-poem, and the smith's sharp-tongued wife supervises the torturers. These make the nails roughly, and as in *Pascon agan Arluth*, Christ has to be stretched on the cross so that all of his joints are dislocated. Even the motif of the further pain caused by the shuddering of the cross as it is erected is voiced again. Less usual is the addition to the (otherwise biblical) mockery by Caiaphas of Christ on the cross of his offer to fetch Christ a woman (a motif we have seen several times), although he refers, too, to the idea of the restored temple again.

There are at the close of the Passion-drama marked variations in the texture of the language which once again draw attention to the pathos of the events portrayed. The Virgin's complaint beneath the cross (in response to Christ's *benen a welte the flogh*, "woman, behold thy son," PC 2925 and John xix: 26) recalls her earlier lyrical speech, with varied line-lengths and a hyper-metrical *ellas*. This second *planctus Mariæ* will itself be recalled with a third,

---

[36]   Nance made this suggestion, but offered other solutions as well. See Murdoch, "Place-Names;" *marghes yow* (Norris misread the text at this point) refers to a Thursday market and we are now on Good Friday. See Anderson, *Drama and Imagery*, p. 106.

at the deposition. Meanwhile the dramatist adds to the details of the final stages of the Passion (the last words on the cross, the vinegar and gall, the death, darkness and earthquake) not only the regrets of some of the torturers, who admit that they have sinned by killing Jesus, but also the story of Longinus (*Longeus* in the stage directions). He is blind, but the blood of Christ in his eyes when he has thrust his spear into Christ's side heals him, and he expresses his belief in a *mea culpa* of eighteen four-syllable lines ending with an expression of what he now knows - seeing is an allegory of knowing, of the opening of the spiritual eyes:

> rak del won sur . map dev os pur
> yn beys gynys
> a vaghtyth glan . vn vap certan
> os the'n das du
> ow *h*am wyth bras . gaf thy'm a tas
> dre the vertu   (PC 3025-30)

> You are, I own,   God's only son
> born here on earth
> of Virgin pure, a son for sure
> of God above
> of my great sin   cleanse me again
> for your great love.

The episode is again well-known in the drama, and before that in Latin legends.[37]

The end of the play is marked by a series of rapid shifts of focus. Already before the Longinus passage the unnamed centurion has appeared, announcing his intention of going to see Jesus. His words are followed by the cosmic events at the death of Christ, however, and then by Longinus, but before he reappears, a brief scene in hell is interpolated in which a thoroughly panicky Lucifer, aware that his gates are going to be attacked, rallies all the devils that there are to help barricade hell against the harrowing. The vigour of this passage is then contrasted with the centurion's speech, expanding the simple assertion of Christ's divinity in the Bible into a lengthy condemnation of those who have killed Christ. Joseph of Arimathea and Nicodemus come and claim

---

[37]   See the introduction to C. M. H. H. Dauven-van Knippenberg, *...einer von den Soldaten öffnete seine Seite* (Amsterdam and Atlanta, 1990), as well the older work by R.J. Peebles, *The Legend of Longinus* (Bryn Mawr, 1911). On the work of Dauven-van Knippenberg, see the *Medieval Sermon Studies Newsletter* 27 (Spring, 1991), 25-7 and 33, with further details. For a Welsh analogue, see G. Jones, *A Study of Three Welsh Religious Plays* (Aberystwyth, 1939), p. 73f.

the body (and there are references to the instruments of the Passion, including the pincers to draw out the nails), and the third and final part of the Virgin's extended *planctus* now forms part of a *pietà* in which the Virgin, again with the anaphoric *ellas* and lines that are metrically distinct from most of the rest of the play bewails her loss but ends with an affirmation that Christ was the son of God. Nicodemus embalms the body (preserving it, he says, for a thousand years), and the three Maries anoint Christ before Joseph of Arimathea seals the tomb. Nicodemus then steps out of character to address the audience, urging them to remember Christ's sacrifice in their own lives:

> bennath ihesu theugh neffre
> > ha henna prest me a pys
> eus pop ol war tuhe tre
> > an guary yw dywythys
> > > ha deug avar
> avorow my agas pys
> > the welas fetel sevys
> > > cryst mes a'n beth cler ha war (PC 3235-42)

> The blessing of Jesus come
> > upon you, now and for aye.
> And now you may set off home,
> > this is the end of the play.
> > > come in good time
> tomorrow, people, I pray
> > to see how Christ rose again
> > > from the tomb, shining and kind.

There is no music this time, as befits the solemnity of what has just been portrayed

The third play falls into three broad sections: the resurrection, the story of Pilate, and finally the ascension. The three themes (with subsidiary themes as well) are all integrated in what is dramatically the most satisfying of the three plays. The resurrection and the breaking open of the prison of hell are shown with a positive parallel, the miraculous release from prison of Joseph and Nicodemus, an episode from the *Gospel of Nicodemus*. The legends of Pilate - the curing of the ailing emperor Tiberius simply by sight of the Vernicle, and the imprisonment and death of Pilate after the seamless robe of Christ has been taken from him - form the centre section. The belief of the emperor and his ensuing cure, with its spiritually soteriological implications, when all he has seen is the image and not the reality of Christ, contrasts with Pilate's failure to believe in spite of his knowledge of Christ himself and his possession of the robe. The theme of belief links also with the contrast of

Mary Magdalene with doubting Thomas - the belief of the Magdalene and the Maries at the tomb, and Thomas, who has to be convinced by the risen Christ. The vigorous removal of Pilate to hell and the rejection by the earth of his body forms a contrastive parallel to the inability of the earth to hold Christ, and the triumphant and lyrical finale of the ascension.

The first section is based to an extent on the *Gospel of Nicodemus/ Acts of Pilate*, another of the most widespread apocrypha of the Middle Ages, which exists in various forms. There is some evidence that the dramatist knew the work in an English version, and it was translated early - there was a copy in Leofric's library at Exeter.[38] The central section reflects another apocryphal legend-complex centering upon the death of Pilate, but linked with the tale of St Veronica and the kerchief with the imprint of Christ's face, and the legend (which appears in other guises and will be encountered again in *Beunans Meriasek*), of the healing and conversion of the Roman emperor. Here it is Tiberius, elsewhere Vespasian. The last section is largely liturgical.

Pilate dominates the first two parts, in fact, although dramatic interest is maintained by more frequent shifts of action than in the other plays between earth, hell and heaven. Any ambiguities in Pilate's role are now resolved in his presentation as completely evil, and his first deed is to incarcerate Joseph and Nicodemus (in the apocryphal gospel and elsewhere only Joseph is imprisoned). The jailer is again given fiefs in Cornwall as a reward. This scene is immediately followed by the harrowing of hell by the Spirit of Christ, based on the second and older part of the Nicodemus-Gospel, but where there is a fairly solemn debate there between hell itself and Satan, here the reaction (and ultimate discomfiture) of the devils is treated in a lively and comic fashion. Lucifer calls for thunder and lightning in defence, once the gates have been shattered, but Beëlzebub points out that a million devils would be useless. Tulfryk, a devil who will play a part later in the Pilate-episode, complains that he had a million souls stewing nicely. The spirit of Christ, however, accompanied *comitatu angelorum*, releases Adam, Eve and the penitent thief Dysmas (who is not always named in the apocryphon). Still following the *Gospel of Nicodemus* closely, we hear too, however, of Enoch and Elijah. These, of course, were taken to heaven in the whole body, and have not been in hell, but they explain how they will combat the Antichrist at the last judgement - the idea was well known, and appears in European vernaculars as early as the tenth century in the Old High German *Muspilli-*

---

[38]   Michael Swanton, *Anglo-Saxon Prose* (London, 1975), p. 139. See William H. Hulme, *The Middle English Harrowing of Hell and the Gospel of Nicodemus* (London, 1907 = EETS/ES 100). The White Book of Roderick (MS Peniarth 5) has a collection of related legends in Welsh.

apocalypse.[39]   After the harrowing, the devils complain bitterly at their impotence in keeping souls in hell, and as an immediate parallel on earth, the next scene shows Joseph and Nicodemus released from their prison by the angels. The whole scene, however, is set in four-syllable lines, allowing it to stand out, and both Joseph and Nicodemus stress the need for right belief, as Eve had done in the harrowing

   The breaking of the prison gates all reflect the resurrection itself. As in the Bible, Pilate places a watch on the tomb of Christ and the soldiers (whose expressions of bravado exceed the brief biblical reference) fall asleep. Christ rises to the sound of the angels singing the hymn *Christus resurgens*, an antiphon repeated regularly between Easter and Ascension,[40] and the liturgical aspects are underlined further by Christ's greeting of *salve sancta parens*, from votive masses to the Virgin, when he meets his mother. This final meeting with Mary harks back to the three meetings (and her *planctus* speeches) in the Passion-play, but now he can assure her that he is in no pain. The soldiers wake up and see Christ has risen, and one of them expresses his determination to find Christ in a speech which has an entire couplet in English as well as other English words:

> me a'n kyf by god ys blod
> kyn fo an harlot mar wod
>   ma mar houtyn y body
> for y dred noth by my hod
> hys red baner ne hys rod
>   the pilat man dryllyn ny.   (RD 543-8)

> I shall find him, by God's blood,
> mad or not, however good
>   the whoreson thinks he is! No,
> for I dread not, by my hood,
> his red banner nor the Rood.
>   With him we'll to Pilate go.

---

[39]   For the relevant passages of the Nicodemus-Gospel, see James, *Apocryphal New Testament*, pp.130-43. Our dramatist presumably followed a recension which contained, for example, the name of the penitent thief. Only David is a significant omission. On *Muspilli* see my *Old High German Literature* (Boston, 1983), pp. 68-72. On Enoch, see Maria-Magdalene Witte, *Elias und Henoch* (Frankfurt, 1987)

[40]   Longsworth, *Ordinalia*, p. 106f. describes the role of the hymn in processions as described in the Exeter Ordinal, and discusses too the use of the *Salve sancta parens* as an introit in masses for the Virgin, p. 107f. Longsworth establishes other liturgical links, including the curious *oremus* of RD 648.

The other soldiers are less sanguine, and decide in the end, as they do in the Gospel, that they will tell the truth. The soldiers, who have seen the resurrection (albeit in a dream) now believe in Christ, and when challenged by Pilate, ask to see Joseph and Nicodemus. When it is discovered that they too have escaped from prison through doors locked by nine keys, the soldiers are confirmed in their belief, and agree only to remain silent when Pilate offers them the familiar land-grant bribes, in this case including Penryn itself.

No special significance attaches to the use of English by the soldier at the tomb in textural terms, though it might again betoken use of an English-language source. The same is true of a significant couplet in the next section, the *quem quæritis* portion, in which the visit of the three Maries to the tomb affirms the resurrection, rather than (as in Mark's Gospel, for example) discovering it as a surprise. The three Maries express their awareness in six-line strophes which vary regular heptasyllables with four-syllable third and sixth lines, frequently climaxing on an expression of sorrow, and with rhymes echoed from strophe to strophe, and they sing (*cantant*) the lines which will be repeated:

> ellas mornyngh I sing mornyngh I call
> our lord ys deyd that boghte ovs al
> (RD 733f., 753f. 779f.)

The provenance of the line is not known, although it has occasioned some discussion. It recalls only the secular song beginning "Mourning, mourning/ Thus may I sing..."[41] The couplet is emphasised further by being sung again, after which the metre changes to eight-line strophes, the fourth and the eighth lines having four syllables. After the third singing, an angel (using once again the six-line strophe) tells them that Christ has risen. The Magdalene expresses her longing to see Christ, also in a new verse form, this time of eight four-syllable lines. These changes in form contribute greatly to the effect of this part of the work, and the entire *Hortulanus* episode in which Christ appears to the Magdalene as the gardener and convinces her by displaying his wounds, is in the same metre. It changes only after Christ announces in Latin the warning *noli me tangere*, when we move from the regular *ababcdcd* rhyme-scheme to a more complex *ababcdedec* pattern of tetrasyllables.

The episode with Thomas is described in John xx, but it is here much expanded.[42] Just as the earlier parts of this play set the various incidents of

---

[41]   In BL MS Harley 2252, included in E. K. Chambers and F. Sidgwick, *Early English Lyrics* (London, 1927), p. 78.
[42]   Eleanor C. Prosser, *Drama and Religion in the English Mystery Plays* (Stanford, 1961), p. 150-77 discusses it.

imprisonment and release against one another, here the belief expressed by the Maries and the reward granted to the Magdalene is set against the doubts of Thomas, who not only disbelieves, but abuses the woman. The other disciples believe what the Magdalene tells them, but Thomas counters every one of them with repeated accusations of folly, insisting that he saw Christ die. The dramatic irony is, of course, that the audience has seen the resurrection. Nothing can persuade him, even when the other Maries are offered as witnesses, and he reminds the Magdalene of her sinful past, something which she accepts, saying that Christ has forgiven her, and associating herself in so doing with the woman taken in adultery in John viii: 1-11 by quoting Christ's final words to the adultress. The linking of this pericope with Mary Magdalene is not quite as specific as in the Digby play, for example. She is also associated with the woman who anoints Christ's feet in the house of Simon the Leper in the Passion play.

Immediately after Thomas' final dismissal of the rest of them as fools (*gokyes*, RD 1136), Christ appears to the apostles, and we are given then the scene in which Christ appears on the road to Emmaeus. Only after this Lucan incident has been presented do we return to the Johannine narrative of Thomas and Christ's showing to him of the wounds. The point of the incident and the unusually heavy stress on and repeated appearances of Thomas is dramatically significant. Thomas is not an unbeliever per se; he mourns constantly the loss of Christ. It is simply that he does not acknowledge the resurrection, although the other apostles, Mary Magdalene and the men from Emmaeus all assure him of the truth. The whole point of a mystery play, of course, is that it underscores belief by a representation of events, or rather: it shows others seeing the actual events, which the audience is then asked to believe. Thomas is immensely important in a play which is mystery as well as drama. Moreover, his failure to believe is psychologically well motivated. Mary is a sinner, the apostles are fools, caught up in some kind of mass hysteria; the travellers are rogues and not to be trusted. And yet he *wants* to believe: he is aware that he cannot believe without seeing Christ, and is close to despair in an expansion of John xx: 25: *ellas ny won pendra wraf* ("alas, I do not know what I can do," RD 1527). When Christ appears to him, of course, and displays the wounds once again, Thomas has to beg for forgiveness, and John xx: 29, which is in a sense the key to the play and to the whole essence of the medieval mystery, is expressed in a straightforward translation:

> thomas rak ty the weles
> ol ow golyow a les
>   yn the golon ty a grys
> the kekemmys na'm guello
> hag yn perfyth a'n cresso
>   ow len benneth me a pys (RD 1551-6)

> Thomas, because you could see
> all my wounds shown openly,
>   inwardly you could believe.
> To all those who do *not* see,
> and who still believe in me,
>   my fullest blessing I give.

By the end of the Thomas-episodes we have covered well over half of the play: after this final appearance to the disciples, Christ says that he will return to sit at the right hand of God, and the stage directions announce *sic finitur resurrectio domini.* However, the Pilate story, which comes next, ties in very closely with what has gone before, and the dominant motif of seeing and believing, which was such a feature of the Thomas episodes, is developed further. The Pilate narrative is unusual in drama, not present in the English cycles and rare elsewhere. It is based on another series of apocryphal writings on the career, death and post-mortem activities of Pilate. This time there are several distinct texts, some of them favourable to Pilate, some extremely negative, and it is the latter group, and in particular a number of Latin texts sometimes attached to the *Acts of Pilate/Gospel of Nicodemus*, and linked with the tales of Tiberius and Veronica, that are of special relevance.[43] Most interesting in our context is the Latin *Mors Pilati*, according to which an ailing Tiberius sends Volusianus., his officer, to fetch Christ, who will heal him. Pilate tries to conceal the crucifixion, but Volusianus meets Veronica with the kerchief and Christ's image. Pilate is tried by Tiberius, but wears Christ's seamless robe, and Tiberius is unable to bring himself to condemn him until it is removed. Pilate commits suicide, but his body is rejected by the Tiber and by the earth, and is eventually put into a well in the mountains, where demons are still to be found. Pilate's soul is taken to hell. There are varied vernacular (though not dramatic) versions of this in English, Welsh and continental sources, and the story in outline was known in England at an early stage. Leofric's library in Exeter contained not only a Nicodemus-Gospel, but a version of one of the Pilate texts, the so-called *Cura sanitatis Tiberii* in English. The source of the Cornish play was perhaps an English version of the *Mors Pilati*, however. The messenger from

---

[43]   The best source of the texts is Aurelio de Santo Otero, *Los Evangelios Apocrifos* (Madrid, 1956), 501-69. For translations see Alexander Walker, *Apocrypha Gospels* (Edinburgh, 1870), pp. 234-6 and James, *Apocryphal New Testament*, pp. 157-61. Achim Masser and Max Siller, *Das Evangelium Nicodemi in spätmittelalterlicher deutscher Prosa* (Heidelberg, 1987) is not only about German, but discusses the whole Pilate-Tiberius-Veronica complex, pp. 35-43, and also on the full legend see Doris Werner, *Pylatus* (Düsseldorf, 1972). The early career of Pilate, which is present in the Passion section of the *Golden Legend*, for example, is not of primary interest here.

Tiberius is here called *Lygth of fout*, which is striking as an English translation of Volusianus. Veronica is far more forceful a personality than in most of the apocryphal writings, and the various jailer and torturers do not appear in Latin versions, though they are quite familiar from other Cornish works.

Of greater significance than source-speculations is the question of integration. Thomas has just been used as an exemplum, so that those who do not see might believe. Pilate has seen Christ, and still refuses to believe, even when the robe of Christ clearly protects him. Veronica has an image of Christ, and that suffices for the emperor to believe and be cured (just as Constantine will be in a very similar situation in *Beunans Meriasek*; here the quite unhistorical adoption of Christianity by Rome plays a minor part only). Pilate's imprisonment and Tiberius' inability to find him guilty so long as he wears the robe is a quasi-parodistic version of the trial of Christ himself. Just as relics such as the kerchief work miracles, so too the body of Pilate, once he is dead, has a supernatural but in this case negative effect, causing sickness, where the image of Christ cures the emperor of his actual sickness (probably leprosy) as well as effecting spiritual salvation. Pilate in the river also contrasts with the Rood in the *piscina*.

Although Veronica is the bearer of the image of Christ, she herself takes on a somewhat unusual role in the trial of Pilate. Where in the Latin legends, the suggestion that Tiberius remove the robe of Christ from Pilate is made either by God or by an unspecified Christian, here it is Veronica who does so, just as she does in at least one of the English versions of the tale, a fifteenth-century *Metrical Life of Christ*.[44] Even when Pilate is condemned, it is Veronica who insists that Pilate should have the most cruel death possible, and to a modern audience she appears overly vindictive. She is, however, entirely justified, even when she says that the most cruel death possible would not serve really to avenge Christ, and that most cruel of deaths (the Cornish insistence upon the idea echoes a point made in the Latin *Mors Pilati*) is in fact suicide, that is, the expression of *desperatio* which leads only to hell. Pilate is more exaggerated in this than Judas even, for Judas was sad in his despair. Pilate has worn the coat of Christ and has still not understood. Just as Judas suffered the fate of his soul having to remain in his body, Pilate's post-mortem activities are even more striking, and contain elements of black humour. His body is entrusted to the jailer and his assistant, Whip-arse (*whyp-an-tyn*) to whom Christ was given in custody - the parallelism is thereby continued. Where the grave was *unable* to hold Christ, the grave

---

[44]   Walter Sauer, *The Metrical Life of Christ from MS BM Add 39996* (Heidelberg, 1977), p. 83. The text is from the early fifteenth century. Evelyn Newlyn, "Pit and Pedestal," pp. 140f. is aware of the difficulties of fitting Veronica into her polarities of women characters.

refuses to hold Pilate. Although in the Latin legends various potential resting places are tried, here the body first refuses to be buried, and then begins to stink. Placing it in the Tiber poisons the water, so that a traveller who washes his hands - as of course Pilate himself had done - dies at once. Eventually Veronica has the body sent out to sea, where devils carry it away with obscene songs and the promise of eternal damnation. Hell has been harrowed to release the just, but Judas and Pilate are damned for all time.

There is no question of this episode being anything other than integrated into a finely-balanced drama. The final section of the play takes up earlier motifs in a magnificent resolution. After the black comedy of Pilate's recalcitrant corpse, the last three hundred lines of the play is a presentation of the ascension from the Mount of Olives which is strongly liturgical, expanding the account in Acts i: 6-11, and picking up Christ's statement that he will go to sit at the right hand of his father. There are various parallels here. The response of the angels, who ask in the spirit of Isaiah lxiii: 1-3 who approaches in red garments (the links are with the liturgy of Holy Week and of Ascension Day), recalls the bafflement of the devils at the harrowing, and the questions of the angels at this new arrival recall also those of Adam to the appearance of Enoch and Elijah. Christ himself recounts the history of the passion, stressing the details of the crucifixion and the crown of thorns, in four eight-line strophes with an addition quatrain (RD 2571-2606). The angels sing the *gloria*, and the key word, repeated time and again, is *myghtern*, "king," so that the red robe is not only that of martyrdom but of kingship. The imagery of the hero is linked with that of the suffering Christ - the crown of thorns and the helmet. The first play in the cycle began with the triune creator forming the world and placing Adam in it, only for him to fall. The conclusion of the last play shows the triumph of Christ as *myghtern den ha dev* (RD 2580, "king, man and God"). The angels stress that salvation is the work of the Trinity as well, and Adam has been restored to heaven:

> arluth ker bynyges os
> a syv ioy gynef gothfos
>   an denses the thos the'n nef
> an tas dev dre'n spyrys sans
> the'n beys danvonas sylwyans
>   a huhon map dev a seyf   (RD 2607-12)

> Dear lord, ever blessed be,
> joy it brings to us to see
>   man brought to heaven again.
> The Father and Holy Ghost
> redeemed a world that was lost.
>   On high the Son will remain.

Christ himself states that he has redeemed man with his own blood. God welcomes him into heaven to sit at his right hand, and the reunited Trinity, which opened the play, now closes it. It remains only for the most important character, the (converted) emperor, to summon the musicians for dancing.

The interweaving of motifs in the final play is balanced and intricate, but what is most striking of all it the manner in which it returns the audience after three days, to the idea of a divine plan for the benefit of man, leaving mankind redeemed, in grace, and in a Christian *imperium*. The audience has moved from the worldly adventures of Adam, Cain, Moses, David and Solomon (through which ran the motif of the cross) to the pain of the Passion, the final glories of the breaking of hell and the return to heaven, with a counter-action in the damnation of Pilate. Additions, such as the narratives of Thomas and of Pilate, which have been seen as padding, are nothing of the sort. Not only do they provide dramatic contrast, but they make a point about the nature of the mystery play as such, the whole of which is concerned at all levels with the question of seeing and believing. The triumphant note on which the *Ordinalia* ends places it in the high middle ages. Man has been saved, and the only really cruel death is suicide in despair. And to avoid despair, all that is necessary is to believe.

CHAPTER FOUR

THE NEED TO REPENT: *THE CREACION OF THE WORLD*

It is appropriate to follow a discussion of the *Ordinalia* with a consideration of a later (incomplete) biblical play, even though the next work in a strictly chronological sequence is the play of St Meriasek, written perhaps fifty years earlier. However, the notion is still encountered from time to time that the play known for convenience (and to mark it out as Cornish) as *Gwreans an bys*, and entitled *The Creacion of the World* in a transcription completed by William Jordan of Helston on August 12th, 1611, is simply a reworking of the first part of the *Ordinalia*. Although there are some quotations from the *Origo Mundi*, implying knowledge in the main of a single role, it is a completely different work, a shift towards what Carl Klimke in his study of the German paradise plays called the learned and tendentious approach to the theme, as opposed to the naive folk-play.[1] *Gwreans an bys* was probably composed in the middle of the sixteenth century, a judgement reached by comparing it with other dramatisations of Genesis from that period in different countries, although the linguistic date is that of Jordan's time, and the work exhibits the features of the later stage of Cornish (*pedn* for *pen* and so on). Themes, characters and dramatic techniques point to the period 1530-50, but it is harder to be more precise; it remains uncertain whether the work retains pre-Reformation ideas because the theological changes were not yet known in Cornwall. In any case, overtly pre-Reformation elements in the work are few, and by no means clear. In *Gwreans an bys* Adam is consigned to limbo when he dies, rather than to hell. Limbo itself is a concept questioned in the *Ten Articles* of 1536,[2] although whether the limbo described here is what the Reformers understood by it is unclear; it may just be part of hell. Like the earlier plays, we find in *Gwreans an bys* elements from those medieval legends dismissed by the Reformers, although even Protestant dramatists kept *some* non-biblical elements, such as the fall of the angels, in spite of the *sola scriptura* precept. Our play contains a small part only of the *Vita Adae*-Holy Rood material - less than in the earlier plays, and essentially only the promise

---

[1]   *Das volkstümliche Paradiesspiel* (Breslau, 1902). The best edition of *Gwreans an bys* is that by Paula Neuss, *The Creacion of the World* (New York and London, 1983); see also Whitley Stokes, *The Creation of the World* (London, 1864) and the modern text first published by R. M. Nance and A. S. D. Smith in 1959, now edited by E. G. R. Hooper, *Gwryans an Bys* (Redruth, 1985). The edition by Davies Gilbert of Keigwin's work and translation (London, 1827) is of curiosity value, although it was the first of the Cornish plays in print.
[2]   A. G. Dickens and D. Carr, *The Reformation in England* (London, 1967), p. 77. But see T. M. Parker, *The English Reformation to 1558* (London, 1966), p. 90f.

of salvation. In fact, there is very little in the work that might have been offensive to the Reformation, such as, for example, an excessive Marianism. What was in the lost second part, of course, we cannot say. To be sure, there is no real sign of the extended Protestant polemic that it is possible to build upon the story, something demonstrated by a very close contemporary in time, but one nearer the theological heart of the Reformation, Jacob Ruf, who wrote in Zurich in 1550 a spectacular play (to which I shall refer again), covering almost exactly the same ground in a manner which is at times remarkably similar.[3]

Of the Cornish dramas, *Gwreans an bys* was not only the first to become known in print; it was, indeed, never lost sight of, and even before Gilbert's unsatisfactory publication from a manuscript in the British Library, references may be found ascribing it often to Jordan as the author, and calling it "a Cornish play or opera" as did the *Biographia Dramatica, or a Companion to the Playhouse,* published in 1812. Keigwin's translation, made at the behest of Bishop Trelawney, is mentioned there, as it is indeed in the catalogue of Harley manuscripts published in 1808.[4]

There are quite specific and immediately apparent differences between this work and the corresponding part of the *Origo Mundi*. The first is size: at over two and a half thousand lines, *Gwreans an bys* is pretty well twice as long as the corresponding portion of the *Ordinalia* play, and although the basic material remains the first part of Genesis, from the creation to the flood, *Gwreans an bys* adds an extensive version of the fall of the angels which corresponds in the *Ordinalia* to a single and brief stage-direction, plus one that has been deleted. Some aspects of the creation and of the temptation of Adam and Eve are different, and the same is true of the Cain and Abel section, which is extended in *Gwreans an bys* - though nowhere else in drama in Britain in the Middle Ages - by a section showing us the wanderings of Cain, and then his death at the hands of Lamech. The last element is found in one of the English cycles, the N-Town plays, but otherwise primarily in

---

[3]   The German-language play has not been translated, nor edited since Hermann Kottinger, *Jacob Ruffs Adam und Heva* (Quedlinburg and Leipzig, 1848), although a new edition is currently in progress by Janice Whitelaw (Stirling). On this and other continental texts (with reference to *Gwreans an bys*) see my paper "Ruf's *Adam und Heva*." Elements of the paradise-play tradition survive beyond the sixteenth century in plays apparently unconnected with biblical material, a point I have made (again with reference to the Cornish work) in "Devils, Vices and the Fall. Dramatic Patterns from the Medieval Mystery to Bidermann's *Cenodoxus,*" *Maske und Kothurn* 23 (1977), 15-30.

[4]   The *Biographia Dramatica,* by David Baker, Isaac Green and Stephen Jones was published in London in 1812 (see II, 129f.), and the play is referred to in similar works of the same period. See the folio *Catalogue of the Harleian MSS in the British Museum* (London, 1808), II, 272. The Harley text is not the main MS. Neuss, CW, pp. lxx-lxxix refers to later copies.

continental drama. Seth's trip to Paradise and the death of Adam are scenes treated in both the Cornish plays, although not elsewhere in England, but even here there are striking differences between the two versions. The story of Enoch is unique to *Gwreans an bys* in insular drama, and is rare in any case, and even the treatment of the flood in this play differs not only from the rest of the English cycles but also from the *Origo Mundi*. Here as in many respects, the later Cornish play corresponds to continental (that is, French, Spanish and German) drama in its presentation of a conflict between the Cainite and Sethite lines, the latter represented by Noah and his family, the former in this instance by Tubalcain, the son of the Cainite Lamech. The lateness of the composition means, too, that there are further differences from the *Ordinalia,* such as the introduction of the allegorical figure of Death. The stanzaic patterns, finally, are more complex in this play than any of the others.

Jordan's 1611 manuscript is Bodley 219 in Oxford, and it is, of course, itself a copy of an earlier version. There are copies from this original in other manuscripts in the Bodleian, in the Gatley collection in Cornwall and in the British Library. Notable features are the absence of a diagram of staging, as we find in the other dramatic manuscripts, the English title rather than a Latin designation, and the fact that the stage directions and names of the speakers are in English. This is clearly to do with the later date of composition, but in one instance Latin *is* used, substituting *deus pater* for *Father* at CW 336. Otherwise the directions point to a prompt-copy, with directions for various props to be held ready for use and comments on the directing of the actors added later.

Paula Neuss has pointed out that of the 178 lines repeated in the play from the *Origo Mundi*, 127 are from the role of God the Father, and there may even be a memory here of a written script on Jordan's part (or that of his predecessor).[5] Some of the lines from the earlier play are amended slightly, and there are some that are not spoken by God. Neuss postulates reconstruction from memory, and certainly in continental tradition in the later Middle Ages standard material is passed on from play to play. I have used elsewhere the example of a play from Catholic Austria, written down in the nineteenth century, which uses lines from the far earlier Protestant Hans

---

[5]   Paula Neuss, "Memorial Reconstruction in a Cornish Miracle Play," *Comparative Drama* 5 (1971), 129-37. She lists the lines as an appendix, CW, pp. 241-5. William Sandys, "On the Cornish Drama," *JRIC* 3 (1865), 5 thought of "Jordan" borrowing from the *Origo Mundi* and from the English cycles. The corollary is to see the text as "the Cornish drama in decline;" thus P. A. Lanyon-Orgill, "The Cornish Drama," *CR* 1 (1949), 42 and (dangerously) in reference works: A. Harbage, *Annals of English Drama*, rev. S. Schoenbaum (London, 1964), p. 98.

Sachs.[6] The quotations, then, are relatively insignificant, and the implications in terms of source are slight. The final point of interest concerning the manuscript is the fact that it finishes where it does. Whether Jordan copied any more is not known, but if he did the text is lost. Only one day remains. The audience is told to return on the following day when it will see redemption (the loan-word is used) granted (CW 2542-4). The structure of the play was, therefore, clearly bipartite, based on the Fall and the Redemption as the two poles of the divine economy. In the absence of a stage diagram (or rather: one of a *plen-an-gwary*) it is not entirely clear how the work was performed. Modern versions of it have used the playing-place format - a modern diagram is provided, for example, by Donald Rawe, who produced the work at Piran Round[7] - but it would work equally well for the later medieval *Simultanbühne*, with heaven elevated, the world and hell beneath; there is no real requirement for stations occupied by significant figures as in the earlier plays. It might as a matter of fact be somewhat easier to stage the fall of the angels elsewhere than in a round.

In the study of *Gwreans an bys* it is of greatest interest to focus upon those elements which are not biblical, especially where they are somewhat unusual. The depiction of the creation of all things followed immediately by the fall of Lucifer and his rebel angels is present in the English cycles and in the great French cycle of the *Mistére du Viel Testament*, but none of these texts is closely comparable with our later play, which has its closest parallels in the Breton *Creation*, and indeed in the late medieval German drama, from Arnold Immessen in the 1480s down to Jacob Ruf in 1550.

The fall of the angels appears in the English cycles, and may have been present at some stage in the *Ordinalia*. The opening statement by God the Father, using the alpha and omega formula from Apoc. i: 8, is present there too, as in the N-Town, Chester and York Creations. In these and other medieval drama, however, we are shown simply the fall of Lucifer, even if the names of the nine orders of angels are given. The York and Chester plays, however, show the two sides, and the *Trébuchement de Lucifer* in the French *Mistére*, for example, has a more expansive version, as does, indeed, the Breton *Creation ar bet*, another sixteenth-century drama, which may be influenced by it. There is a full treatment also in the pre- and post-Reformation paradise-plays by Arnold Immessen and Jacob Ruf in German. The notion of a prior fall of one of the angelic choirs (comprising angels from all the orders), which is replaced by the creation of man, remains familiar

---

[6]   "Creation, Fall and After in the Cornish *Gwreans an bys*," *Studi Medievali* 29 (1988), 689f.

[7]   Donald Rawe, *The Creation of the World* (Padstow, 1978), pp. 137-41 and frontispiece. See also Paula Neuss, "The Staging of *The Creacion of the World*," *Theatre Notebook* 33 (1979), 116-25.

even after the Reformation. *Gwreans an bys* is striking in presenting a genuine conflict in heaven, rather than a simple arrangement of sides. Although we find in the *Mistére*, for example, angels praising Lucifer, here we have a counterpoint of argument between angels of Lucifer and angels of God (thus designated), before Lucifer is eventually overthrown. Stress is laid by the loyal angels, for example, on the fact that God made Lucifer (just as Adam will be made) and that he can therefore be unmade; but Lucifer's supporters rally to him until he is eventually cast out, even though his own speech of defiance is, as usual, based on the death-song of the King of Babylon in Isaiah. His call for silence (*Pays, I say*, CW 113) matches God's silencing of him (*Taw, Lucyfer*, CW 284), and recalls the *silete* commands of the early dramas, but it is notable that Lucifer is despatched to hell without the possibility of redemption (CW 286f.)[8] The stage-directions call for a dramatic fight between Lucifer and the archangels, with devils running *into the plain*, which might imply use of the *platea* at some stage, and the image of Lucifer chained in hell (CW 331) concludes the opening section, when God decides to replace Lucifer with man. Adam is created in Hebron - another tradition of some antiquity - and the actual creation is performed by the Trinity. The motifs of the *Trinitas creator* and of the so-called Trinity-formulas are familiar in Cornish from *Pascon agan Arluth*; the link with the fall of Lucifer is slightly different, however:[9]

> Gallas Lucifer, droke preve,
> Mes an Nef tha dewolgowe.
> Ha lemyn un y lea ef
> Me a vyn heb falladowe
> Un dean formya
> In valy Ebron devery,
> Rag collenwall aredy
> An le may teth anotha.
> (CW 336-43)

> Gone is Lucifer the snake,
> out of heaven to dark hell.

---

[8]   For the *silete* commands, see for example the fall of the angels in the early Vienna Passion-play: R. Froning, *Das Drama des Mittelalters I.* (Stuttgart, 1891), p. 305f. On the traditions of the fall of the angels (not just in German), see Paul Salmon, "Der zehnte Engelchor in deutschen Dichtungen und Predigten des Mittelalters," *Euphorion* 57 (1963), 321-30.

[9]   The formula is in *Pascon agan Arluth* and the *Ordinalia*, and the idea is a medieval commonplace. Adam's creation in Hebron is also familiar, linked with his supposed burial there; see v. Erffa, *Ikonologie* I, 76-87

> Now, without fail I shall make,
> to take and fill his place well,
> a new-formed man
> in the Valley of Hebron.
> And the man shall fill, anon,
> the place from which he was banned.

There are elements of the creation of man which *do* match those in the *Ordinalia*, such as the naming of the beasts by Adam, after Eve has been created already. The actual temptation of Eve, however, leading to the Fall of man, differs from that in the *Ordinalia* in some respects. In the earlier play a stage direction tells us simply that the devil takes the form of a serpent; here the matter is developed far more fully. A diabolical council in hell discusses prior to the temptation two points: that Eve should be tempted first, and that, since the devil is so ugly that he would frighten Eve, another tempter must be found. The decision to approach Eve first is a commonplace of medieval Latin exegesis, sometimes linked with pseudo-etymologies such as the derivation of *mulier* 'woman' from *mollier* 'softer', and the devil's decision to use the serpent can also be traced back a long way. There is an interesting early analogue in the Irish poem *Saltair na Rann* in the eleventh century, in which the devil actually spends some time debating with the serpent before the latter agrees to conceal him; in *Gwreans an bys* the serpent, although it does try to get away from Lucifer, has a more passive role than in the Irish work.[10] Here it is bullied, rather than persuaded. The reason for the choice of the serpent, however, is made specific; it has the face of a woman. This will not frighten Eve, and in a symbolic sense it will reflect her own self. The idea of the serpent with a woman's face is common enough after its probable first appearance in the *Historia scholastica* of Peter Comestor, both in literature and in iconography (the Sistine chapel has a celebrated example), although paintings often show the serpent either realistically or with a devil's face. Certainly in later Genesis-plays the snake usually has a woman's features; the two-day Lucerne Easter-play, for example, again a near-contemporary of the Cornish work, calls for the serpent to have a "woman's face, crowned, otherwise to be like a poisonous serpent."[11] In the Cornish work, we have, however, already been shown the

[10] David Greene, Fergus Kelly, Brian Murdoch, *The Old Irish Adam and Eve Story from Saltair na Rann* (Dublin, 1976), I, 32-5 and II, 75-7. See also Olin H. Moore, "The Infernal Council," *Modern Philology* 16 (1918), 1-25

[11] Klimke, *Paradiesspiel*, p. 34. The play is from 1583. Occasionally reference is made to the serpent merely having "a human head": see my *Recapitulated Fall*, pp. 159-61. In a Breton poem, however, the serpent has the head of a young girl (*a guis vr verh iouan*): Hemon, *Christmas Hymns*, p. 75. There is a detailed study of the female-headed serpent by

serpent, and this is unusual. At the creation of the animals, the serpent actually appears (*a fyne serpent made with a virgyn face, and yolowe heare upon her head*, CW at 409), so that Lucifer, when discussing the fall, can refer to it as one of God's creations. Lucifer has also been referred to as a snake or a worm (*preve*, CW 336) before the fall. Given that the actual scene of the creation of beasts is unusual, the appearance of the future tempter so early is of some interest. As a rare parallel, Ruf's *Adam und Heva* has an extended naming scene in which Adam, when naming the serpent, actually comments that it will cause problems for man. The Cornish text is more subtle in the introduction of the creature. Once the diabolical entry is effected, however, what is noticeable is not the similarity with Eve (a point sometimes stressed), but the supposedly angelic nature of the creature. It has to be stressed, however, that the serpent as such is merely a serpent, and is most certainly not a female character. It is only an instrument, and we are made well aware that Lucifer is using it. Condemned to crawl on its belly, as in the Bible, it is in fact Lucifer who crawls away, as the stage-directions make clear. The serpent is just an animal. A separate tradition, again of some antiquity, has the temptation brought about by the devil in the guise of an angel, echoing II Corinthians xi: 14, and found for example in the apocryphal Adam and Eve tradition, where Eve is tempted for a second time by the devil in such a disguise. At all events, here Eve takes the beautiful creature through which Lucifer - who after all *was* an angel - both sings and speaks, to *be* an angel. Eve is suspicious at first, and remains nervous for some time, even when assured that the creature has just left heaven in a great hurry, *gans hast pur vras* (CW 557), which is perfectly true.[12] The ironies of the passage have been pointed out by Paula Neuss, as when the serpent goes on to note that only the good come from heaven. Eve is, nevertheless, strongly tempted by the notion that she can become the equal of God. Perhaps it is because she does want to believe it that she asserts - as she does in the *Ordinalia*, albeit later - that the advice to take the fruit came from an angel. Already before she eats, she decides to share the fruit with Adam, but (a point not found elsewhere in the Genesis tradition) she promises Adam that the fruit will bring financial rewards. Adam recognises the fruit in spite of Eve's assurances that the origin was angelic. It is once again a commonplace of

---

J. K. Bonnell, "The Serpent with a Human Head in Art and in Mystery Play," *Journal of the Archaeological Institute of America* 21 (1917), 255-291. Newlyn, "Pit and Pedestal," p. 151f. is unconvincing in her attempt to see the presentation of the serpent as misogyny; it is and remains an animal, and in fact the issue is to make sure that Eve is not afraid. Neuss includes in her illustrations the relevant scene of the St Neot Creation Window.

[12]   See Neuss' introduction, p. xxv. Rosemary Woolf, *The English Mystery Plays* (London, 1972), p. 117 discusses the angelic disguise, as does Eric Smith, *Some Versions of the Fall* (London, 1973), pp. 82-8. The point is that Eve ought to be able to see through the disguise.

biblical hermeneutic that Eve persuaded Adam with unrecorded words of blandishment, but various different approaches are used in the literary adaptations of the story. The *Ordinalia* has a truncated version of what has been called the romantic interpretation, namely that Adam eats when threatened with the loss of Eve's affection.[13] The version in *Gwreans an bys* is dramatically far more satisfying. Just as the serpent had, in gesture at least, resisted the devil, and Eve in words and gesture had made a slighter stronger effort to resist, Adam's efforts are more forceful still, and Eve has to make considerable efforts to win him over. Having tried quasi-innocent cajolery, insisting upon the truth of what the supposed angel told her, Eve displays next a well-drawn display of injury when Adam accuses her of stupidity, implying that Adam would be perfectly happy if he *did* reap the benefits she has been telling him about:

> Yea, yea, me a gevyth oll an blame
> Tha worthis ge lemyn Adam,
> Pynagell for ytha an game.

> Saw a pony dewyow gwyres
> Ny veas malbew serrys,
> Me a wore hena ynta. (CW 809-14)

> Oh yes, now I'll get the blame
> from you Adam, just the same,
> whatever end to the game!

> But if we were gods, not men,
> damned if you'ld be angry then!
> *That* much I know for certain.

Adam tries to reason with her and to calm her down at the same time, but her response is an even more dismissive sulk:

> Yea, y thosta ge dean fure,
> Ny vynny orthaf cola...(CW 822f.)

> Oh yes, you are the wise man,
> don't want to listen to *me*...

---

[13]   See J. M. Evans, *Paradise Lost and the Genesis Tradition* (Oxford, 1968), p. 203.

and at this point it is Eve - rather than Adam - who threatens to walk away; she has the ascendancy, and is now able to say very simply that she believed *an eal ega in wethan* (CW 827, "the angel in the tree") and can deliver her ultimatum: if Adam does not eat he will lose her love. In her new-found persuasiveness her last comments leading up to the Fall are not aggressive, but wheedling, the wife who knows she is going to get her way, though she slips in a reminder of the consequences if Adam continues to resist:

> Meir, kymar an avall teake
> Po sure inter te hath wreage
>   An garenga quyt a fyll,
>   Mar ny vynyth y thebbry. (CW 833-6)

> Look! Take this apple so fair
> or else the love you now share
>   with your wife will disappear
>   if you refuse to eat it.

Adam capitulates and eats the fruit, but the whole is far more complex than in the earlier work, showing a gradual movement from the self-centred fall of Lucifer to the latter's bullying of the serpent, the extended but simple persuasion of Eve, and the far slower persuasion of Adam, with a cumulative irony as Eve constantly reminds us (and Adam) that her interlocutor was an angel.

The interrogation of the couple by God matches that of the *Ordinalia*, but the conclusion of that passage is again rather different. Lucifer is now identified with the serpent, cursed by God, and bewails his fate; however, he does have the apparent comfort that all of Adam's children will come to him in hell. This passages places into better relief the plea by Adam - which is also present in the earlier play - for some of the oil of mercy. God does indeed promise them a redemption, but only after hardship. Interestingly, God's promise of the oil of mercy coincides biblically with the protevangelical verse Genesis iii: 15, which is normally interpreted as a promise that the Redeemer will crush the devil. Adam admits to God's justice, and the whole structure of the passage is more logical than the earlier version, although some parts are very close; it is almost as if the earlier play has been corrected and made consistent. But they are not the same play; there is no sign in *Gwreans an bys* of Adam's bargaining for land, but instead we have a new character, the morality figure of death, appointed God's messenger. His brief words are a statement to the audience, underlining the point of the fall. Death also underscores the role of the devil's deceit by an external comment on the play, referring to things "you have seen together here" (CW 1004). The real burden of his comment is that had the couple not sinned, they would not have had to

83

face death. The inclusion of this anthropomorphic figure, furthermore, provides an indication of the lateness of the drama. He has a greater role in the Breton *Creation*, and appears in plays of the fall regularly from the beginning of the sixteenth century. Frequently his role is limited, but effective, and this is true of Ruf's *Adam und Heva* once again, in which he has one speech only. In Gil Vicente's *Historia de Deus* in 1527, indeed, the mere appearance of *Morte* at the moment of fall is sufficient, although he does have some dialogue later. Only rarely does he have a fuller role.[14]

The treatment of Cain and Abel differs from that of the *Ordinalia*, but is again of some interest. The motif of Adam's blessing is not present - and the absence of that small motif indicates that the later play is not following and expanding upon the earlier - but Cain does show his true colours at once when he states that he has no intention of making a proper sacrifice. Abel's double blessing (by mother and father, OM 470-3) contrasts with the double curse on Cain in the later play. In the *Origo Mundi* Cain offers less than his proper tithe (the emphasis on tithes by Adam and his children, and Noah as well, is absent from the later play in any case), but here he resorts to active trickery. Worse, he tells us so:

> Ye lysky ny vannaf ve,
> An eys nan frutes defrye.
> Taw, Abell, thymo, pedn cooge!

> Me a guntell dreyne ha spearn
> Ha glose tha leskye heb bearn,
> Hag ara bus brase a vooge. (CW 1086-91)

> I've no intention to burn
> either the fruit or the corn!
> So shut up, Abel, thick-head!

> Thorns and brambles I shall take,
> burn them with cow-dung to make
> a great bush of smoke instead.

Where the earlier Cain is a rationalist - asking what benefit the sacrifice will have for anyone - this Cain is openly and deliberately devious. Cain's offering of thorns and brambles, rather than a simple withholding of his tithe, or offering inferior corn, may echo the *Golden Legend*, where the same motif is found. Traditional exegesis, faced with the problem of why God chose one

---

[14]   I have discussed the point in "Jacob Ruf," p. 117 and "The Breton *Creation*," p. 172f.

and rejected the other sacrifice, gets round the problem with a reference to Cain's presumed state of heart and unwillingness to sacrifice; here his intent is perfectly clear. The Breton creation-play takes this a stage further, even, and has Satan prompt Cain with the notion that he, Cain, has worked hard for his corn, and that God does not need it. In a far more extensively developed section, the Breton play has Cain refusing to sacrifice at all, so that there is no problem as to why God accepts that of Abel only. Satan then prompts Cain to murder his brother. *Gwreans an bys* diverges from the Bible (and the *Origo Mundi*) in that there is no reference to God rejecting the sacrifice; Abel's own satisfaction in the smoke produced by his offering so enrages Cain that he takes the jawbone of an ass and kills his brother. This is the murder-weapon in a number of versions of the story, though once again not in the *Ordinalia*, the whole tone of which is different. The somewhat curious realisation of Gen. iv: 10 in the *Origo Mundi* in which a voice apparently does call from the earth, at least according to the stage-direction, is not present in the later play (although Neuss adds it in her text). The real point, however, is the evil of Cain; he expresses no regret at Abel's death, but rather reiterates the point that God has no need of their belongings. Abel's last words, however, were a prophecy of retribution, and God the Father does - as in the Bible - confront Cain. Both Cornish plays pick up the point of Cain's *desperatio*, his conviction that his guilt is greater than God's mercy. This is unlike the Breton play, where Cain does beg for mercy and the mark is seen as a positive gesture, which indeed it is, since it is to prevent Cain from being killed. The French *Mistére* interpolates here a debate between Justice and Mercy. The sign placed upon Cain by God so that he will not be killed is unusual in the Cornish play, however, namely the Greek letter omega, described somewhat confusingly in the English stage directions not only as a *marcke* but also as *the worde omega*. Literary and iconographic traditions vary, although the mark is frequently seen as a horn;[15] the Greek letter is unusual, and most dramatic versions fail to specify the mark. What value has to be placed upon the stage direction is questionable, however, since later on the mark is referred to as being *in corne tha dale* (CW 1371, "in the horn of your forehead") and may be a horn after all.

Both the *Ordinalia* and *Gwreans an bys* have Cain repeat to Adam the evasion about not being his brother's keeper, but the development of the narrative is quite different. In the *Origo Mundi* Adam and Eve lament their misfortune, the former linking it with Eve, and blaming all misfortune on his relationship with her. The later play has once again a quite different angle;

---

[15]   The mark is discussed by Emerson, "Legends," and by v. Erffa, *Ikonologie* I, 381 (usually depicted as horns). Neuss indicates in her notes, p. 225 that an *omega* would look like a pair of horns, which is a plausible explanation. There may be an overlap with Ezechiel ix: 4, where the mark is the Greek letter *tau*.

Adam curses Cain formally and banishes him, before succumbing to his own grief, whereupon Cain declares his intention of becoming a wanderer. It is then left to Adam to break the news to Eve, and the pair comfort one another on the loss of the sons. Adam does not blame Eve on this occasion, but rather laments his own fate in general. Eve then adds *her* curse. The speech in which she does so is simply a parallel to that already given by Adam, and has been added for structural balance - there are verbal echoes - and each parent adds the curse of the other to his or her own curse. Indeed, both make the point that there will be no more joy for them, expressing in effective counterpoint the sorrows of the parents at the death of their son (CW 1196-1210 and 1251-1279) But Cain is impenitent, leaving with the words *malbew yddrag es thyma* (CW 1287 "I don't repent a scrap"), a point he makes several times, using the same phrase a few lines later, with the added coarse interjection *bram an gathe* (CW 1303, "cat's fart") for example.[16] This is in spite of the fact that his wife/sister Calmana also reproaches him, in terms similar to those used by Adam and Eve, and although she leaves with him, she laments the loss of her family. Calmana, who is not present in the earlier play, is an interesting cameo part. Her half-dozen or so speeches (which contain one full line of English) present her as a sorrowing but dutiful wife, a vivid non-biblical female part. The name is traditional from the *Historia scholastica* onwards (with Delbora as the wife either of Abel or occasionally of Seth), and both women are present in other late Genesis-plays, such as that by Ruf, and somewhat earlier in the *Mistére*, where they are the first to discover the murder. Adam and Eve in both Cornish plays swear that they will have no further children. Where in the *Ordinalia* play a seraph is sent to Adam to command that he and Eve should have another child, in *Gwreans an bys* God himself tells Adam, as soon as the vow is uttered, that he and Eve should have another child and that the new child - Seth - will be loved by God. When Seth is born, God affirms that he will be the father of learning.

The story of the death of Cain at the hands of Lamech, which now follows, is not particularly common, and is found mainly in later dramatisations (although the N-Town plays have the incident). It is there in the *Mistére*, in German plays such as the *Egerer Fronleichnamsspiel* and in Ruf, and in some

---

[16]   The text is difficult at this point, and Stokes, Neuss and Nance differ from one another; see Neuss' notes, p. 226. But the despairing defiance of Cain in the face of his mother's curse is clear. Newlyn, "Pit and Pedestal," p. 150 highlights Eve's words and links the curse issued by Eve with God's curse on her; but there are no verbal links, and indeed, God strictly speaking only curses the serpent. The counterpoint and cumulative effect of the parental curse is far more significant. Newlyn also attributes the paucity of women characters in medieval Cornish plays (p. 153) to "attitudes towards women and women's marginal status in the culture," whereas the dramatists are bound by their biblical sources and are unable to introduce new characters; but it is notable that here the dramatist precisely *does* add in Calmana a well-drawn figure who is not mentioned (though she is implied) in the Bible.

late Spanish dramas, including one by Lope de Vega, although the Breton play breaks off at Lamech's entrance.[17] Two separate narrative elements at issue here. The first is the death of Cain itself, and the other the development of Lamech and the diverging lines of patriarchs, the good Sethites and the evil Cainites, the merging of which will later on lead to large-scale corruption and the flood. The Cornish Lamech (who does not appear in the *Ordinalia*) presents himself as an evil man, worse even than Cain. He declares himself to be an oppressor of the weak (a very unusual motif), but also the proto-bigamist. This point is made by many Latin exegetes, in spite of the complex matrimonial arrangements of later and more respected patriarchs. The Cornish dramatist develops this point by making Lamech into an all-round womaniser:

> Moy es vn wreag thym yma
> Thom pleasure rag gwyll ganssy.
> Ha sure me ew an kensa
> Bythqwath whath a ve dew wreag.
>
> Han mowyssye lower plenty
> Yma thym; nyngens dentye.
> Me as kyef pan vydnaf ve;
> Ny sparyaf anothans y,
> Malbew onyn a vo teag   (CW 1449-57)
>
> Not just one wife - I have more
> to give great pleasure to me.
> I'm the first - of that I'm sure -
> to marry two wives at once.
>
> And I have girls a-plenty,
> they're never over-dainty!
> I pick them when it suits me.
> Damned if I'll keep off them, see,
> especially pretty ones!

[17] See my "Creation, Fall and After," pp. 701-5; the background to the narrative is found in Emerson, "Legends of Cain," pp. 874-7. The best study is that by Edmund Reiss, "The Story of Lamech and its Place in Medieval Drama," *Journal of Medieval and Renaissance Studies* 2 (1972), 35-48, who discusses also the patristic origins of the episode. On the theme in art (it is also in the St Neot window), see Sandra Hindman, *Text and Image in Fifteenth Century Dutch Illustrated Bibles* (Leiden, 1977), p. 17f. and plates 16f. and v. Erffa, *Ikonologie*, I, 392-4.

Lamech is blind, but still a huntsman. The influence of a narrative version of the story such as that by Peter Comestor or the *Golden Legend* is clear in that Lamech explains that he shoots animals only for skins, and his long speech is clearly a dramatisation of the prose version, since statements of that sort are irrelevant to the plot. More important, however, is the reference to Cain, who is still alive, and is *yn defyth...yn myske bestas*, "in the desert among beasts" (CW 1479). When Lamech has already been led to the woods by his servant for the hunt, Cain claims to be:

> Yn cossowe hag in busshes,
> Avell beast prest ow pewa. (CW 1518f.)

> in the woods and the bushes
> living always like a beast.

The dramatist reiterates too, however, the crucial question of despair; Cain is too proud - the *superbia*-motif - to seek God's mercy, and therefore *is* damned. This point is developed in the *Legenda aurea*, for example, in which Cain is condemned both for despair and for failing to trust in the efficacy of the sign, which will prevent his death; at the same time, the sign is perceived there to be part of his condemnation, so that Cain will live in fear for a long period. In our play Cain fails to trust God's promise regarding the mark, and it is while hiding in a bush (again a point made in the *Golden Legend* and elsewhere) that Lamech's servant sees him and assures his master that this is indeed a beast (and an especially ugly one into the bargain). Lamech realises slowly that this is Cain, identified again by the mark *in corn tha dale* "in the horn of your forehead" (CW 1624) which Lamech was unable to see. Once Lamech realises what he has done, his reaction is an interesting one: at once he blames the servant (*ow boya*, "my boy" CW 1650). In some versions this role is taken by his son, although that seems not to be the case here. Consumed with anger, Lamech kills the servant, thus fulfilling (one reading of) the sword-song in Genesis iv: 23. The actual death of Cain is extended, however, and prior to Lamech's killing of the servant, Cain not only repeats that God will not forgive him and he will seek no forgiveness - *desperatio* once again - but he states that he himself killed Abel because Abel would not show him proper reverence as the elder brother. This is a precise parallel to the fall of Lucifer, who in medieval theological writings (most notably the apocryphal Adam-books) refuses to worship the image of God in Adam because he is the elder creation. And as Lucifer was despatched to hell, so too Cain (and also Lamech) are taken down into hell.

The play shows us several instances of action taken in defiance of God. Lucifer is guilty of outright rebellion and the desire to replace God; the protoplasts break one commandment out of a desire for knowledge; Cain acts out of petulance, taking out on Abel his anger at God's rejection of his insincere sacrifice; Lamech's act is a mixture of farce and accident; and subsequent acts of rebellion against God (which lead to the flood) are merely petty wickednesses. Adam's sin, however, is not like the rest. Lucifer and Cain declare that their sins are so great that God will not forgive them:

> Ny amownt whelas mercye... (CW 428)

> There's no use seeking mercy

> Ny vanaf tha worth an Tase
> Whylas mercy...   (CW 1522f.)

> I shall not seek our Father's
> mercy...

The same may be assumed of Lamech; Adam, however, is penitent, acknowledging guilt but looking also for the oil of mercy, and when Eve shows signs of beginning to despair, he talks her round:

> Ow fryas, gwella tha geare,
> Gas tha ola hath ega.
> Gwren grasse thagen maker
> Agan lavyr in bysma;
>   Ny andyllas, ha moye. (CW 1306-10)

> My wife, be of better cheer,
> dry your eyes, no more sorrow!
> Let us thank our Maker dear
> for our labours here below,
>   for we deserve them, and more.

The role of Adam as comforter and advocate of penance - an almost priestly role - is not unusual in medieval adaptations of Genesis.[18]

What happens to the soul of Abel in this play (unlike the *Origo Mundi*) is unclear. Adam's death, however, is approaching, and he sends Seth to paradise to obtain the oil of mercy. The outlines of the Sethite/ Holy Rood material differ from those of the *Ordinalia*, however, and the dramatist of

---

[18]   The pattern of rebellion is made clear in J. M. R. Margeson's *The Origins of English Tragedy* (Oxford, 1967), p. 10. On the role of Adam as priest, see my "The Origins of Penance: Reflections of Adamic Apocrypha," *Annals of the Archive of Ferran Valls I Taberner's Library* 9/10 (1991), 205-27.

Gwreans an bys was either following a different text of the Holy Rood material, or was remembering it only imperfectly. At all events it does not play such an extended role in the later play. This is partly because the later play stops at the flood, of course, but it is worth recalling that in the *Origo Mundi* there is even a reference to the oil of mercy at the very time of the creation (OM 325). The notion of the burned earth and withered grass on the road to paradise is present, but where in the *Ordinalia* Seth sees the single tree, stripped of its bark, as in the Holy Rood *Legende*, in *Gwreans an bys* it is not absolutely clear whether Seth sees one tree or two. Certainly he sees the dry tree with the serpent at the top (*a vadn*, CW 1809), and this is described as the tree of the fall, that is, presumably, the tree of knowledge. Seth looks again and sees a tree reaching from hell to heaven, and in this is the Virgin with a child. He notes incidentally that he can see his brother Cain (though not Abel) in hell - something not voiced in the earlier work. In the earlier play, there is clearly only one tree, though Seth has three glimpses of it - to see the tree, the serpent round it (rather than on top of it), and the child (but not its mother). The stage-direction of *Gwreans an bys* need not be definitive, but the text, too, seems to imply a tree of knowledge *and* the tree of life:

> Ther he vyseth all thingys, and seeth two trees: and in the one
> tree sytteth Mary the Virgyn, and in her lappe her sonn Jesus,
> in the tope of the Tree of Lyf, and, in the other tree, the
> Serpent which caused Eva to eat the appell. (CW at 1804)

The later play has perhaps added the Virgin to make clear that this is the promised Redeemer. It is one of the few Marian points in the work, although it is in essence soteriological, rather than concerned expressly with the Virgin. As with the earlier work, Seth is given three seeds, but they are to be placed in Adam's mouth and nostrils on this occasion, and from them a single tree (rather than the three rods of the *Ordinalia*) will grow. One final difference is that *Gwreans an bys* introduces the point (found in the *Vita Adae*, the *Gospel of Nicodemus* and the Holy Rood legends) that the redemption will come after 5,500 years.[19]

In apocryphal writings, those who die before the harrowing of hell go to hell itself, and in works like the *Gospel of Nicodemus* the first to be released at the harrowing are Adam, Eve and Abel. In *Gwreans an bys* Cain is in hell (devils carried him away, and Seth saw him in his vision), and we have heard that Lamech is destined for hell, too; but Abel is not mentioned, and so, too, when Adam himself dies, he does not go to hell, as he and Abel do in the *Origo Mundi*. Adam has a death-bed speech (in which he refers to his 66

---

19   See the *Vita Adae*, Sparks, *Apocryphal Old Testament*, p. 158 and the *Gospel of Nicodemus*, James, *Apocryphal New Testament*, p. 127.

children - the number varies, but this version may perhaps be based on the *Vita Adae*),[20] and Death himself then appears. Adam expresses his thanks to this functionary for ending his weariness. But where in the earlier play devils carry the soul away, here Lucifer himself declares that Adam will go not to hell but to limbo; the devils wanting to carry Adam off are met with the words:

> Na, na, ny wreth in della!
> Yma ken ornes ractha.
> Yn Lymbo, barth a wartha
> Ena ef a wra trega,
>   Del ew ornes gans an Tace. (CW 2015-9)

> No, no, you will not do so;
> it is arranged that he go
> to the highest point, Limbo,
> dwelling there whilst here below,
>   as God the Father ordained.

Cain is in the lowest point of hell (*in pytt*, CW 2035), but Adam is in the upper reaches of hell, and when a devil asks why Adam cannot be tormented the same way as Cain, Lucifer tells him that it is to do with repentance; Cain not only refused to repent and gave no thought to God's mercy, but he even rejoiced. He will suffer, but Adam and those who, while not yet *sub gratia*, repent thoroughly, will *not* suffer the great pains of hell. An angel carries Adam to limbo, which is, however, still a part of hell. The motif has its origins, perhaps, in the *Vita Adae* tradition, once more, where an angel takes Adam's soul at his death, charged by God to keep it in custody until judgement day. The idea is present in the Latin and also in the various vernacular versions of the *Vita Adae* as well. Interestingly, in the near-contemporary *Historia de Deus* of Gil Vicente, Abel is sent to limbo and is

---

[20]   In the Adamic tradition (see the full translation of the *Vita Adae* in R. H. Charles, *Apocrypha and Pseudepigrapha of the Old Testament*, Oxford, 1913, II, 139) Adam has thirty sons and thirty daughters, plus Cain, Abel and Seth. Here, as Neuss speculates, CW, p. 231, the number of sons is given as 32, probably having added in Cain and Abel, though it also mentions them separately. The number of daughters matches that. It is odd that Seth is not named. Frequently the number is greater, and even medieval sources (such as the *Collectanea Bedae*) admit that different traditions were known: see James E. Cross and Thomas D. Hill, *The Prose "Solomon and Saturn" and "Adrian and Ritheus"* (Toronto, 1982), p. 88f., with examples. The *Legenda aurea* notes that opinions differ as to whether Adam had sixty or a hundred children.

there joined by Adam.[21] What is striking in the Cornish play, however, is the explanation that Adam is not to be punished in the deepest part of hell because he did repent: that repentance is perhaps more important than the idea of limbo as such.

Not only the use of apocryphal writings like the *Vita Adae* or the Holy Rood legends (or rather, of motifs found in them), but the idea of limbo has been cited as a key element in placing our work before the Reformation, which rejected the concept of any mid-way stage between heaven and hell. How swiftly this somewhat detailed theological concept actually took hold, however, is quite another matter, and certainly the stress on proper contrition (as underlined by Lucifer's somewhat out-of-character homily) is not at variance with Reformation thought and its insistence on the principle of *metanoiete*, which is accompanied by the free gift of grace. We may note, too, that limbo in the work appears to be conceived as a part of hell, albeit one of its upper reaches. This whole section concludes with the psychopomp-angel reiterating the notion that the redemption will not be long, a point found in other Genesis-plays.

Only later Genesis-plays deal in any detail with the patriarchs, and even here (as in non-dramatic reworkings of the theme) it is quite normal to move directly from Cain and Abel to the flood. The complex material in Genesis iv and v is rarely covered, apart perhaps from the episodic development of the death-song of Lamech the Cainite. The biblical narrative provides two lists of patriarchs, in fact deriving from the same original, but as they stand offering two distinct lines, one descended from Seth, the other from Cain, a wicked and a good generation. The *Ordinalia* ignores them, moving straight to Noah after the death of Adam, and the English cycles also miss out the generations. Only later continental plays include them - the French *Mistére* has a complex series of scenes showing both lines, and Ruf's *Adam und Heva* makes a theological point with them, varying the names in accordance with the Zurich Bible to make clear that the Cainite Lemech is different from the Sethite Lamech. *Gwreans an bys* shows us Enoch the Sethite in a separate scene, but this is linked with the Lamech story. The point is made in medieval commentary that where the evil Lamech the Cainite is the seventh in line from Adam, Enoch, seventh in the Sethite line, is correspondingly good. This is spelt out in the *Golden Legend*, and if the source of our play is something like that version, it would account both for the insistence of Lamech on his own

---

[21]   See the *Vita* xlviii, Sparks, *Apocryphal Old Testament*, p. 160. Vicente's Portuguese *auto* is in his *Obras Completas*, ed. M. Braga (Lisbon, 4th. ed., 1968), II, 188f. Jenner, "Cornish Drama II," p. 67 and Neuss, CW, lii, both comment on limbo. It is odd that the *earlier* play has no reference to it. In the Digby play of the Magdalene Christ rescues Adam from *lymbo*, which simply means "hell:" *The Digby Plays*, ed. F. J. Furnivall (London, 1896, repr. 1967 = EETS/ES 70), p. 92, v. 975.

The Creacion of the World

wickedness, and on the inclusion of Enoch, who announces his special piety.
The customary interpretation of Gen. v: 24 is that Enoch entered heaven in
the whole body, and this now happens in the play, developed into a vision of
paradise on Enoch's part, followed by a brief homily placed into his mouth.
Enoch recalls the fall, and warns mankind not to transgress the laws of God.
There is a long tradition of vision-literature associated with Enoch, and his
role as a preacher goes back to the New Testament, of course, in Jude xiv,
which refers to Enoch as the seventh from Adam. The words spoken by him
here, in fact, sound rather like the continuation in Jude (xvii-xxii), complete
with the promise of eternal life. In Ruf's German-language play Enoch has a
similar role, warning the people, and in the French cycle there is a separate
section in which *Enoch, qui fut ravy en Paradis terrestre* makes a general-
tropological point to Noah, well before his actual translation.

What *Gwreans an bys* does *not* do is develop the gradual coming-together
of the two generations until the whole world becomes evil. Instead, Seth
announces in an extended apocalyptic speech which runs on easily from the
vision of Enoch the increase in wickedness, and foretells the coming of the
flood by reference to the stars and planets. This whole section is of interest,
portraying Seth as a scholar and custodian of the history of the world; the
motif is found at an early stage in the apocryphal *Vita Adae* tradition, when
Eve instructs Seth to inscribe the history of the world on stone and on clay,
so that one will survive whether the destruction of the world is by fire or
water. The idea is also encountered that the books are preserved in pillars,
and the idea as such goes back as far as Josephus.[22] That Jared, who is
Enoch's father and Seth's great-great-grandson, should be involved is
extremely rare, however. His role appears to be to collect all kinds of books -
two copies of each - in order to preserve one way or another a continuation
of the history of man. As Neuss indicates in the notes to her edition, the only
parallel to this idea seems to be in John Trevisa's translation of Higden's
Polychronicon. There is perhaps also a pre-echo here of the preservation of
life in the ark. In the French *Mistére* the two pillars (*des coullonnes de pierre,
de marbre et de terre* means really only two) are erected by the sons of the
Cainite Lamech, which is equally unusual.

With this motif, the Cornish dramatist moves directly to Genesis vi: 6,
God's regret that he made man at all, and the play moves therefore - less
abruptly, it is true, than in the *Ordinalia* - to the flood. The rest of the two
generations are therefore omitted, although the presentation of Noah's building
of the ark differs considerably from other versions. Where the English cycles,

---

[22]   *Vita Adae* L, Sparks, *Apocryphal Old Testament*, p. 160f., Josephus, *Antiquities of the Jews* II, tr. William Whiston (Halifax, 1859), p. 27. Jenner, "Cornish Drama II", p. 68 refers to the *Historia Scholastica*. For a full discussion of the point, see Neuss, CW, p. 233, with details of the *Mistére* version.

93

for example, simply present Noah and his family, as indeed does the *Origo Mundi*, the later play confronts Noah with the Cainite generation, in the shape of Tubalcain, who is once designated Tabell in the stage-directions; since spellings alternate, it may even be that another member of the family of the Cainite Lamech, perhaps Jubal or Jabel, as well as Tubalcain is implied. There is, it is true, no mention of the useful skills of the Cainites (as in Gen. iv: 21f.), and they are simply presented as scoffers. This happens too in Ruf's play, where it is sustained and lengthy. In *Gwreans an bys* there is a careful dramatic counterpoint in which Noah gathers the beasts on God's command, and his sons make the ark, enumerating the items as they bring them along. While this is going on, Tubalcain provides a commentary of mockery, laughing at Noah as he does so for foolishness of constructing a boat so far from water:

> Marthe ew genaf a un dra:
> Y vosta mar ucky, Noye.
> Praga ew genas she omma
> Buyldya lester mar worthy
> > In creys powe, tha worthe an moare? (CW 2295-9)

> One thing really puzzles me,
> Noah, that you are such a fool
> to build - what stupidity -
> a ship so solid and true
> > inland, so far from the sea!

Noah explains to him carefully that the flood is coming, but the whole passage really makes a moral point to the audience, with Tubal(cain) acting as a foil for Noah. He picks up the notion of repentance, which has been voiced at several points, and his injunction to Tubal(cain) and the rest of the scoffers is couched in the words of Matthew iv: 17:

> Hag eddrag thothef yma
> Bythquath mabe dean tha vos gwryes.
> Rag henna gwrewgh amendya;
> Ages foly byth nehys.
> Yn urna der vanar da,
> Mara pethowgh repentys,
> > An kethe plage a wra voydya (CW 2340-46)

> And He has now repented
> of ever creating men!

> And your ways must be mended
> and folly cast off again.
> And when all is well tended,
> if you repent - only then
> will the misery be ended.

The parallels with a relatively distant continental play such as that by Ruf cannot be pursued too far, since there is no question of direct linking. Nevertheless, Noah's speech at this point and the response, is close, and the two plays share an approach which is not found in earlier plays, that of Noah as the preacher - Tubal dismisses him in Cornish literally as *progowther* (CW 2347) in the passage which follows that just cited.[23] The preaching, however, is to no avail; the mockers resort to abuse, and are not heard again once Noah and his family enter the ark.

The flood itself is treated in relatively brief terms. There is, it is true, a little play with Noah's wife, who is not the shrew that she sometimes can be in the English (though not the continental) tradition, but who does dither, reluctant to leave things behind. In neither Cornish version is the unnamed lady as vigorous as in the Chester plays, say, where she refuses to leave her gossips, although there is a very slight resemblance to the Wakefield plays, where she again resists to the very last minute. Already docile in the *Origo Mundi*, she has in *Gwreans an bys* only one six-line speech.[24] The sons underscore the folly of the mockers, but the actual flood is treated very quickly; the raven is sent out with the dove, and the latter returns with an olive branch; Noah assumes (and this is a traditional point in medieval commentary once again) that the raven is feasting on carrion, those destroyed in the flood.[25] The flood itself is swiftly over in the play, however, and the bulk of attention is placed upon the sacrifice to God to celebrate the safety of Noah and his family, to which God's response is the rainbow. Dramatically, this makes for an effective ending. It is noteworthy that the emphasis in the Noah section is not on the flood as such, but on the possibility up to the last of repentance. There is nothing of this in the *Ordinalia* play, and *Gwreans an bys* represents a quite different tradition.

---

[23]   See Murdoch, "Jacob Ruf", p. 123, and "From the Flood to the Tower of Babel," *Ériu* 40 (1989), 77 (citing the *Cursor Mundi* as well as our play).
[24]   See K. Garvin, "Note on Noah's Wife," *MLN* 49 (1934), 88-90; F. L. Utley, "The One Hundred and Three Names of Noah's Wife," *Speculum* 16 (1941), 426-52; A. J. Mill, "Noah's Wife Again," *PMLA* 56 (1941), 613-26.
[25]   For a list of medieval examples, see Murdoch, "From the Flood," p. 83. The idea was still current in Luther's period.

Although we do not have second day, we are left with a good idea of what that day's drama will contain. Having shown us the creation and fall of man, and the near destruction of the wicked society, the second and last day's action clearly picks up the notes of redemption found at various points - in the Seth episode and indeed with the rainbow. The audience is invited to return the next day when they will see the other side of the divine economy of history, the redemption. Where the emphasis on the first day has been primarily upon loss - by Lucifer, by Cain, by Lamech and by the wicked generations, quite apart from the fall of man itself - with relatively few references to salvation, the next day will contain more:

> Dewh a vorowe a dermyn;
> Why a weall matters pur vras,
> Ha redempcyon granntys
> Der vercy a Thew an Tase,
>   Tha sawya neb es kellys. (CW 2542-6)

> Come tomorrow in good time
> and see great matters take place
> and redemption granted then
> by God the Father's great grace
>   saving the lost souls of men.

The actual performance for the day ends with a summons to the minstrels to play for dancing.

We have no idea, of course, why the text breaks off, nor whether Jordan ever copied the second day. His final statement in the manuscript - "Heare endeth the Creacon of the worlde *with* noyes fludde wryten by William Jordan" - has a certain finality about it. Perhaps he did not have the rest of the play before him. If indeed the second day contained more overtly Catholic elements than the first day (perhaps with what was later felt to be an undue emphasis on the Virgin, though there is no hard evidence to suggest this), it might not even have been preserved long enough for Jordan to know it. At all events, the play stands at the end of the tradition of biblical adaptation in dramatic form in Europe, comparable most readily with the French *Mistére* and to an even greater extent with works like Ruf's *Adam und Heva*, however remote in real terms. *Gwreans an bys* looks in some ways like a Protestant drama, and certainly it stands at the very least on the fringe of the Reformation. As we have it, only the reference to limbo and the retention (which is neither full or completely clear) of the Sethite episode, and perhaps also the reference to frankincense in the final stage-direction (though hymns are called for as well, which looks more Protestant) might place it before the reforms, and even Jacob Ruf, firmly in the Protestant tradition, infringed

Luther's precept of *sola Scriptura* with the addition of legend material. The role of Noah as the preacher urging repentance upon the mocking world is striking, and of course it was a major tenet of the Reformation that the whole world had fallen again into a state of corruption, for which the expanded narrative of the wicked generations and the flood was a useful analogy, rather than being a vehicle simply for wonder and light comedy with the ark and Noah's wife.

What was in the second day of this play is not known, but the overall pattern is clearly very different from that of the *Ordinalia*, the emphasis of which is firmly upon God's mercy to fallen man. There is unlikely to have been any of the Old Testament typology found in the *Origo Mundi*; there is simply no room for Isaac, David, Moses in the later work. The second part presumably showed the Passion. The first play of the *Ordinalia* sequence - with its extended use of the Holy Rood legend, far more than could have been developed in *Gwreans an bys* - reminds us constantly of the promise of grace, and the final plays present it to us. All the audience has to do is believe, and the importance of Thomas and of Pilate is paramount. Even without the second day's play, *Gwreans an bys* is different. The emphasis here is on the individual's need for repentance and the avoidance of *desperatio*. Clearly the two attitudes are not contradictory, and the difference is one of emphasis and of texture. The earlier play shows us the miracle of the divine economy by presenting incidents even in the Old Testament section whose outcome is positive for the most part and often christological: the saving of Isaac, David and the temple. What stays in the mind in *Gwreans an bys* are the darker tones, even though the redemption is still promised at the end. The dogged refusal of Cain to repent and the supposed uselessness of trying to do so, Lamech the double-malefactor, and the destruction of a world not willing to listen to the preaching of Noah. But it is not, of course, a pessimistic work, even in the text that we have. It does demand, however, that man, who is created in the image of God, and who is reminded of this at the end, should love his maker and listen to God's word:

> Ymadge dean gwrega shapya:
> Mar an kerowgh dell gotha
> Why a wra orthaf cola. (CW 2525-7)

> The image of man I made.
> If you love me as you should,
> You will listen to my word.

The stress on tithing is gone in *Gwreans an bys*, and even those overt works that are in the play because they are there in the biblical source are interpreted strictly according to the spirit in which they are offered. Abel demands that

97

the sacrifice should be made well (*leall*, 'faithfully' CW 1094) for God's own sake, and God himself accepts Noah's sacrifice because it is from a good heart (CW 2494-8). The solifidian Reformation would have been hard-pressed to object to the presentation of good works and the stress on the word of God in the play, even if it effectively put an end to the practice of mystery-plays in general as a means of communicating that word. *Gwreans an bys* is about personal penance and change of heart, not just about seeing and believing.

That we have only half a work, however, is a sad and inexplicable irony, just as it remains an irony of a different sort that a work like this, written at the end of the whole tradition of biblical drama, should have been copied out in a modernised and somewhat inconsistently spelled Cornish in the year in which, as far as drama is concerned, Shakespeare was still writing, and which in theological terms saw the commanding and unifying publication for Britain as a whole of the English King James Bible.

CHAPTER FIVE

CHURCH, STATE AND SALVATION: THE PLAY OF SAINT MERIASEK

Amongst the many saints associated with Cornwall, St Mereadoc is typical in one respect: not very much is known about him. The name Mereadoc(us) is that found in Latin texts, perhaps from Welsh Meiriadog. In Breton the name is Meriadek, and it changes in Cornish to Meriasek, the form that will be used here. His cult in Britain is highly localised, with a single dedication, admittedly one of some antiquity, in Camborne, and his country of origin (though it was probably Wales) is uncertain. We have some late Latin hagiographic material, but even potentially verifiable details, such as his elevation to the bishopric of Vannes, cannot be confirmed, and we are not even sure of the century in which he lived. Yet his life provided one of the masterpieces of religious drama in late medieval Britain, a two-day dramatic cycle in Cornish of around four-and-a-half thousand lines of strophic rhymed verse dealing (uniquely) with a non-biblical saint. This makes it more surprising that it is not better known. The text was discovered at the end of the 1860s by W. W. E. Wynne in a small paper manuscript among the Hengwrt collection, and it is now in the National Library of Wales as Peniarth 105. Wynne communicated his discovery to Canon Robert Williams, publisher of the first major Cornish dictionary, who printed the opening lines in 1869, and on whose suggestion the work was edited by Whitley Stokes. His full text and translation appeared in 1872. Since that time it has been put into Unified Cornish with an accompanying translation (not all of this version has appeared in print) and has been published in English prose and verse, and re-edited with a translation. It has also been performed on various occasions.[1]

The manuscript has a colophon indicating that the copying was completed in 1504 by a priest (he is styled *dominus*) with the name "Rad Ton." The first part of the floridly written name may be Rad(ulphus) and the second the surname Ton(ne), but no firm identification can be made. The title and many

---

[1]   The best edition (with a translation), by Myrna Combellack-Harris, is not yet in print: *A Critical edition of Beunans Meriasek* (Diss. PhD, Exeter, 1985). I have used the older edition by Whitley Stokes, *The Life of St Meriasek* (London, 1872). There is a prose translation by Markham Harris, *The Life of Meriasek* (Washington, 1978) and one into verse by Myrna Combellack, *The Camborne Play* (Redruth, 1988). Yogh is used irregularly in the text, mainly for *dh/dd*, here resolved as usual as *th* (which, when it appears as such in the work, can represent the voiced or the unvoiced sound). It can also represent *y* (as in BM 2747), and on rare occasions *gh* (as BM 154). See Stokes' introduction, p. xiiif. Other italicised resolutions in citations are by Stokes.

stage directions are in Latin, and there are added secondary stage directions in English, apparently referring to an actual performance. The first few pages appear, finally, to be in a later hand, and the Cornish of the first couple of hundred lines contains some late features, where the rest is clearly Middle Cornish. In the manuscript, too, are diagrams for the layout of each day's performance, as in the *Ordinalia*. Various stations are indicated on a round once more, thirteen for the first day, fifteen for the second, with heaven at the top and hell nearby.

The title of the play in the manuscript is in Latin: *Ordinale de sancti Mereadoci episcopi et confessoris*, but it is customarily referred to by a Cornish phrase used at the end of each day's action, *Beunans Meriasek*, "The Life of Meriasek." The name shows the shift of *d* to *s/z* seen in place-names, and recent commentators note the nickname "merry-jeeks" applied to the people of Camborne, this showing presumably the continued change of that sound. Although we have a date for the copy, we are less sure of the date of composition, although it seems unlikely to be much older, and the last decades of the fifteenth century have been suggested. The language points to this, but a firmer clue is afforded by the reference to *rose noblennov* (BM 2881), "rose nobles," a coin introduced by Edward IV in 1465.[2]

Although it celebrates a saint with a cult in Cornwall and in Brittany, from which country he came, according to the play, to Cornwall, Meriasek's life is very much a standard late *vita*, not a martyr's passion, but the life of a bishop of noble birth, who associated with the secular ruling class. His life is set in an age of conversion, but within an established ecclesiastical context. In the surviving material in Latin and also in the drama, we hear of his precocious and pious education, of healing miracles, withdrawal as a hermit, reluctant acceptance of preferment and holy end. Many of these elements (as well as others, such as the refusal to marry a king's daughter), are hagiographic commonplaces, and details of Meriasek's life can be linked with other saints, with or without a Cornish connection. His battles with pagan tyrants recall St German, for example, but there are correspondences with the early episcopal *vita* that serves virtually as an archetype for the Celtic saint, that of St Samson of Dol, in whose church Meriasek is elevated to the See of Vannes. Many of the same features, plus the calming of tempests and the

---

[2] On the "merry-jeeks" see Janet Thomas, *The Wheels Went Round* (Redruth, 1987), p. 7f. There is an illustration of the manuscript, with the colophon, in Stokes. Charles Thomas, *Christian Antiquities of Camborne* (St Austell, 1967), p. 25 sees "Master Ton" as making this (prompt-)copy of a work of which a cleric linked with Glasney, either Nans or Alexander Penhylle (who exchanged the benefice of Camborne and Illogan with John Nans for the provostship of Glasney) had been the compiler-author. Thomas dates the work to the period between 1493 (when Penhylle came to Illogan) and 1504 (when the manuscript was written).

subduing of beasts may be found in the *Vita S. Samsonis Dolensis*.[3] Other
hagiographic commonplaces echo the life of Christ, be it healing the lame, the
blind and the possessed (Matt. xv: 30f., xii: 22 and xx: 33f., xvii: 14 etc.),
calming the seas (Mark iv: 37-41) or living in the wilderness. The role of the
saint as mediator between Christ and men because of the imitation of Christ
by the saint is important. Meriasek's visit to Cornwall in the play, finally,
echoes the Celtic saint's *peregrinatio*, travel for the purpose of conversion,
and the movement of saints between Ireland, Wales, Cornwall and Brittany is
very familiar.

Brittany figures largely in the story, and what we know of Meriasek comes
from sources originating in Brittany, although they are in Latin rather than
Breton. The Breton hagiographer Albert le Grand (whose work was followed
by the Bollandists in the *Acta Sanctorum* in 1698) used in 1636 three lessons
from the *Vannes Proper* of 1630, and a text from a lost manuscript containing
various saints' lives, from the chapel of St Jean du Doigt, just north of
Morlaix. Early in the present century, Canon Gilbert Doble discovered and
printed a life of the saint from a late copy of a fifteenth-century *vita*, probably
from Tréguier, and perhaps identical with Albert le Grand's lost manuscript.
Incidents included in the play are found in these lives. In the material from
Brittany, for example, a grateful duke grants three feasts in ackowledgement
of the saint's help: on July 6 (the feast of St Noyale, patroness of Noyale-
Pontivy, the centre of the cult in Brittany), on September 8 (the Nativity of
the Virgin), and on September 29 (Michaelmas). The Cornish play gives the
second of these as August 8, but the consistent Marianism in the work and the
fact that the legend of the Virgin retold in the play is included in the *Golden
Legend* and elsewhere on September 8 seems to indicate that September was
the original and August an intentional or unintentional change - the Cornish
text also mis-spells the name of Noyale. Whether the Mary-narrative was
linked with Meriasek before it reached Cornwall is unclear, however.
Speculation on the nature or language of the source(s) of the Cornish work is
unlikely to be productive, and no absolute assertions can be substantiated.
Parallels may be found between elements in the play and medieval texts such
as the *Legenda aurea*, but beyond this we cannot go. Nor are we likely to
find a "real" Meriasek: a Bishop of Vannes with that name is not known, and
even the Bollandists, who place him in the seventh century, speculate that the

---

[3]   See Walter Berschin, *Biographie und Epochenstil im lateinischen Mittelalter* II
(Stuttgart, 1988), 231f. The *vita* is in the *Acta Sanctorum*/July (vol. VI), pp. 573-91 (1729).
The modern edition is by R. Fawtier, *La vie de Saint Samson* (Paris, 1912), and a translation
by Thomas Taylor (London, 1925, repr. Felinfach, 1991).   See also J. C. Poulin,
"Hagiographie et politique: la première vie de Saint Samson de Dol," *Francia* 5 (1977), 1-26,
and E. G. Bowen, *Saints, Seaways and Settlements* (Cardiff, 2. ed. 1977), pp. 167-9.

year of his birth provided by le Grand, namely 758, might be either 587 or 578.[4]

Absent from the Latin sources is any specific link with Cornwall. The idea that the saint travelled to Cornwall might have been added once the cult had been transplanted from Brittany, and it has been suggested that the *vita* of another Cornish saint, Gwinear or Fingar may have been influential. Gwinear is sometimes seen as a companion of Meriasek, and King Teudar, who also appears in the Cornish play, appears in his *vita*.[5] Nevertheless, there is evidence of the existence of a chapel, a holy well, and even of "Meriasek's rock" in Camborne, and the church there has certainly been dedicated to Meriasek for a long period. The cult of the Breton saint might have been imported after pilgrimages to Tréguier. As far as the dramatisation is concerned, we may recall, finally, that Master John Nans, who became Rector of Camborne in 1501, had previously been Provost of Glasney.

Beunans Meriasek is, however, not only about Meriasek. It is also a play with incidents from the legendary life of St Silvester, and it contains as well the representation of a miracle brought about by the intervention of the Virgin Mary. The interlocking of these three apparently discrete stories is one of the most striking features of the text. Although it has been seen as a hotchpotch, with extraneous material included as padding, the play has a number of overarching themes. The principal of these are the relations between Church and State, the combatting of evil and the conversion of unbelievers, healing in the physical and soteriological sense, and the role of saints (and the clergy) as intercessors, with special emphasis on the Virgin. Internal motifs and linguistic devices link the three narrative strands more firmly.

The *dramatis personae* of the work form a series of hierarchies. Indeed, the three saints themselves present a progression in which Meriasek, as a bishop, is the lowest-ranking figure. Next comes a better-known saint, Silvester, whose story as given here relates closely to a widely read and politically significant work, the so-called *Donation of Constantine*. Silvester

---

[4]   See the *Acta Sanctorum/* June, vol. II (1698), pp. 36-7. Gilbert H. Doble, *Saint Meriadoc, Bishop and Confessor* (Truro, 1935), has the relevant Latin material. See also his *Cornish Church Kalendar* (Long Compton, 1933), and Thomas, *Antiquities*, pp. 21-40. Catherine Rachel John, *The Saints of Cornwall* (Redruth, 1981) discusses Meriasek, p. 44f., with photographs of his statue at Stival-Pontivy. For general references see *Butler's Lives of the Saints* [1756-9], rev. ed. by Herbert J. Thurston and Donald Attwater (London, 2nd ed., 1956), II, 493; Andrew Bond and Nicholas Mabin, *Saints of the British Isles* (Bognor Regis, 1980), p. 91f. as well as Farmer, *Dictionary*, p. 276. Louis Réau, *Iconographie de l'art Chretien* (Paris, 1955-9), III/2 shows the reliquary at St Jean du Doigt. On the Breton bishoprics, see John T. McNeil, *The Celtic Churches* (Chicago and London, 1974), p. 150 and *Histoire de la Bretagne*, ed. Jean Lumeau (Toulouse, 1969).

[5]   See W. H. Pascoe, *Teudar. A King of Cornwall* (Redruth, 1985), with reference to various saints' lives. On other aspects of the Meriasek story, see Thomas, *Antiquities*.

is not a bishop working with dukes, earls and kings, but a pope working with an emperor, and where Meriasek can affect local events, Silvester is very much on the world stage. Above both comes the third saint, the Virgin Mary, who works in harmony with Christ himself. The Virgin dominates the play in several respects, and we are made aware of her importance by heightened and usually anaphoric verse. Both Meriasek and Silvester have a special devotion to the Virgin, and such devotion becomes a theme in itself in one part of the play.

The range of characters is striking for its breadth and for its moral variety. The secular hierarchy extends from the emperor Constantine and his court to kings, dukes and earls in Brittany and Cornwall, and further on down to the sailors, artisans, and the poor and suffering who come to Meriasek to be healed. But even lower than the lepers (in moral terms) are the tyrant kings and their retinues, jailers, soldiers and torturers. The range is matched by the celestial and infernal characters. In accordance with medieval dramatic simultaneity we see not only human characters but the inhabitants of heaven and of hell. Christ, the Virgin, Peter and Paul represent the former, whilst the infernal forces take the shape of demons, who appear on stage from time to time.

The hagiographic play reaches by the end of the middle ages a high level of sophistication, and in *Beunans Meriasek* the interweaving of three apparently discrete plots distinguish the work from more rectilinear dramatisations. Just as there may have been more Cornish saint plays, there is much evidence for lost hagiographic plays in English, permitting full-length studies of the saint play in English, even though the extant material is limited, apart from some fragments, to two complete plays only, both of them concerned with biblical saints. The play of St Paul in the Digby manuscript is not really comparable with our play in that it is limited in theme and very brief (about 700 lines); but the other saint play in the manuscript, that of Mary Magdalene, although still shorter than *Beunans Meriasek*, is comparable in some respects. The play takes two days, and goes beyond the Bible. There are even points of contact in thematic terms, as when angels feed the penitent Magdalene in the desert at Christ's behest. There are, of course, differences - the Digby play introduces morality figures, such as the seven deadly sins. But the main difference is that the play of the Magdalene is biblical. For comparable non-biblical hagiographic drama we need to look to the continent, where numerous saint plays *have* survived.[6] Thus in German

---

[6]   See *The Saint Play in Medieval Europe*, ed. Clifford Davidson (Kalamazoo, 1986), especially pp. 31-122. See also David L. Jeffrey, "English Saints' Plays," in: *Medieval Drama*, ed. Neville Denny (London, 1973), pp. 68-89; R. M. Wilson, *The Lost Literature of Medieval England* (London, 2nd ed. 1970), pp. 209-33 and 85-103; Glynne Wickham, *The Medieval Theatre* (London, 1974, repr.1977), pp. 95-104 and his "The Staging of Saint Plays

there are plays of St George, but there are none extant in English, even though we know that such plays were performed. In England as on the continent prose and metrical legendaries do exist, many deriving from the *Golden Legend*, and even in Breton we can point to one admittedly late vernacular adaptation from the *Legenda aurea*, a prose life of St Catherine printed in 1576, the *Buez an itron Sanctes Cathell*. Nicholas Roscarrock, of course, had a life of the Cornish St Columba, which is now lost.

French in particular has a large number of plays concerned with saints, some of them from the early middle ages. Of greatest interest here is a cycle of dramas comparable with the *Mistére du Viel Testament*, but devoted to the miracles of the Virgin. Amongst these is a play of St Silvester, but not the separate Mary-miracle in the Cornish play, which appears to be unique in drama. Plays of Silvester are not uncommon, and there are independent French and German plays. In Breton there is one large-scale play roughly contemporary with ours, dealing with a saint with a cult in Cornwall, the mother of St David of Wales: *Buez Sanctes Nonn hac he map Deuy* ("The Life of St Non and her son, David"). The sixteenth century saw the printing of Breton plays concerning St Barbara (*Buhez Santes Barba*) and from the same period, perhaps, comes the drama of St Winwaloe (*Buhez Sant Gwénolê*), the founder of Landévennec monastery and patron of Landewednack and Gunwalloe. There are also several later Breton saint plays. Although there are no direct Cornish links in the early Breton plays, it is hardly difficult to point to correspondences between Breton and other continental saint plays, and there are sometimes quite strong overlaps in point of detail. The early education of St David in the *Buez Sanctes Nonn* is a case in point, although there is a scene in which Christ learns his letters in the widespread medieval apocryphal *Protevangelium Jacobi*. There is another (fortuitous) dramatic parallel in the initial refusal of St Bernard de Menthon to marry, in the French play of his life. However, these correspondences are almost invariably commonplaces, found also in the non-dramatic lives of the saints.[7]

---

in England," in *The Medieval Drama*, ed. Sandro Sticca (Albany, 1972), pp. 115-8. In his *Early English Stages*, 1300-1600 (London, 1959-81), III, Wickham stresses its early appearance, and demise at the Reformation. His comments on our play, p. 217 are confused, however. Studies of medieval drama in England bracket *Beunans Meriasek* too glibly with the Digby plays: thus Christine Richardson and Jackie Johnston, *Medieval Drama* (London, 1991), p. 5.

[7] See Lynette R. Muir, "The Saint Play in Medieval France," in Davidson, *Saint Play*, pp. 123-80. The French Silvester play (with a repeated rondel to the Virgin) is in the *Miracles de Nostre Dame*, ed. Gaston Paris and Ulysse Robert (Paris, 1876-93), III, 187-240. For Breton materials, see Roparz Hemon, *La langue Bretonne et ses combats* (La Baule, 1947), pp. 199-224. The most relevant Breton plays are edited by E. Ernault, "La vie de Sainte Nonne," *RC* 8 (1887), 230-301 and 406-91 and "L'Ancien mystère de Saint-Gwénolé," *Annales de Bretagne* 40 (1932), 2-35, 104-41 and 318-79. On German see David Brett-Evans,

The first day of the action of *Beunans Meriasek* opens with the child Meriasek in Brittany. The only son of noble parents, he is sent to school with the blessing of the Virgin Mary, and the scholarship and piety of the child is contrasted with the inability to learn and preoccupation with food of his fellow pupils, all under the control of a less than sober master. In spite of family resistance, Meriasek chooses the priesthood and rejects the proposed marriage to a king's daughter. He works healing-miracles through his prayers of intercession to Christ and the Virgin. He then travels to Cornwall, calming a storm at sea, as did St Samson (who is depicted in a thirteenth-century window at Dol calming a devil-sent tempest), establishes a church at Camborne, finds a holy well, and heals more of the sick. In Cornwall, however, he encounters the pagan King Teudar, who argues against the basic tenets of Christian belief, appeals to Meriasek's high birth, and (with Gospel echoes again) tries to tempt him with riches. Teudar then pursues Meriasek, who hides by a rock which later bears his name, *carrek Veryasek*, and which provides circumstantial evidence of the truth of the tale. Meriasek returns to Brittany, where he tames a wolf, another echo of other saints' lives as well as foreshadowing Silvester, who tames a dragon.

The second saint in the work appears in the first day's play. This is Silvester, the fourth-century pope, and the story is that found in the eighth or ninth century *Donation of Constantine* (although it of earlier provenance), according to which it is his curing of Constantine of leprosy, rather than the vision at the Milvian Bridge, which brings Christianity to the Roman empire. After Constantine has rejected a cure involving the blood of children following an appeal from their mothers, Silvester (in hiding from persecution) is summoned after Christ has sent saints Peter and Paul in a dream to Constantine, and he heals and converts the emperor and his empire with him. Constantine himself then leads Silvester to the papal palace. Christ's active participation is rare in the work, but the points at which he appears are significant. The drama now returns to Meriasek, who is living as a hermit in Brittany. Just as Constantine sought Silvester on a mountain, Meriasek is also found on his hill-top retreat near Pontivy, the saint's cult-centre in Brittany, by the Earl of Rohan. Asked to help remove a group of bandits, he does so by prayer which causes a forest fire and terrifies them into conversion, much as the fear of leprosy had led to Constantine's conversion. In gratitude, the earl grants three festivals in the parish of Noyale-Pontivy, and the first day ends with a return to Cornwall, and the defeat of King Teudar by the Christian Duke of Cornwall. In this action none of the three saints is involved,

---

Von Hrotsvit bis Folz und Gengenbach (Berlin, 1975), II, 9-37. Christ learning his letters is found in the *Proto-Gospel of James* and the *Infancy Gospel of Thomas*: see James, *Apocryphal New Testament*, p. 77f. Glasney, of course, had a school attached: see Orme, *Education in the West of England*.

but there are echoes here of the period of conversion; the so-called Alleluia victory described in Bede's *History of the English Church* comes to mind.[8]

The second day opens, after a brief statement by Constantine on the conversion of the empire, with Meriasek restoring the sight of Earl Globus, and then curing a demoniac. It is decided that Meriasek should become the next bishop of Vannes, and Pope Silvester agrees - thus two of the saints in the play are specifically linked and the chronological setting established. A reluctant Meriasek argues against the desire for riches (recalling the Teudar episode), but eventually gives way. This is another commonplace. He remains devoted to the Virgin, and continues to heal the sick.

This section of the play is followed by a third narrative. this time a miracle of the Virgin herself, entitled in the manuscript *de filio mulieris*, "of the son of a woman." The only son of a woman devoted to the Virgin goes away to fight for the Christian King Massen, but who is captured by a pagan tyrant. He is to be hanged because he refuses to renounce Christ, and the prayers of the mother to the Virgin seem to be unanswered. Accordingly she takes from the church the image of the infant Christ as a hostage for her own son. Mary intercedes with Christ in heaven, and she is permitted to release the woman's son, after which the woman restores the statue. As a contrasting action we are shown the tyrant's men holding a black mass, although the various demons who appear seem designed really to point out to the audience somewhat gleefully the fate that awaits their worshippers after death. The rewards of good and evil are contrasted throughout, and the tyrant's men complain about not being paid by their lord. The miracle, however, causes a change of heart in a jailer and his boy, who turn against their former master.

The story is followed by a brief return to Meriasek, who drives out demons, another Christ-like activity done in imitation of and through Christ, who commands Gabriel to take food to the ageing Meriasek after the latter has prayed to the Virgin. A second episode from the life of Silvester is introduced, the removal of a dragon, a literal as well as an allegorical defence of Christianity, since the conversion of the empire is blamed for the beast's arrival. The play closes with the final miracles and death of Meriasek, when his soul is called for by Christ. The dying saint sets his feast-day as the first Friday in June (actually June 7) and refers to Camborne, although he dies in Brittany. After a final blessing in the names of Meriasek and St Mary of Camborne, the observers are invited to drink with the play, and music is played for dancing.

Repeated individual themes unify the separate elements. Thus Meriasek (who has already tamed a wolf) removes a group of bandits, while Silvester

---

[8]   Bede, *A History of the English Church and People*, tr. Leo Shirley-Price (Harmondsworth, 1955), p.58f. (= I, 17-22). See also Henry Marsh, *Dark Age Britain* (Newton Abbot, 1970), p. 78.

copes with the threat to the land of a dragon. In both cases the Church assists the state after an appeal by the secular authorities, and both may be seen as allegories of the triumph of good over evil. It is more important, however, that both make clear how the Church is vital to the order of the State. At the same time, in the case of Silvester as of Meriasek, the State is instrumental in *establishing* the ecclesiastical hierarchy. Within the framework provided by these two cases, shown to be happening at the same time, the tale of the holy hostage underscores a different point as a pious legend addressed to the emotions, a sentimental story concerned with individual intercession. But even that story is placed within a larger conflict, in part political, between (in the celebrated terms of the *Chanson de Roland*) the Christians who are right and the pagans who are wrong. Yet another element links that legend with the rest of the work: the role of the mother, itself necessarily part of the thoroughgoing Marianism of the play. The hostage story shows a mother protecting her son by appeals through the Virgin to *her* son, Christ. An appeal by the mothers of the children who are to be sacrificed in a quack cure for leprosy proposed for Constantine causes the emperor's change of heart. Not their sacrifice, but Christ's willing one, provides the cure and the salvation. The role of Meriasek's mother is smaller but not insignificant: her only son goes to Christ instead of remaining in the world, and his devotion to the Virgin is as strong as that of the woman whose son is captured. All the mothers in the play experience at least a potential loss. But Mary has lost her real son (rather than the image) in a different sense, and because of that sacrifice she and her saints are able to redeem other potential losses.

The Marianism of the play is striking. The blessings issued by Meriasek or Silvester are usually in the name of the Virgin or of Christ as the Virgin's son, and the intercession by the saints is frequently to Christ by way of the Virgin, not only in the hostage section. The frequent use of patterned Marian prayer establishes itself early in the form of longer anaphoric strophes:

> Marya my*gh*ternas nef
> a vagas c*r*ist gans *th*e leth
> maria drefa *th*e luef
> *then* mab a skyentoleth
> marya whek peys genef
>
> byth na*n*geffa an iovl keth
> warnaf power
> nan beys ov escare arall
> ham kyke yv escar teball
> p*ur* ysel me an temper (BM 154-63)

Mary, queen of heaven's way,
　　with whose milk once Christ was fed,
Mary, raise your hand today
　　to bless a struggling child's head.
Mary, dearest, with me pray
　　that on me the devil dread
　　　no power wield -
nor the world, my other foe -
and that the flesh, a great woe,
　　can be tamed and made to yield.

Meriasek's prayers are, of course, directed at Christ as well; thus when he
appeals in Cornwall for the healing of the sick he does so in a ten-line strophe
with a simpler rhyme-scheme, but again with internal echoes and anaphora:

Ihesu arluth neff han beys
　　yehes dywy re grontya
ih*e*su arluth me ath peys
　　le*m*men sav an keth tusma
maria mam lue*n* a rays
　　peys theth vap arluth ragtha
maria mam ha guerhays
　　gueres ov pesy gena
sevugh inban a t*u*s vays
　　fatel omglowugh o*m*ma　　(BM 700-9)

Jesus, lord of earth and sky
　　grant that ye be healed again!
Jesus, lord, to thee I cry,
　　ease the sorrows of these men.
Mary, mother, maiden high
　　with thy lord son plead for them!
Mary, virgin mother, I
　　ask you now your help to lend.
Rise up now, good folk! come! try!
　　Are your sorrows at an end?

Silvester also baptises Constantine in the name of the Virgin and her son, and
the anaphoric pattern recurs in the prayers of the oppressed Christians.

The central expression of Marianism is, of course, the hostage narrative.[9] This miracle is not unknown elsewhere, but other versions are metrical or in prose, although there are a few pictorial representations of the story. Unlike the other strands in the play, this part is independent, and is given a separate heading, with the added comment that it is taken from a collection of stories about the Virgin. In spite of Nance's edition under the title *An venen ha'y map* ("The woman and her son"), it is the son who is in the foreground, and in contrast with some other versions of the story, he is an active character. Both the woman herself and her son express devotion to Mary in the style already seen. After the woman has taken hostage the statue of the infant Christ, the scene shifts to heaven, where Mary does intercede with Christ to have the son released - this version is careful to avoid any possibility of what might be interpreted as blackmail. The Virgin asks Christ to allow her to work the miracle in view of the genuine devotion of the distraught mother. Mary is permitted to rescue the young man herself, and he then has a six-line anaphoric prayer of thanks:

> Maria gorthys reby
> maria guyff nynsen vy
> > genes the vones ledijs
> maria thyso mur grays
> maria na ve the rays
> > gon guyr y fyen dyswreys
> > (BM 3699-704)

> Mary, all honour to thee,
> Mary, I was unworthy
> > that thou shouldst have been my guide.
> Mary, thanks to you I bring
> Mary, but for your saving
> > I know that I should have died.

The mother echoes this when she returns the Christ-child to the church. The movement from iconic devotion to a focus on the celestial saint interceding directly with Christ emphasises the important theme of intercession itself.

---

[9]   I have discussed the section (with further bibliography) in "The Holy Hostage: *de filio mulieris* in the Middle Cornish Play *Beunans Meriasek*," *Medium Aevum* 58 (1989), 258-73. I note the problems with the text by R. Morton Nance and A. S. D. Smith as *An venen ha'y map* (Cornish Language Board, 1969), especially their decision to omit the contrastive and balancing lines by torturers and devils, BM 3245-43. On Marianism see Marina Warner, *Alone of All Her Sex* (London, 1976). On Mary in the play, see Newlyn, "Pit and Pedestal," pp. 144-7.

The devotion to Mary in this episode contrasts too with the scenes in which the subordinates of the pagan tyrant king (a cruder version of Teudar) celebrate a black mass in language which is neither heightened nor liturgical. It is on the other hand significant that two on-stage observers, a jailer and his boy, react to the miracle and comment positively. The external audience has just seen a kind of black mass, and now they observe how the Mary-miracle that they have just been watching causes the rejection of the tyrant, with a noteworthy curse:[10]

> Ay turant ke war the gam
> molleth du the vap the vam
> yma ree ov leferel
> heb ty vyth nag ovlya
> delyfrys *der* varia
> fetel yw dyogel
> hagis boys wy de vlamya
> war vohogo[g]yon cruel (BM 3737-44)

> No, tyrant, your race is run!
> God's curse on your mother's son!
> Already the tale is known,
> and is plainly told to men.
> Mary set him free again
> (for without doubt he is gone)
> and now yours is all the blame,
> for the cruelty you have shown.

Conversion and right belief constitute another basic theme in the play. The drama puts forward basic Christianity throughout, either in debate or in the action. Meriasek, for example, argues with King Teudar in a theological disputation which stands out once more in the formal sense, the strophes balancing each other. Teudar appeals to Meriasek as a man of noble birth to reject Christian mysteries such as the Virgin birth. Teudar declares this impossible, but Meriasek counters with the familiar image of the sunbeam which passes through glass.[11] Teudar then questions how God could be killed, and this time Meriasek presents a concise *summa*:

---

[10]   See James Whetter, "Cornish Swear-Words and Terms of Abuse," in his: *Cornish Essays 1971-1976* (St Austell, 1977), pp. 13-16.

[11]   Yrjö Hirn, "La verrière symbole de la maternité virginale," *Neuphilologische Mitteilungen* 29 (1928), 33-9. See in particular Andrew Breeze, "The Blessed Virgin and the Sunbeam through Glass," *Barcelona English Language and Literature Studies* 1 (1988), 53-64.

Der pegh adam age*n* tays
  eff hay lynnyeth o da*m*pnys
sav an devgys a vynnays
  arta y vones pre*n*nys
    the saluascon
an map a fue co*n*cevijs
ha densis a kemereys
rag na ylly an devsys
      gothe pasconn (BM 881-90)

By our father Adam's sin
  he and all his kind were damned,
but the godhead wanted then
  that mankind should be redeemed
    to salvation!
The son was conceived - he had
to take on the shape of men
for he could not, as God,
    suffer passion.

The Latin loanwords in the passage suggest a learned source, and the same point was made in *Pascon agan Arluth*. Faced with this unswerving faith, Teudar attempts to buy Meriasek off, to become one of his "bishops" (BM 896 uses the word *epscop*), something which foreshadows Meriasek's later resistance to becoming a real bishop. The argument comes down at the last to a straightforward conflict between the worship of God and the all-purpose medieval paganism that takes the names (though nothing else) of its supposed deities (including *Mahound*, "Mohammed") both from Islam and from classical mythology, and is equated with devil-worship and a militant antagonism towards Christianity.

The *theology* of conversion does not arise in the sections devoted to Silvester and to the Virgin. In the first case, Silvester makes the point by his action after Constantine himself has already earned grace by his mercy towards the children. Even in the dragon episode, it is Silvester's actions that speak, although in other versions of the saint's legend he does indeed dispute on the subject. It may be that Meriasek has subsumed this aspect of the Silvester story, and it is certainly noteworthy that Meriasek's debate with Teudar comes in a passage which has no parallel in the sources from Brittany. In the hostage section, conversion, insofar as it is an issue at all, is the result of direct observation rather than of argument.

Meriasek's refusal to become a "bishop" for Teudar is taken up in his reluctance to accept the bishopric of Vannes. The motif is another hagiographic commonplace, and in some versions of his legend (such as that in the *Legenda aurea*) Silvester also refuses initially to accept the Papacy. Meriasek makes clear from the start his attempt to avoid the world and its blandishments. When seeking Meriasek's help, his kinsman, Count Rohan appeals to his sense of *noblesse oblige* and points out that this is not incompatible with piety; indeed, Meriasek's behaviour might bring shame upon his family:

> Meryasek nynsos fur
> gorthya du ty alse sur
> kyn fy reoute an beys
> meth yv gans ol the cufyon
> the vones omma dyson
> avel begyer desethys (BM 2016-21)

> Meriasek, you are quite wrong!
> You could still sing the Lord's song
> and as a nobleman rule.
> It shames all your kindred dear
> that you should spend your time here
> seated on a beggar's stool.

But Meriasek continues to resist the world, even though he does help the count (who effectively shrugs his shoulders and pursues the point no further). More interestingly, one of the supposedly shamed kindred, dubbed simply *agnatus* ("relative on his father's side") underlines the connection between the saint's life and the Gospel. The parallel is with Christ's temptations in the desert, one of which was with riches. *Agnatus* comments:

> Na temptyogh na moy an den
> reys yv the crist cuff colen
> thy lel servye (BM 2048-50)

> You must tempt the man no more.
> Christ's dear heart has a need for
> loyal service...

The question of riches is picked up again when Meriasek uses the proffered bishopric to criticise those preoccupied with the income of a benefice rather than with the account they will have to settle after their deaths. His reluctance to accept reward, too, contrasts with the soldiers and torturers of the tyrant in the hostage section, who complain about not being paid, but who will - as we see - certainly receive the wages of devil-worship.

The elevation of Meriasek has to be approved by Pope Silvester, and although he does so readily it is noteworthy that at this point he also offers a blessing followed by a doctrinal statement which stands out for its unusually elaborate form and rhyme. After his blessing, Silvester presents to the audience what is effectively a brief homily on the nature of sin:

> Mercy du prest yv parys
> the vap den mar an wyla
> nynsyv y voth boys kelys
> an peth a ruk the prenna
> insol bethugh glan yesseys
> avodyogh pegh in bysma
> ha rag an pehas us grueys
> kemerogh luen edrega
> ha bethugh war
> na drelogh *the* pegh na moy
> ha why a thue sur then ioy
> us in neff nangeves par   (BM 2743-53)

> God's mercy is always free
> (if they but choose) for men.
> He has no desire to see
> them once saved and lost again.
> Now hurry, confess fully,
> turn in the world from all sin,
> and for those sins that maybe
> burn you still, repent, and then
> ever beware!
> Return to your sins no more.
> You shall gain the joy for sure
> of heaven beyond compare.

Silvester's homily underscores the dogmatic point made by Meriasek, whose resistance increases when the income is named (*iij cans puns...in blethen ha moy inta*, "300 pounds a year and more" BM 2820f.) Meriasek comments adversely on the whole practice of accepting an ecclesiastical post for money alone, something which was indeed being satirised on the continent at the same time in works like Sebastian Brant's *Narrenschiff* ("The Ship of Fools", 1494). It takes the combined efforts of Earl Globus (whom Meriasek has healed), the Earl of Vannes and the Bishop of Cornouailles to persuade him, and it is not surprising that Meriasek appeals once again for help to the Virgin:

Maria wyn gueres vy
maria the orthys gy
    erbyn ov both ledijs off
maria mam ha guerhes
maria da y wothes
    an charg peys da my nynsoff (BM 2970-5)

Mary, blessed one, help me,
Mary, now away from thee
    unwillingly I am led.
Mary, Virgin Mother, you,
Mary, know that it is true:
    this charge brings me only dread.

He is led to the church for the consecration, and even here appeals against his elevation, doing so this time in the name of the Passion of Christ in a thirteen-line stanza which enumerates the sufferings (including the familiar notion of the crown of thorns having pierced the brain). The passage is interesting, too, in that although Meriasek's first resistance echoed Christ's temptation, this ultimate sacrifice of his own wishes for the good of others is associated with Christ's sacrifice for men by the saint himself.

The drama contains, then, not only invocations of Christ and the Virgin, but also analytic theological statements aimed at the unbelievers in the play, and at inner and outer audiences. Other parts of the play, however, make the point of the necessity of right belief in a more direct way, by force rather than by argument, and right invariably prevails. Wolf, dragon and robbers are subdued, the persecution of the Christians is triumphantly overcome, the son of the unnamed woman is released from captivity. If the tyrant king is discomfited rather than vanquished, King Teudar in the first day's play very clearly *is* defeated. Although he drives Meriasek out of Cornwall, this proves his downfall, even if this does not involve any of the principal characters. We are shown instead a battle that is entirely in the spirit of the *chansons de geste*, and an unnamed Duke of Cornwall defeats the pagan king. A battle is no place for a saint. Teudar is, incidentally, seen as an interloper in Cornwall, even though he has established his palace at Lestowder ("Teudar's home").[12] Teudar is, furthermore, urged on by demons: one of these is Beëlzebub, and although the name Jupiter is given to another, the reference to *tassens an berth north*, "holy father from the north" (BM 2328, and see BM 3427) is clearly to Isaiah xiv: 13 and the King of Babylon/Lucifer. Apollo and Sol are also named, but other devil-names are perhaps scatological. The Duke and Teudar indulge in an extended flyting, in which Teudar mocks

---

[12]   In St Keverne; see Pascoe, *Teudar*, p. 41f.

Christ and refers to himself as an emperor, while the Duke dubs him a stable-boy. Words give way to actions, however, and Teudar is defeated, even though he claims the support of other kings, including King Mark. The primary stage-direction says simply *Hic praeliabunt* "they fight now", but the secondary (and later) comment in English adds details of the props required - *gonnys*, "guns." Presumably this involved some lively business. Christ is the instrument of victory, however:

> gorthyans the crist caradov
> grontia dym an vyctory   (BM 2497f.)

> Thanks be to Christ, our dear lord
> for granting me victory.

The dramatic implications of this scene as the conclusion to the first day need no underlining, but a victory over a pagan king in a battle the primary cause of which was the latter's treatment of Meriasek shows us the State in triumph on behalf of the Church.

The relationship between State and Church links Meriasek and Silvester in particular, and it has been noted how the State both seeks the aid of the Church, and avenges its representatives. It is of incidental interest that the major protagonists are all on one social level: even Teudar accepts and reminds Meriasek of his noble birth. The State-Church relationship is at its clearest in the Silvester scenes, and given the political overtones it is not hard to see why the play could no longer be performed a mere generation or so after its composition; not only had the Marianism and intercession theology become unacceptable, but the role of the Papacy and the attitude towards it of the temporal ruler could hardly be played in post-Reformation England.

The Constantine of the play is not, as indicated, the historical emperor, but the central figure of the legend expressed first in the so-called *Donation of Constantine* in the eighth or ninth century, a fiction in which the curing of the emperor's leprosy leads to his grateful granting of temporal privileges on a massive scale to Silvester and the Church. The legend is found too in the *Legenda aurea* and its derivatives, and there is a fine visual expression of its implications in the oratory dedicated to the saint in the church of the Santi Quattro Coronati in Rome. One fresco shows Constantine on foot leading Silvester on horseback into the city, and later the emperor is shown standing below the enthroned saint, offering him the papal tiara, both making the relative levels of authority clear. In our play, Constantine does not expressly give to Silvester all the primacies mentioned in the *Donation*, but he leads Silvester into the city and to his palace, insisting that the laws will now be those of Jesus (BM 1858-65). The *Donation* itself may not have been a direct source, although the reference to the laws of Christ is close to the original. By

115

the time of the Cornish play it had been shown by scholars such as Lorenzo Valla to be a forgery, and in the 1530s an English translation with comments on its authenticity appeared in London. The full force of the Silvester legend and its implications for the supremacy of the Church over the State is not drawn out in the Cornish text, but both the Silvester and the Meriasek sections underline the interdependence of the two: the concept of a secular state is a long way off.[13]

The most significant theme of the play, however, and one which subsumes several of the others, is that of soteriology. *Beunans Meriasek* presents a whole series of images of salvation. This is not surprising, of course, given the relationship between many of the standard elements of hagiography and the Gospels. The link between physical and metaphysical healing becomes clear implicitly and explicitly in the various miracles performed by the saints on earth and in heaven. The miracles of Meriasek echo Christ's healing of the lame, the possessed and the blind, and one case may be selected, namely the restoring of the sight of blind Earl Globus in the second day's play. The name, unlike many of the others, cannot be linked with an historical or legendary figure, and is presumably a speaking one; *globus* can in classical Latin mean "the world" and also "group, clique, following."[14] It is safe to assume that the Earl represents mankind, and the link with Christ comes in what was, in Cornwall and elsewhere in the middle ages, probably the most famous healing miracle, though it is not biblical, namely the restoring of the sight of the blind centurion at the cross, who is named either Longinus or Longus. The healing of Earl Globus resembles that of Constantine in that he offers money for a cure, only to be told that the wealth of the world is of no use, a motif repeatedly associated with Meriasek. Like Teudar, Globus is surprised when Meriasek fails to respond either to money or to the appeal to

---

[13]   Translation in Henry Bettenson, *Documents of the Christian Church* (London, 2nd ed., 1963), pp. 135-40 (abridged). See H. Grauert, "Die konstantinische Schenkung," *Historisches Jahrbuch* 3 (1882), 3-30. See also the entry on Silvester in the *Liber pontificalis: The Book of Pontiffs*, tr. Raymond Davis (Liverpool, 1989), pp. 14-26. The mountain Serapte or Syraptim is Soracte elsewhere (as in the *Legenda aurea* for December 31). The legend was dramatised in the *Miracles de Nostre Dame* and also in German. The Rome frescoes are in Maria Giulia Barberini, *I Santi Quattro Coronati A Roma* (Rome, 1989), pp. 55-7. The English version of 1534 was printed by T. Godfray in London: *A Treatyse of the donation...vnto Syluester pope of Rhome by Constantyne...& what truth is yn the same grau[n]t...* The translator was Bartylmewe Picern, and the reference is to Mount Soracte.
[14]   Harris, *Meriasek*, p. 136 rejects Nance's suggestion that *globus* means "worldly," and comments that it cannot mean "world" in classical or medieval Latin. In fact Cicero uses it precisely in that sense ("ille globus, quae terra dicitur" in the *Tusculan Disputation* and the Republic), while it can also mean "coterie, group." The Middle Ages also knew the world to be a globe, even if the word is not recorded in that sense until 1553. See C. S. Lewis, *The Discarded Image* (Cambridge, 1964), p. 140, as well as Rudolf Simek, "Die Kugelform der Erde im mittelhochdeutschen Schrifttum," *Archiv für Kulturgeschichte* 70 (1989), 361-73.

his noble birth. Meriasek, indeed, does not intercede with Christ for the actual cure until Globus *himself* invokes Christ, in a two-stanza speech in which he asks first to be saved for the sake of the Passion, and which refers to the piercing of Christ's side - the Longinus allusion. The second and emotionally more forceful strophe is marked by its unusual form:

> gans gu lym in tenewon
> del russons y y guana
>
> Der an golon
> y woys dyson
> may tevera
> gueres de*n* dal
> oma heb fal
> oth ihe*s*u rag kere*n*sa (BM 2604-011)
>
> with a sharp spear in the side
> as he was then pierced right through
>
> into the heart.
> His blood did spurt
> down from above.
> Heal a blind man
> here, if you can,
> for Jesus Christ and his love.

With Silvester, the primary miracle is the cure of Constantine, following his mercy towards the children. The echo here is of the Holy Innocents, into sermons for which feast the story of Silvester is sometimes incorporated, as for example in Myrk's *Festial* in English. The healing of leprosy by sacrifice is not uncommon as an allegory of salvation in the Middle Ages, and one thinks of Hartmann von Aue and his *Der arme Heinrich*, in which the blood of a young girl, though freely offered, is not required as a cure for leprosy because Christ intervenes.[15] One sacrifice is enough when man is *sub gratia*, and the repetition either of that of Christ or of the Innocents is unnecessary. In the hostage section, too, the soteriology is clear. The son is rescued from physical imprisonment, but the whole episode is a symbol of redemption. The

---

[15] On the medical aspects, see Frank A. Turk and Myrna Combellack, "Doctoring and Disease in Medieval Cornwall; Exegetical Notes on Some Passages in *Beunans Meriasek*," *CS* 4/5 (1976-7), 56-75. The passage with the pagan doctors still contains difficulties, however. There is a translation of Hartmann's work in R. W. Fisher, *The Narrative Works of Hartmann von Aue* (Göppingen, 1983).

captivity of the devil is an equally familiar motif, the notion being that the world is in the snare of the devil until the trap is sprung by Christ. The point this time is a release from prison rather than from illness, and the opening of the prison doors by Mary on the word of Christ echoes the harrowing. The infant Christ as hostage recalls the incarnation, but the woman whose son is taken appeals to Mary as the *mater dolorosa*, sorrowing for the sacrifice, by which, however, other men are saved.

Various source-suggestions, mostly unconvincing, have been made for the play.[16] Probably the best that can be said is that *Beunans Meriasek* combines material that may also be found in a range of other medieval writings, and that analogues range from whole narrative units (such as the story of the holy hostage) to occasional historical names. The Latin prose hagiography of Mereadoc has been referred to already, and the Meriasek parts of the play clearly derive from something along these lines. The reference to the festivals, including one linked firmly with the cult-centre in Brittany, is a specific link to this type of source, the hagiography found otherwise in Brittany, but the dramatist does misdate one of the feasts. The age of the story of Meriasek as a whole is perhaps indicated by his consecration (albeit as Bishop of Vannes) at Dol Cathedral (which gave way to Tours as the Breton metropolitan see in 1199), but beyond this, a precise (or perhaps more significantly an immediate) source is unknown. It is possible that some motifs from the Silvester legend have been transferred to Meriasek, or have been borrowed from another saints life. At the same time, elements may have been reduplicated. Thus the roles of Constantine (before his conversion), Teudar and the unnamed tyrant are all similar. It does, of course, remain unclear where the idea of the saint's visit to Cornwall came from, unless it was adapted from another saint's life. King Teudar might also have historical antecedents, although any link with the Tudors seems highly unlikely except on an accidental basis. There may be a link between King Massen in the hostage episode and Macsen Wledig, the literary reflection in the *Mabinogion* of the historical Magnus Maximus.[17] There are, as might be expected, Breton echoes as well, perhaps of Conan of Rennes, an early Duke of Brittany, but some names have no parallels - Globus is an example. Of the

---

[16]   Ellis, *Cornish Language*, p. 40, cites an earlier comment that it is translated from a Breton play, but although he appears not to believe this himself he offers no alternative views. Halliday's comment that it is "based on a Breton play in Latin," *Legend*, p. 15, is opaque. See Thomas, *Antiquities*, pp. 23-25 for a clear view. His reference to a "compiler-author" is also sensible.

[17]   Jenner referred to the *Dream of Macsen Wledig* in "Cornish Drama II", p. 60f. See *The Mabinogion*, tr. Jeffrey Gantz (Harmondsworth, 1976), pp. 118-22. On the "real" Macsen Wledig see Stephen Johnson, *Later Roman Britain* (London, 1980), pp. 68, 101-2. He refers also to Vortigern as the proud tyrant, p. 116, and the Alleluia victory and St Germanus, p. 116 (with reference to Nennius).

unnamed characters, the tyrant king of the hostage section (who has strong overlaps with Teudar), recalls - especially given the link with the *Breuddwyd Maxen* - the various "proud tyrants" found in the pages of Nennius, Gildas or Bede; but trying to identify the tyrant king of a fifteenth century drama as Vortigern, say, is as fruitless as trying to find the real fourth-century emperor Constantine in our play.

Some version of the legend of St Silvester was known to the dramatist, specifically one incorporating the *Donation*, although the version here lacks circumstantial detail, and the immediate source (if not a dramatisation of some sort) might well have been a version from a legendary. If so, the play has adapted the material considerably, and the same is true of the Mary-legend, which is also found in the *Legenda aurea*, but the tale is indeed well-known, especially in Britain, where there are iconographic representations in the fifteenth century, and where one of the French versions locates the tale. It is found in Latin (Caesarius of Heisterbach, Vincent of Beauvais, the *Legenda* itself), French (Gautier de Coinci), Spanish (the *Cantígas* of Alfonso the Wise), English (Myrk's *Festial*) and German (the *Passional*). Some of these are derived from the *Legenda aurea*, of course. It is possible that the source was something like the collection of Mary-miracles prepared by Johann Herolt, known as the Discipulus, the so-called *Promptuarium* of 1435. None of the versions noted is an exact match, and none is dramatic, however.[18]

If the dramatist did not compile from various sources, which seems the most plausible conclusion, the best candidate for a single source might be a legendary of some kind, arranged perhaps according to the propers of the saints, probably in Latin, and probably from Brittany (for the Meriasek material itself). Even so, the reference to the Mary-miracles might still mean that this part of the play came from a different source. What has to be stressed is that the time in which the play is set is quite consistent, and to criticise the work for anachronisms is to mistake it for an historical document.[19] The introduction of the emperor Constantine places us willy-

---

[18]   I have discussed analogues in "The Holy Hostage," with bibliographic references. To underline further the widespread nature of the legend we may add: E. A. Wallis Budge, *One Hundred and Ten Miracles of Our Lady Mary* (London, 1933), pp. 98-106 (Ethiopic); Mary Ellen Goenner, *Mary-Verse of the Teutonic Knights* (Washington, 1944), p. 100f.; Evelyn Faye Wilson, *The Stella Maris of John of Garland* (Cambridge, Mass., 1946), p. 206; C. G. N. de Vooys, *Middelnederlandse Marialegenden* (Leyden, n.d.), I, 86f. (from a MS. of the late 15th century). For collections of Mary-miracles, see: "Miraculorum B.V. Mariae quae saec. VI-XV Latine conscripta sunt index," *Analecta Bollandia* 21 (1902), 241-360, see p. 327f. (Nr. 1295); Mary V. Gripkey, *The Blessed Virgin Mary as Mediatrix in the Latin and Old French Legend Prior to the 14th Century* (Washington, 1938), pp. 1-61 and 131-218.

[19]   Jenner, *Handbook*, p. 31 refers to "mad anachronisms," a point taken up by T. D. Crawford, "Stanza Forms and Social Status in Beunans Meriasek," *OC* 9 (1979-85), 487. That the guns are a later embellishment is pointed out by Harris, *Meriasek*, p. 135f.

nilly in the fourth century, and the reflection, at least, of Magnus Maximus, whose claim to the purple from a British starting-point failed when he was defeated at Arles in 388, puts the hostage story in roughly the same period. Since Meriasek, whose dates are frankly not known, is presented as a contemporary of Silvester, the audience (medieval or modern) is not faced with any anachronisms; the notion of "chronological discrepancies" applied to the play by a recent critic is not remotely applicable. The reference to fighting with guns is clearly a late addition in the stage directions (as is the use of a gun to fire from the dragon's mouth). What is more important is that *Beunans Meriasek* transports the audience back to a period of tension between the forces of paganism and an established but not yet universal Christianity, back to the age of the saints.

Both the biblical plays and *Beunans Meriasek* have large casts. The subdivisions here of the hierarchies are important, and simply to divide the characters into upper and lower classes (as has been done) is both misleading and inadequate. The tripartite division dictated by medieval dramatic simultaneity overrides other considerations: there is a clear distinction between the heavenly characters (Christ, the Virgin, angels and saints) and the infernals. The earthly characters divide into believers and unbelievers, although some of course shift from the latter to the former. The unbelievers are presented in a hierarchy as well (with the demons below them), ranging from King Teudar (who claims imperial status), through the tyrant king down to their minions, the jailers, torturers and menials. With the latter belong the followers of Constantine before his conversion and the robbers in the Meriasek section. Beside these unbelievers, there is a kind of pagan ecclesiastic hierarchy, including supposed bishops in the second major Silvester scene. The idea of a pagan bishop is present throughout - Teudar offers to make Meriasek into one - but we may note that those who taunt Silvester about the dragon do repent, as does Earl Globus, who was presumably an unbeliever before his encounter with Meriasek and the confession that leads to his cure. The hierarchy of believing characters - the most important - also divides into representatives of Church and State, and ranges from pope to hermit, from emperor to leper. A distinction between classes is possible only in broad terms, and while attention is paid to the notion of aristocracy, some characters cannot be fitted into such a scheme at all, such as the woman and her son in the Mary-legend. The question of characterisation in a medieval play is always problematic, and modern criteria are not always useful. Nevertheless, although Meriasek is *a priori* a good character, he has quite specific and consistent attitudes, such as his reluctance to have anything to do with the world, even though in the end he is persuaded of his God-given role as bishop. There is individuality in Constantine's change of heart, and dramatic tension in the scene with the pleading of the mothers, whose request for mercy to their children leads to divine mercy for the emperor himself. Even the unnamed *mulier* of the hostage story is individualised by her complete (if somewhat aberrant) devotion to the Virgin. Clearly, some characters are little more than functional - *Calo, Primus tortor*, and so on - but sometimes even jailers and soldiers act individually.

The formal (surface) variation in the strophes using different permutations of rhyme, line and stanza length, seems not to be character-based. T. D. Crawford concluded that "lower-class characters are marginally less likely to use short lines,"[20] but the relatively rare four-syllable lines and are used for effect by the whole range of characters; there are examples by Conan (BM 407), Teudar (BM 2438) and a cripple (BM 4246), but both Christ and St Paul have passages with a short-line element. Attention needs to be paid primarily to the texture of the speeches and the use of a given strophic form at a particular point in the play. Linguistic contrasts can be found, too, just as in the *Ordinalia*. In the hostage section, the anaphoric prayers to the Virgin contrast in style and content with the devil-worship of the tyrant's men or the words of the demons, although these sometimes have formulaic openings:

> Thum dy iovyn in y fath
> me a offren lawen cath
> ny yl boys guel legessa
> me as droys a voruelys
> le may fue an iovle elys
> degens ytte om hascra
> pen bogh ha gaver pelys
> ov du lemen thyn grassa   (BM 3411-9)

> To my god, Jove, in his face
> a tom-cat I'll sacrifice -
> the best mouser I could find.
> Bought it in Morville. I paid,
> and the devil blessing made.
> May he take these gifts of mine:
> stag's head, a goat that's been flayed -
> my god, now to us be kind!

In general the speeches of the torturers are more of a warning than a source of comedy both in the Silvester and hostage sections, however. In the latter, indeed, their discontent at not being paid forms a nice counterpart to the attitudes of Meriasek concerning preferment, and an ironic pendant to the fact that they will be paid in hell. Indeed, almost the only genuine comedy in the

---

20   "Stanza Forms," p. 485. He does, however, correctly indicate the use of short line stanzas at points of high tension, p. 486.

play comes with the school scenes at the start. There is a certain amount of burlesque ribaldry in the scenes with the quack-doctors and the emperor, and a relatively rare example of the same kind of tone as that adopted by, say, the Butler in the *Origo Mundi* comes from one of Constantine's followers in these early scenes. He is dubbed *Calo*, "menial," and he assures the emperor that killing a few children is no problem, since he will (and has indeed already begun to) beget more:

> Pan gol us awoys latha
> an chett*is* mowes ha mav
> in vn noys mar lefara
> me a russe dywhy ix
> an keth sort ma
> mar mynnogh arluth brentyn
> me a dregh y vreonsen
> hag an dewoys knak oma (BM 1645-52)

> What loss would it be to kill
> these chits? Girls and the boys too!
> In one night - I know full well -
> I could make nine more for you
> of the same brood!
> If you like, my noble lord,
> I'll set their throats to the sword
> and snick! we'll have all the blood!

The passage in which this speech occurs, though, needs to be looked at as a whole. It is part of a lengthy scene composed of roughly uniform stanzas (with some metrical variation) giving us a fairly rapid cross-dialogue between the menial, the torturers (equally happy to kill children as to sacrifice bucks and goats), the Justice (one of Constantine's men), and Constantine himself, who first goes along with his men, but then, caught between this bloodthirstiness and the pleas of the mothers, gives way and releases the children.

Too much critical attention has been paid to the apparently discrete nature of the three narrative strands in the play, and not enough to the way in which they are unified, nor to the overall dramatic effect. The alternation and balance of scenes is careful, though, and there is almost a continuous spectacle, and a considerable degree of tension. This comes first in Meriasek's decision to take the cloth, and interest is maintained with the perilous sea voyage and the shift to Cornwall, followed by the adventure in the disputation with and flight from Teudar, who is left apparently triumphant. Meriasek's healing miracles point on to the more important healing of

Constantine (where there is also tension on the lives of the innocents), and then, in an empire which is now Christian, the Breton lords can solicit the help of Meriasek against the robbers, and a Christian duke can defeat, satisfyingly, the pagan Teudar, avenging Meriasek's flight and providing a rousing conclusion to the first day, which is thus opened and closed with Meriasek. The conversion of Constantine and establishing of Silvester set the tone for the first main part of the second day, the conversion of Globus and the elevation of Meriasek. The integration of the Mary-play of the hostage has caused problems, but it should be seen as an *exemplum* within a sermon of the form *de sanctis*. Certainly there are strong thematic links (soteriology, the mother, the power of the Virgin) and one wonders whether the introduction of the story is connected with the Feast of the Nativity of the Virgin, one of those granted to Meriasek. The second Silvester episode links with Meriasek and both the wolf and the robbers, but it serves to confirm Christianity in the empire, while providing dramatic action. The second day is concluded with Meriasek (and so, therefore, is the work as a whole), his holy dying providing a fitting conclusion to a work which began with his childhood.

Critics have begun to emphasise the unity of the work, although even relatively recently it has been asserted that "the linkage of the Meriasek and Silvester sub-plots is quite superficial; the third sub-plot is not linked with the others at all." [21] Leaving aside the begged question of what then constitutes the *main* plot, the various narrative elements precisely *are* linked by repeated motifs, and the Earl of Vannes sums up the content in a valedictory speech in which he steps out of character (as the Duke of Cornwall had done at the end of the first day) to become an epilogue:

> Pes in hanov du avan
> mens us oma kuntullys
> bevnans meryasek certan
> genen revue dysquethys
> in keth dethyov ma dywy
> trestia inno a rella
> ha lel pesy warnotha
> ihesu re grontias detha
> age desyr eredy.   (BM 4548-56)

---

[21]   Thus Crawford, "Stanza Forms," p. 486. Jenner was unhappy about the various elements, and A. L. Rowse, *Tudor Cornwall* (London, 1941), p. 26 calls the work "a very long and ill-constructed play." Harris argues to the contrary in the introduction to his translation, as does Ronald W. Vince, *A Companion to Medieval Theatre* (New York, 1989), p. 62.

> Peace, now, in God's name on high,
>   to all gathered here today!
> Meriasek's life we have tried
>   to bring to you in our play
>   over the two days just past.
> Whoever puts trust in him
> and loyally prays, finds then
> Jesus has granted to them
>   all that they desire at last.

The stage-plans in the Peniarth manuscript give an idea of the layout, which is like that for the *Ordinalia*, with (presumably) elevated stations for the major characters, who come down and speak: there are references to Constantine's tower and to the *platea*, and the verbs *descendit* and *pompabit* recur. The first day calls for a *capella*, presumably the chapel of St Mary in Camborne, in centre stage. The directions give a good idea of production, too, and the work has indeed been performed in Cornish and English. Possibly the original performances would have been on the saint's day, in June, when the weather would have permitted an outdoor presentation.[22] The primary stage directions are in Latin, and are usually simple directions - *ad palacium pape procesconant* (at BM 4180) - for example. Occasionally they do make serious demands, as in the scene with the robbers, where the instruction calls for fire upon their heads - *Hic ignis venit super illos* (at BM 2091). The secondary stage directions are for the most part in English, and are clearly those of a stage manager. Partly directing, they are concerned mostly with props, some of which are quite ambitious, ranging from "holy water aredy" (at BM 4253) to the workings of the dragon: "her a gonn yn y dragon ys mvthe aredy & fyr" (at BM 3947). Sometimes they have been added to Latin stage-directions, expanding what is to happen and indicating props once again:

> tranceat ad montem Mereadoci And hys squyer ledys hym
> and a staff yn hys handde (at BM 2435)

Possibly the most interesting is the reference to a named player, indicating that our text is a working one:

> And John ergudyn aredy a horse bakke yt was ye Justis wt
> constantyn ffor to play ye marchont (at BM 1865)

---

[22]   See Darryll Grantley, "Producing Miracles," in: *Aspects of Early English Drama*, ed. Paula Neuss (Cambridge, 1983), pp. 78-91. Rowse, *Tudor Cornwall*, p. 26 refers to the production on the saint's day.

This is in the section concerning Meriasek and the robbers, and clearly the player who had taken the small part of Constantine's sheriff now took the equally small part of the merchant, and perhaps others as well.

The play ends on a serious, but not a tragic note, since Meriasek's soul has already gone to heaven. Both days end with a benediction in the name of Meriasek and St Mary of Camborne, and on both the final invitation is to "drink with the play," and for the musicians to strike up for the dance. The parallels with the *Ordinalia* are clear. This play is the celebration of a saint, and it ends with celebration as such; the life and death of Meriasek are a cause for rejoicing.

The saint play could not and did not survive in England (with the not entirely relevant exception of the once again biblical interludes of John Bale), a country in which the entire theological and political premisses of *Beunans Meriasek* were soon to be dismissed. The stress on the intercession of the saints, the role of the Virgin (especially in the context of an iconic representation), the overt political supremacy of Rome (still a favoured pilgrimage goal well into the fifteenth century even from England) and indeed the very "identification of the church with the whole of organised society" which was "the fundamental feature which distinguishes the Middle Ages from earlier and later periods of history" - all these gave way, even in Cornwall, as the sixteenth century progressed. Although a book of hours of the Virgin published in Paris in 1526 referred to the special indulgences granted by Pope Sixtus IV for prayers said before the image of the Virgin, and noted those granted at the request of Elizabeth of York, the wife of Henry VII, the English text of the *Donation of Constantine* with its refutations had appeared by 1534, and two years later came the Henrician *Proclamation Restricting the Number of Holy Days* and also the *Ten Articles*, which stressed the justification by faith alone and warned against excessive attention to "images of Christ and Our Lady" and against the idea that "any saint is more merciful or will hear us sooner than Christ."[23] *Beunans Meriasek* is a triumphant assertion of the tenets of medieval Christianity, a unified and by no means merely epigonal work, demonstrating clearly the sustained power of the saint play to the end of the Middle Ages. All the same, *Beunans Meriasek* represents a high point just before the end. It is a fortunate survival, the more so when its quality is measured against the Digby plays, the French or even

---

[23]   The material from the *Horae Beatae Mariae Virginis* of 1526 was highlighted ironically in the *Edinburgh Magazine* 3 (June, 1786), 407f. On the Reformation material, see Dickens and Carr, *Reformation in England*, pp. 73-7. The quotation on Church and State (from R. W. Southern) is used as a starting point by R. L. Storey, "Episcopal King-Makers in the Fifteenth Century," in: *The Church, Politics and Patronage in the Fifteenth Century*, ed. R. B. Dobson (Gloucester, 1984), pp. 82-98. The collection contains other material of relevance to the Church/State balance in *Beunans Meriasek*.

the Breton survivals. It is, of course, an important part of Cornish literature; but it is as part of a British and indeed of a broader European tradition that it merits critical attention.

CHAPTER SIX

NEBBAZ GERRIAU... SURVIVALS AND REVIVALS

William Jordan's transcription of the play of the Creation in 1611 is a beginning as well as an end. The preservation of Cornish writings in the seventeenth and eighteenth centuries became inexorably a rescue act, made in the awareness that the language as a cultural medium was nearing its end. It is an irony that Cornish came into print for the first time when it was really too late. The surviving late texts, genuine examples (albeit in an inconsistent orthography) of contemporary Cornish and exhibiting the linguistic signs of the last stage of the living language, are not particularly impressive, almost a scrapbook of oddments: some religious and other translations; a folktale preserved effectively for pedagogic and linguistic reasons; a few rhymes, including one for a dead king and one about pilchards; a folksong; some sayings and proverbs, riddles and a tongue-twister; and a handful of self-conscious pieces by the scholars who were trying to save what they could of the language. At this late stage Cornish often looks in upon itself, a standard feature of a language under attack.

The final stages of Cornish literature - and here we must extend the meaning of "literature" to include any written monuments, however slight - consists of three separate, but overlapping stages, the third of which is "final" only in the chronological and not in the conclusive sense. They also straddle the linguistic division between middle and late Cornish. The first of these stages falls within the sixteenth century, not far from the time at which *Gwreans an bys* was actually composed, and here we have very little indeed to go on: odd words and phrases, probably some liturgical translations (though no authorised prayerbook), and a translation of a group of sermons. Next comes the age of the scholars, who consciously preserved what they could of Cornish in an antiquarian spirit and themselves at different distances from the spoken language. This stage is difficult to define, since fragments of far earlier Cornish were still being noted into the nineteenth century. The third stage is the age of the revivalists, and a bridge between them and the earlier antiquarians is provided by the more thorough scholars of the nineteenth century, such as Jago, Williams, Norris and Stokes. The publication in 1904 of Henry Jenner's *Handbook of the Cornish Language* was a milestone, however, and it was followed by the foundation of the Old Cornwall Society in 1920 and the establishing of a *gorsedd* with bards, along the lines of the Eisteddfod in 1928. The language revival work of Robert Morton Nance and A. S. D. Smith, and the establishment of a modern Cornish standard (however debatable the linguistic principles may be) led to the publication of new

127

writing in Cornish, and in spite of debates on and variations in orthography, the writing of Cornish continues, albeit on a limited scale.

The sixteenth-century material apart from the Creation play is hardly literary. Two monuments come into question, a selection of phrases noted by Andrew Boorde in 1542, and the so-called *Tregear Homilies*. The odd sentences in the *Image of Idleness* (as the later one in Broome's *Northern Lasse* in 1632, which appears on the title page of Jenner's *Handbook*) need not concern us, but Boorde's work is of general historical interest. His *Fyrst Boke of the Introduction of Knowledge* was dedicated to Princess (later Queen) Mary, and appeared in 1547, though it had been written earlier, as "the earliest example of the complete tourist's handbook written in English," with practical tips and useful phrases. His comments on Cornwall are not flattering:

> Cornwal is a pore and very barren countrey of al maner thing, except Tyn and Fysshe. There meate, and theyr bread, and dryncke, is marde and spylt for lacke of good ordring and dressynge...there ale is starke nought, loking whyte & thycke, as pygges had wrasteled in it...

Not only is their beer hogwash, the people are characterised by a propensity to litigiousness, and we are told too that the people speak either "naughty Englyshe" or "Cornyshe speche," with the addition that "there be many men and women the whiche cannot speake one worde of Englyshe." Similar comments recur in the early years of the seventeenth century, sometimes with fragments of the language, such as the numbers, in the writings of Richard Carew, whose *Survey of Cornwall* appeared in 1602, of John Norden, whose *Speculum Britanniae* was a little later, and of others.[1] The Cornish phrases included by Boorde contain the numbers up to thirty (we are told that no Cornishman numbers higher than that, though we are given the words for "hundred" and "thousand.") The rest of the passage consists of sentences of greeting and farewell, asking for food and for the bill:

---

[1] Boorde's work was edited by F. J. Furnivall (London, 1870 = EETS/ES 10), and see pp. 122-5. It is also in *RC* 4 (1879-80), 262-4 edited by Stokes, with a modernised version by Nance in *JRIC* 22 (1928), 366-381, and adapted in his *Cornish for All* (St Ives, 1949), pp. 48-55. On Boorde, see Antonia McLean, *Humanism and the Rise of Science in Tudor England* (London, 1971), p. 104f., and for the later references, Ellis, *Cornish Language*, pp. 73-5. Fudge, *Life*, p. 27 points out that Norden (whose *Speculi Britanniae Pars...Description of Cornwall* was published in a later edition, London, 1728) refers to Cornish as the language of the home, and indicates the social preëminence of English. Pool, *Death of Cornish*, p. 7 refers to the "crucial decision" not to provide a Cornish Bible and Prayer-book.

> Syr, your rekenyng is .v. pens
> *Syrra, iges rechen eu pymp in ar*

and for the distance to London ("thre houndred myle").

The interest in the *Tregear Homilies* is also historical and linguistic, although the document is a difficult one. In 1555 (by which time the Cornish rebellions were all over),[2] Bishop Edmund Bonner published his *A Profitable and necessarye doctryne*, a handbook on faith, the creed, the sacraments and on specific prayers. A second part, published separately, contained thirteen homilies primarily by other hands. The unpopular Bonner and his colleagues were disgraced on Elizabeth's accession, and it is reasonable to suppose that the text was translated into Cornish before 1558. The Cornish manuscript, which was not noted until 1949, forms part of the papers of Sir Richard Puleston of Worthenbury, in Flintshire, now in the British Library. The homilies were described in 1871 as being in Welsh, although the translation is headed *Homelyes XIII in Cornysch*.

Although the title page of the first part of Bonner's book refers to sermons by Edmund Bonner simply being attached, the second part (printed, like the first, by John Cawood), has a separate title page reading:

> Homelies sette forth by the righte reuerende father in God; Edmvnde Byshop of London, not onely promised before in his booke intitled A necessary Doctrine, but also now of late adioned, and added there vnto, to be read within his diocese of London, of all persons, vycars, and curates vnto theyr parishioners vpon Sundayes, & holydays.

The specific reference to the diocese should be noted. This second part contains an index of the thirteen sermons, the titles of which do not match exactly those in the body of the text, and an introduction by Bonner, although few of the sermons are his. All but the thirteenth are signed at the end: nine bear the name Io. Harpesfeld, two that of H. Pendilton, and only the fifth has the initials E. B. John Harpsfield was archdeacon and chaplain to Bonner, and was made Dean of Norwich by Mary. He was, like Bonner, unpopular, and played a leading part in the Marian persecutions. The first description of the Tregear manuscript confuses him with his brother, Nicholas. Henry Pendleton was an academic theologian and preacher, whose footnote in history appears to be that he was fired at by a would-be assassin when preaching at Paul's Cross in London in 1554.

---

[2]   See S. T. Bindoff, *Tudor England* (Harmondsworth, 1950), pp. 155-7 on the "Prayer-Book rebellion" and the subsequent Act of Uniformity.

The first four homilies, the sixth, and the ninth to the twelfth are by Harpsfield on topics including the creation, the supremacy, and the doctrine of transubstantiation. Pendelton's name appears at the end of the seventh and the eighth, on the church and on authority. The fifth piece, signed with Bonner's initials, is "of Christian loue or Charitye." The thirteenth, which is much longer than the rest, is unsigned, and rather different in style. It is not, curiously. the source for the final Cornish homily, although it matches it in relative size and theme (the doctrine of transubstantiation). Bonner's book ends with a page of verses in Latin and English not in the Cornish. The sermons are provided with marginal references in both versions.

Clearly there is work to be done on the relationship between the originals and the Cornish texts. A glance at the Cornish indicates also a profusion of English words left untranslated: "circumstaunces" and "aduisement" in the original can both be picked out easily enough from the manuscript photograph in Ellis, and there are many literalisms. Only the problematic final sermon in Cornish, which may also be from a different translator and in a different hand, shows the sound-change of *mm* to *bm* that distinguishes the final stage of Cornish from its predecessors. Unlike the final sermon in Bonner's collection, it has a greater number of Latin quotations than the rest. The Puleston papers as a whole do not help much, as most of them are clearly to do with Wales. The theme of the last homily is one which preoccupied the (Counter-)Reformation, and the works of theologians such as Stephen Gardiner might come into question, though how, when and why the last sermon was replaced is difficult. It would be more interesting to know something of John Tregear, who is styled simply *clericus*, or the provenance of the manuscript, but the reasons behind the translation of a work in the name of an unpopular bishop well away from his own diocese, during Mary's brief reign are hard to guess.[3]

---

[3]   The sole edition of the Cornish is by Christopher Bice, *The Tregear Manuscript/ Homeliyes XIII in Cornysche* (cyclostyled, 1969), with studies by R. M. Nance, "The Tregear Manuscript," *OC* 4 (1950), 429-34, and "More about the Tregear Manuscript," *OC* 5 (1951), 21-7, as well as his "Something New in Cornish," *JRIC* NS 1 (1952), 119-21. There is a picture of the first page in Ellis, *Cornish Language*, plate 4. There are two extracts in the *Kemysk Kernewek* (below, note 29). On the language, see George, "Computer Model," p. 40. The MS is now BL Add. 46397. The Puleston papers were first described in the *Report of the Royal Commission on Historical Manuscripts II* (London, 1871), appendix, pp. 65-8. Our text is a paper quarto. Bonner's work was issued in two parts in 1555, printed by Cawood (Cawodus, Cawodde) with the title *A profitable and necessarye doctryne, with certayne homilies adioyned thervnto set forth by the reuerend father in God, Edmonde byshop of London for the instruction and enformation of the people beyng within his Diocese of London, & of his cure and charge.* It is available in the Ann Arbor University Microfilms collection of English Books 1475-1640 (reels 176 and 645, nos. 3282 and 3283a). On Bonner, see Carolly Erickson, *Bloody Mary* (London, 1978), p. 452; see p. 398 on Pendleton, as well as D. S. Brewer, "Observations on a Fifteenth-Century Manuscript," *Anglia* 72 (1954), 390-99.

Moving to writings in Cornish which clearly show the sound changes of
Late Cornish, what we have has survived thanks largely to a group of
gentlemen-scholars in West Penwith, in specific small towns and parishes:
Newlyn, Paul and Mousehole, Ludgvan, Penzance, Marazion, St Buryan, St
Leven, St Just. Further, within a broad period we can delineate different
levels of association with the living language, different aims and skills. Of
the various scholars and antiquarians involved, reference has been made
already to William Scawen, Vice-Warden of the Stannaries, who died in 1689
and who owned the manuscript of *Pascon agan Arluth*. We know, too, of
others, like Richard Angwyn of St Just in Penwith, who died in 1675, and
who seemingly wrote well in Cornish. Reference has been made already both
to the oration held at Valladolid, and to Nicholas Roscarrock and his Cornish
saint's life.

In particular, however, mention must be made of John Keigwin of
Mousehole, (1641-1716) as translator of the medieval biblical texts, some of
whose work was commissioned by the Cornish Bishop of Exeter, Sir Jonathan
Trelawney. Keigwin provided, incidentally, a translation into Cornish of the
letter of Charles I thanking the Cornish people in 1643 for their services in the
Civil War and preserved in English on tablets in a number of Cornish
churches.[4] Keigwin was a scholar of the language, and presumably in contact
with the spoken tongue, but did not leave any original literature. For the
seventeenth and eighteenth centuries, the leading producers of writing in
Cornish were the members of the Boson family in Newlyn, Nicholas, Thomas
and John, whose works are preserved in a variety of manuscripts, most
notably those kept by other antiquarians with an enthusiasm for the
preservation of Cornish, William Gwavas (1676-1741), Thomas Tonkin (1678-
1742), William Borlase (1696-1772), Henry Ustick (1720-1769) and the
Welshman Edward Lhuyd (1660-1709). Details of the careers of some of these
will be given later, but for the moment they are of interest as intermediaries,
especially William Gwavas, a lawyer from Penzance, who was taught Cornish
by John Boson. And yet the Bosons were not native speakers of Cornish.
That is made clear in Nicholas Boson's important piece *Nebbaz gerriau dro
tho Carnoack,* "A Few Words about Cornish", in which he tells us that his
mother refused to allow the servants to speak anything but English to him.
He and his kinsmen (the relationship is not entirely clear, though Thomas was
perhaps Nicholas' cousin and John Nicholas' son) did learn Cornish, of

---

[4]   See Pool, *Death of Cornish*, p. 11f. on Keigwin, and on the letter. On the family,
see John Burke, *The Commoners of Great Britain and Ireland* (London, 1834-8), IV, 287-91.
The English text and details of the churches are in J. Charles Cox, *County Churches:
Cornwall* (London, 1912), pp. 45-7.

course, wrote in it and taught others, but the attitude of Nicholas in particular to the language requires consideration.

The Bosons were at least in touch with the language, and some further small pieces by other writers have also survived from a time when the language was still being spoken. The next group of writings in Cornish, however, moves inexorably further away. The scholars who preserved the writings of the Bosons and others composed in Cornish themselves, but were far from being native speakers. William Gwavas was a barrister, born in Suffolk, who lived mainly in Penzance and spent much time arguing over fish tithes (part of his inheritance) with the fishermen in Newlyn and Mousehole. He wanted to learn Cornish, and corresponded not only with John Boson, but with others, such as James Jenkins of Alverton, near Penzance, by whom two brief pieces of verse survive. But although he was in contact with those more fluent in Cornish, his own literary productions - effectively only a few verses - are at a greater remove. Thomas Tonkin, from Trevaunance in St Agnes, was an antiquarian of wide-ranging interests, but is further from the Bosons since he got much of his material from Gwavas. Tonkin corresponded with the next celebrated scholar, Edward Lhuyd, whose native language was Welsh, and who was essentially an Oxford antiquarian. But he was interested in Cornish, printed a grammar with a long preface in Cornish, and sent a copy of his poem on the death of William III to Gwavas.[5] Lhuyd's Cornish, then, is that of a scholar writing self-consciously.

We have, then, a particular linguistic situation, in which even the areas of discourse are being reduced to local matters and themes, with a group of antiquarians trying to preserve scraps of native Cornish literature. In the Boson family we see a kind of last-ditch attempt to write a modern Cornish, acquired only in the face of clear opposition. Then comes the increasingly self-conscious and sometimes linguistically inward-looking material by Gwavas and Lhuyd, and finally a few scraps and remnants gathered even later, some of them garbled and barely recognisable. Not until the revival in the twentieth century does a literature as such appear again, and even here we often encounter material which is as much about the language as much as in it.

It is to the Bosons, however, that we owe the biggest debt, and especially to Nicholas Boson, from whom came the most important of the monuments,

---

[5]   Pool, *Death of Cornish*, pp.16-7 describes the life of Gwavas (with a copy of the portrait in Truro Museum) and of Tonkin. On Lhuyd, see Brynley F. Roberts, "Edward Lhuyd", in *Proceedings of the 7th International Congress of Celtic Studies*, ed. D. Ellis Evans etc. (Oxford, 1986), pp. 1-9. On Tonkin, see H. L. Douch, "Thomas Tonkin," *JRIC* NS 4 (1962), 145-80. The two major manuscripts by Gwavas are described in CWBF: the Gatley MS (named after its donor) is a notebook kept by Gwavas. See further Jenner, "Cornish Manuscripts I," and "The Cornish Manuscript in the Provincial Library at Bilbao in Spain," *JRIC* 21 (1922-5), 421-37.

the folktale *John of Chyanhor*, "John of the Ram's House" (in St Levan). An incomplete version of the story appears in the hand of John Boson with a translation in the main manuscript belonging to William Gwavas (BL Add 28,554), and the work was used even then as a teaching device, as indeed it still is. John Boson instructed Gwavas to read what he had written so far, and when Gwavas had mastered it, he would continue. The whole story appeared in printed form in Edward Lhuyd's *Archaeologia Britannica* of 1707 (on pp. 251-3), with an English translation and a version in Welsh, still divided into sections, but using special symbols for the dental spirants (*th, dh*) and other sounds. The whole was reprinted by William Pryce in 1790 as a specimen of modern Cornish, and again, also from Lhuyd, in the late 1930s in Germany, described by its editor as "a modest folktale." Most recently it has appeared in Unified Cornish as a teaching text in versions by Nance, and (with linguistic annotations) by John Page. Lhuyd noted that the tale had been written "about forty years since," so that it seems likely that this version was composed by Nicholas Boson, but the content is both widespread and of some antiquity.[6]

The tale is that of the "Servant's Good Counsels," placed into a Cornish context. John of Chyanhor goes east from St Levan, not far from Land's End, to find work. He works for three years, and in each of them accepts instead of the agreed three pounds in wages a piece of wisdom (*point a skeeans*). The pieces of advice (sometimes found separately in other folktales), consist of the injunction not to leave an old road for a new one, not to stay in a house where there is an old man with a young wife, and finally not to act when angry. By sticking to the old road to Marazion John is able to save some merchants who are robbed when they try a new road; the merchants, but not John, lodge in a house where the young wife and her lover, a monk, murder her old husband and blame the merchants. John, who has stayed next door, observes the deed, and cuts a piece of the monk's garment, his evidence exculpating the merchants. Returning to his wife, he thinks he hears "another man in the bed," but restrains himself from attack, and finds that the other occupant is his own young son, of whom he knew nothing. Celebrating with a cake given him by his erstwhile master, John discovers the nine pounds due to him baked into it.

---

[6]   Text (with notes) from the Gwavas MS and from Lhuyd, CWBF, pp. 14-23. Lhuyd's text and translations are in Pryce, *Archaeologia Cornu-Brittanica*, pp. 55-64 (with Lhuyd's orthography), and in Gilbert's *Creation*, pp. 201-15; amended reprint in Ludwig Mühlhausen, *Die kornische Geschichte von den Drei guten Ratschlägen* (Berlin, 1938), pp. 9-12 with a German translation and notes, pp. 13-18, plus translations of two Irish versions. A brief introduction discusses these Irish parallels, and gives a history of the textual background. Unified Cornish editions are by R. M. Nance, *John of Chyannor* (Penzance, 1969), who used it in his *Cornish for All*, and John Page, *Jowan Chy an Horth Examined* (Redruth, 1982).

Versions of the story are known all over Europe, with analogues in Irish and Breton. The basic narrative, in which the characters are functional and undeveloped, has been adapted for local interest, with place-names inserted ranging from St Levan to Exeter. The quest of the central figure and the triad of prohibitions, his gaining of wisdom and ultimate reward, are all standard elements.[7] The language of Boson's version is straightforward for the most part, and the narrative method that traditional for the folktale, with an opening formula *En Termen ez passiez*, "Once upon a time," and a paratactic accumulation of consecutive actions with linking anaphoric "and." In what form Boson first met the story (from the servants?) is, of course, not known. At all events, it survived in English, sometimes in bowdlerised form. In the later nineteenth century William Bottrell printed a more circumstantial version (as "Tom of Chyannor"), and in 1891 Joseph Jacobs gave an English version of Lhuyd's text, with Welsh names; he changed the third piece of advice on the grounds that the "man in the wife's bed" was unsuitable *virginibus puerisque*. A far earlier version is that in a widespread medieval collection, the *Gesta Romanorum*, where the central figure is the emperor Domitian (improbably depicted as a wise Christian), and the order of the points of wisdom is changed.[8]

In his essay on the Cornish language, *Nebbaz gerriau...* Nicholas Boson refers also to having written a piece for his children called *The Dutchesse of Cornwall's progresse to see the Land's end & to visit the mount*. Extracts survive in a manuscript written by Lhuyd (now in the Bodleian, Ms Carte 269), and the few passages in Cornish in the surviving text were copied separately by William Borlase, whose manuscript also includes the song refrain "Hal-an-tow", which is not Cornish. The Cornish extracts, to do with the locality and folklore of the extreme west, include a verse for inscription on a hurling ball, a protestation of support for the Duchess of Cornwall, and most famous of all, a couplet with a prophecy regarding the towns of Penzance, Newlyn and Paul (in Lhuyd's version of the text and translation as emended by Oliver Padel):

> Eue Rateera war mean Merlin
> Ra leske pawl, pensans & Newlyn

---

[7]   See V. Propp, *Morphology of the Folktale*, tr. L. Scott (Austin and London, rev. ed., 1968. See Stith Thompson, *Motif-Index of Folk-Literature* (Bloomington, 1966), sections J21.2, J21.3 and J21.5.1 on the prohibitions.

[8]   W. Bottrell's *Traditions and Hearthside Stories of West Cornwall* of 1870 is in a facsimile selection (Felinfach, 1989), see pp. 51-67. Joseph Jacobs, *Celtic Fairy Tales* (originally 2 vols., 1891 and 1894, repr. London, 1970), pp. 125-8. The *Gesta Romanorum* was translated by Charles Swan, revised by Wynnard Hooper (London, 1877), pp. 177-80 (= CIII).

There shall land on the stone Merlin
Shall burn Pawl, pensans, & Newlyn.

The distich seems to be old - there are earlier references to it - but its context
is unclear. Another verse in the piece (in lines which are again longer, than
the heptasyllables of earlier Cornish) is a moralising distich of which Lhuyd
gives one version and Borlase two, but which remains difficult. Borlase's final
version has the added note "this is the Right reading", although the metre is
also somewhat ragged:

> Na ges travith a dale talves en Bes
> Buz gen dew benignas do gwell gun Cres

Lhuyd gives Boson's translation:

> This world hath nothing worth our love
> But to make peace with God above.

It is unclear whether this is an original Cornish composition or a translation
of an epigram or prayer from another source.[9]

Most interesting of Nicholas Boson's writings is his essay *Nebbaz gerriau
dro tho Carnoack*, his "Few Words about Cornish," written perhaps around
1700. The order of the English and Cornish versions is unknown, and the
work is problematic linguistically, existing as it does in only one manuscript,
copied (apparently with difficulty) by Henry Ustick (1720-69), vicar of
Breage, near Helston. The piece begins with the comment that Cornish is on
the wane, and unlikely to survive, given its restriction at the time of writing
to small areas in the west. It goes on to talk about the people who can speak
Cornish, about inscriptions in the language, and about Boson's own knowledge
and the fact that his mother had forbidden the servants to speak anything but
English to him as a child. This leads to his most significant point, the
prognosis of the fate of the Celtic languages in general, and indeed of their
putative disappearance. even of Breton and Welsh. Boson says of Cornish
that it will be supplanted by *an Sousenack nobla* "noble English", and he
notes further that "the Cornish...is but coarse & insignificant in Comparison
of the English" (CWBF, p. 30). He respects the Cornish language, but
acknowledges, in a passage which is admittedly extremely difficult to
understand, the preëminence of English. Davies Gilbert and Matthew Arnold
would make similar comments more than a century later.

---

[9]   Text and notes in CWBF, pp. 8-14 (with other bibliographic references, most notably
to R. M. Nance, "Cornish Prophecies," *OC* 4 (1951), 443-53 on the Merlin piece, which is
much reprinted. Padel notes its appearance in Carew's *Survey* in 1602.

Nicholas' kinsman Thomas is of lesser significance. From him we have a seven-line inscription (containing the date 1705) for a hurling-ball given to William Gwavas, who copied and translated the piece. John Whitaker (1735-1808), who was rector of Ruan Lanihorne and who wrote notes on his parish, quotes a sentence about the sport of hurling as current as late as the end of the eighteenth century, and inscriptions are common.[10] Thomas Boson's writings, preserved by Gwavas, are otherwise mainly translations - of the Old Hundredth (claimed in a note as "David's *first* song") in John Hopkins' version, unrhymed, and of the Paternoster, Creed and Ten Commandments. It might be noted that Jenner listed, including the Boson versions, ten versions dating back to 1632 of the Lord's Prayer (two of them by Keigwin, written in "ancient" and "modern" Cornish), eight of the Creed (again with two by Keigwin), and seven of the Commandments. Parts of Genesis and Matthew are present in Cornish, too, in the Gwavas papers, translated by various hands, and the youngest of the Bosons, John, translated not only the Commandments, Paternoster and Creed, but Genesis I and a verse of Matthew.[11]

John Boson also produced a number of occasional verses, one of twenty-six lines in rhymed couplets on what Jenner rightly terms the "not very poetical subject" of curing pilchards for export. The subject matter is certainly rather technical, describing the oil-pressing process, but the rhyming has to resort (as Tonkin noted in his manuscript) on at least one occasion to an English word:

> Gorra spladn en Balliar Pedden ha Teen,
> Gobar ha Tra broaz Enz rag Varshants feen
>
> Stack head to tail in the barrel all bright,
> fine merchants will make their profit alright![12]

John Boson also wrote a brief piece of Cornish comic bawdry in eight lines of advice to Arthur Hutchens, who had to collect a sum of money in far-off London:

---

[10]   See John Holloway, *The Oxford Book of Local Verses* (Oxford, 1987), p. 63 for an inscription from St Columb Major and Minor in English. A modern inscription in Cornish for St Ives, by Nance in 1922, is reprinted in *Kemysk Kernewek*, p. 63 (see below, note 29).

[11]   Jenner, *Handbook*, 42-4 lists translations, and the Bosons' translations are in CWBF, pp. 38-42 (Thomas) and 51-7 (John). R. M. Nance comments on "The Cornish of William Rowe (Wella Kerew)" in *OC* 2/11 and 12 (1948), 32-4 and 25-7.

[12]   CWBF, pp. 43-5, with details of the technical aspects. See also R. M. Nance, "The Pilchard Rhyme," *OC* 3 (1938), 169-74.

Kymero 'wyth goz lavrak pouz
  goz argan, ha guz aur.
Ma Ladran moz en Termen Noz
  Reb vor Loundres Tur.
An hagar musi na ens vâze
  Th-ens en Kinever Tol,
dha meraz rag an peth es moaz
  Komero 'vyth goz Kal. (CWBF, p. 58)

Mind your breeches! Pockets tight!
  for silver and gold watch out!
There are thieves in London Town at night
  near the Tower and round about!
The naughty ladies are really bad
  in every street they flock.
They're out for anything to be had -
  so watch out for your cock!

Less vigorous are six lines of moral advice in the context of a lawsuit involving Gwavas, and enjoining mercy to the poor, and two pieces which link death and Cornish. Both are epitaphs, one on James Jenkins of Alverton, by whom some verses have survived, and the other on Keigwin. The latter is brief, praising Keigwin's prowess in the classical languages and French, as well as Cornish, but four triplets, see Jenkins as its last master:

Lebbn duath Tavas coth ny en Kernow
Rag kar ny Jenkins gelles durt an Pow
Vor hanow taz ny en Eue tha Canow. (CWBF, p. 48)

Cornwall now Mourn thy Tongue just lost and gone
Jenkins, our Cornish Bard is fled among
The Saints to sing his Everlasting song.

That eighteenth-century translation of the *englyn* is fairly free, but the loss of the language, seen as irrevocable, is the real point, and it is reiterated in an additional quatrain destined for Jenkin's tombstone. That Henry Ustick, who copied out the lines of the tombstone quatrain, should have thought they applied to Keigwin is not surprising.

Gwavas and Tonkin collected a number of other pieces, and a number of these literary fragments appeared in print at the end of the eighteenth century in William Pryce's *Archaeologia Cornu-Britannica*. Some were reprinted in, for example, Davies Gilbert's edition of *Gwreans an bys* - and some have been edited separately in recent times. A few have not been printed in full. James Jenkins of Alverton, for example, the object of John Boson's epitaph verses, left at his death in 1710 about three dozen lines in rhymed couplets, passed from Gwavas to Lhuyd to Tonkin, and then printed by Pryce. It is unclear whether there are two separate poems or a long poem (of five stanzas, in Jenner's view). The latter assumption seems reasonable, but metrically and thematically the piece is difficult to analyse. Jenner saw it as an "irregular ode." The first part, which has been taken as a separate piece, seems to consist of nine short rhymed couplets (though the last is problematic), distinguishing between good and bad wives and thoughtful and thoughtless children. A second part, in longer couplets, addresses the wise man, telling him how to treat a good wife, and that he should build a solid house. This fragment provides little upon which to judge the literary expertise of Jenkins, however, and a similar literary judgement has to be made on John Tonkin of St Just, whom Jenner describes as "a solitary Whig in a nation of Jacobites" for having written in about 1693 a poem of fourteen unpretentious quatrains on James II and William of Orange, beginning *Menja Tiz Kernuak buz galowas*, "If Cornishmen would listen...," and noting William's welcome in Cornwall. Tonkin (a tailor, who is not to be confused with the antiquary Thomas Tonkin) also wrote a somewhat shorter moralising poem. His work is in regular quatrains, rhymed *aabb*, and (mostly) with seven syllables, though often with anacrusis.[13]

Other pieces salvaged by Gwavas, Thomas Tonkin and others are slighter still. The rector of St Just, William Drake, who died in 1636, sent notice to his colleague Thomas Trethyll, vicar of Sennen, to marry a couple whose banns had been called, in six lines of rhymed verse, copied out by his son, and another single strophe survives on an idle weaver:

> Why ladar gweader,
> Lavarro guz pader,
>   Ha ro man do higa an cath:
> Gra owna guz furu,
> Hithow, po avorou,
>   Ha whyew boz dean dah whath.

[13] Jenkins' text is in Pryce, *Archaeologia* (unpaginated in the reprint); as Jenner notes, *Handbook*, p. 35f., there is a line missing. See R. M. Nance, "James Jenkins of Alverton," *OC* 4 (1938), 268-73. The full text is also in Ellis, *Cornish Language*, pp. 108-110. Jenner analyses the metre in his *Handbook*, p. 188f. For Tonkin, see R. M. Nance, "Kanna Kernuak," *OC* 1 (1925-31), 41f. (original text of the William and James poem from the Gwavas MS, BL Add. MS 28 554). Ellis, p. 92, misquotes Jenner and reverses Tonkin's loyalties. Jenner describes and cites Tonkin's work, *Handbook*, pp. 36 and 189.

You weaver - thief, rather -
should say your "Our Father,"
  not sit there and play with your cat!
If you mend your ways,
in a matter of days
  you may be a good fellow yet!

A number of the survivals belong to the realm of folklore: a riddle; the so-called "Fisherman's Catch" collected by Thomas Tonkin in 1698 from St Agnes, referring perhaps to an octopus when it mentions a great "nine-tailed fish"; a brief poem from Ludgvan; and finally a rhyme collected again in St Agnes on married life and the rapidity with which the hugging and kissing stops, which has parallels in English and may again be a translation.[14]

Gwavas, Tonkin and Lhuyd collected a number of mottoes, proverbs and sayings that Pryce printed, not always accurately, several of them relating to fishing and tinning, beside a nice tongue-twister along the lines of "if there's cheese, we'll have some cheese, please." In literary terms, though, the most interesting of the pieces printed in Pryce is what Lhuyd saw as a genuine Cornish *englyn*, an epigrammatic rhymed triplet which he cited in his Cornish grammar as an example of the form. He refers to it in a letter to Tonkin in March, 1703, giving a slightly different version, noting that he had it from the clerk at St Just. Pryce also prints a third, again different version from Tonkin. It has even been claimed as a three-man song, although there is no evidence in support of this. There is a elegiac irony about the piece, here cited from Lhuyd's letter; *tavaz* can mean "tongue" and "language:"[15]

An lavar koth yw lavar gwir,
Na boz nevra doz vaz an tavaz re hir;
Bez den heb davaz a gollaz i dir.

A saying old, but a saying grand:
a tongue too long gets out of hand,
but the man with no tongue lost his land.

---

[14]   The weaver-rhyme is in Pryce, as is a riddle on barley, "the substance born in spring which makes a parson fall over at the year's end." For the St Agnes catch, see Ellis, *Cornish Language*, pp. 92f., and also Jenner, *Handbook*, p. 38, and Peter Kennedy, *Folksongs of Britain and Ireland* (London, 1975), p. 207. On a Ludgvan poem ascribed to James Harry. see Ellis, p. 100, and the rhyme from William Allen is discussed there, p. 99f. There is a detailed commentary by R. M. Nance, "William Allen's Cornish Rhyme," *OC* 4 (1938), 325f.

[15]   Lhuyd and Tonkin provided translations but I have attempted my own. Pool's *Death of Cornish*, p. 31 ends with the triplet, as did Nance's *Cornish for All*, p. 36.

Gwavas himself composed verses in Cornish, usually in eight-syllable rhymed couplets, some of it to do with his long-standing lawsuit involving the fish tithes for the village of Paul, owned by the Gwavas family, plus six lines addressed to a neighbour, Nicholas Pentreath, and eight lines on a legal judgement. These are clearly occasional pieces, as is an unpretentious sestet on the Marazion bowling-club. Several epigrams of three or four lines complete his contributions. Lhuyd himself provided one poetic offering, the elegy on the death of William III and the accession of Anne, written in imitation of the Welsh heroic triads, and sent to Tonkin with a Latin version in the letter containing the *englyn* about the loss of land. Entitled *In Obitum Regis Wilhelmi 3tii Carmen Britannicum, Dialectu Cornubiensi; Ad Normam Poetarum Seculi Sexti* ("A Song on the Death of King William III in the Cornish Dialect of Celtic, on the Model of the Poets of the Sixth Century"), a five-line introduction to the ancient language is followed by nineteen triplets of decasyllables:

> An Mihtern William val eal yw gwryz;
> An urma mi wel porth nev ageryz;
> Pella ni olav mwy vel reg colyz.

> King William is at the angels' side;
> I see the gates of heaven open wide;
> and my lamenting I shall lay aside.[16]

The content and style of most of these later pieces are essentially English. Their period was the age of the epigram (and also of the epitaph), and the rhymed triplet (usually a pentameter) a favourite form, used by Pope, Dryden and many others; indeed, Lhuyd's and Gwavas' verses call to mind (although the metre is not quite the same) the output of minor poets like Thomas Shipman.[17] Lhuyd was a Welsh speaker, and although he contributed a long preface to his grammar in Cornish (in Pryce, with a translation), contemporaries noted that there was a great deal of Welsh about it. We are dealing with Cornish works that are in all senses artificial, even if the writers were closer to the living language than are we, or, for that matter, the German scholar who wrote letters in Cornish to Edwin Norris in 1859 and 1861!

---

[16]   See Jenner, *Handbook*, p. 35; Keigwin apparently translated it into English. I cite Pryce (read *Portam* in the accompanying Latin translation, however).

[17]   Thomas Shipman is cited as a fortuitous example of a not very good poet: *Carolina or, Loyal Poems* appeared in 1683 in London (repr. New York, 1971). For some equally unpretentious poems of advice in the same vein as those by Gwavas, see *Sacred Poetry of the 17th Century* (London, 1835), I, 310-11.

Only one early song is known, recorded by Tonkin as coming from "one Chygwyn" and printed in Pryce, with another version in the Gwavas papers presumably written by Edward Chirgwin himself. Tonkin notes that it was sung in 1698. It begins

> Pelea era why moaz, moes fettow teag,
> Gen ackas pedden dew ha ackas blew mellen?
> Moas than ventan, sarra weage,
> Rag delkiow seue gwra moesse teag.

The song is known in English with the title "Where are You Going my Pretty Maid" or "Dabbling in the Dew." The interlocutor asks the maid where she is going, and is told that she is going to the well, and that strawberry leaves make maidens fair. The maid is asked for her reactions should she be laid on the ground, brought with child and so on, and she responds with encouraging pertness. The version cited is that written down by the singer, but the Tonkin version adapts the second line, which reads "with your dark head and your golden hair" and presumably seemed contradictory, to read "with your fair face" (*bedgeth gwin*). On the other hand, the convincing suggestion has been made that the girl has indeed a sunburnt face and yellow hair, and it is precisely to make her complexion fashionably pale that she is using the strawberry leaves. The servant-girl, whose tanned skin indicate her status as an outdoor worker, wants to be a lady. There is more doubt whether the song is Cornish or a translation. That this is the earliest version in any language has been used as an argument for a Cornish original, but the form is like many other English folksongs, and we have nothing in Cornish to compare it with. It is unlikely that the question will be solved, but at least we have an example of verse sung in Cornish of the seventeenth century.[18] Whether or not this early survival is original, efforts have been made to translate or reconstruct other songs. What weight can be put on the stated aim of "reclaiming the lost music of Cornwall" is difficult to determine, but a variety of older English-language folksongs have been translated, including the famous and enigmatic Padstow May-Day song. There is evidence, however, that one song noted in English in the mid-nineteenth century among Cornish miners working in Germany also had Cornish words. "The Sweet Nightingale" has in recent times been translated (back?) into Cornish by Richard Gendall as "An eos whek." Once again it is hard to determine precisely what belongs

---

[18]   Quoted from R. M. Nance, "Edward Chirgwin's Cornish Song," *OC* 4 (1938), 210-13. Tonkin's version is in Pryce. Nance considers the original to be English, as does Kenneth Jackson, *A Celtic Miscellany* (Harmondsworth, 1971), p. 317. For counter-arguments, see Kennedy, *Folksongs*, p. 236 and Inglis Gundry, *Canow Kernow* (3. ed., Redruth, n.d.), p. 28.

to Cornish literature or folk-tradition, but it is interesting that we have two parallel cases, either or both or neither of which may be Cornish in origin.[19]

An epitaph on Dolly Pentreath, composed by someone called Thom(p)son in Truro claims that she was 102 at her death; whether, or in what sense, she was the last speaker of Cornish, the literary survivals have now effectively finished. John Davey of Boswednack, who died in 1891, could apparently still recite Cornish verses, learned from his father, but the one example we have, a local jingle, required great ingenuity by Nance to make sense of it in 1922, and four years later Nance published a paper entitled "A New-Found Traditional Sentence of Cornish," in which he resolved some remembered gibberish that had been passed on through generations into a Cornish sentence.[20] The urge to collect and preserve all these scraps goes on, and has its latest expression in what we might call tea-towel Cornish, presented as a few words from the past as something of quaint interest for tourists.

It is a curiosity that the demise of Cornish as a language of everyday discourse was actually welcomed in some respects, notably in the nineteenth century, when the medieval literary works were printed and edited for the first time. The comments of Davies Gilbert on what he felt was a welcome end to the Cornish language are frequently cited, but how widespread this view was is usually neglected. The preface to *Gwreans an bys* in 1826 begins:

> No one more sincerely rejoices, than does the Editor of this ancient mystery, that the Cornish...language has ceased altogether from being used by the inhabitants of Cornwall.

In spite of the outrage expressed by Cornish language enthusiasts since, Gilbert was aware that here had been a long and gradual deterioration, and he went on to justify his comment in a passage rarely cited by his critics:

> whatever may have been its degree of intrinsic excellence: experience amply demonstrating, that no infliction on a province is equally severe, or irremediable, as the separation by distinct speech from a great and enlightened Nation, of which it forms a part. A separation closing against it most of

---

[19] For "The Sweet Nightingale" see Kennedy, *Folksongs*, pp. 218f. and 233 and Gundry, *Canow Kernow*, p. 20f. The antiquity of the Padstow song is discussed in Bob Stewart, *Where is Saint George* (London, 2. ed. 1988), pp.62-71. "Hal-an-tow" is, contrary to appearance, not Cornish, and is either "heel and toe" or the Dutch nautical *hal aan touw*, "haul on the rope."

[20] R. M. Nance, "John Davey, of Boswednack, and His Cornish Rhyme," *JRIC* 21 (1922-5), 146-53; "A New-Found Traditional Sentence of Cornish," *ibid.*, 22 (1926), 281-7. The Pentreath epitaph is cited in Ellis, *Cornish Language*, p. 120.

the avenues of knowledge, and wholly intercepting that course
of rapid improvement which eminently distinguishes the present
age from all other periods in the history of man.

Let us be fair to Gilbert: he is *not* glorying in the death of Cornish, but
making an appropriate statement for his age, and he affirms the value of a
literature of which his edition, though poor, was still the first. Matthew
Arnold, praised for stimulating interest in Celtic literature as much as Gilbert
is vilified, said:

> It may cause a moment's distress to one's imagination when
> one hears that the last Cornish peasant who spoke the old
> tongue of Cornwall is dead; but no doubt, Cornwall is the
> better for adopting English, for becoming more thoroughly one
> with the rest of the country.

Arnold saw the homogeneity of Britain as of paramount importance, and even
urged Welsh writers to use a language with a larger audience, seeing writing
in a minority language as a waste of talent.[21] Not until the later part of the
nineteenth century was it suggested that Cornish might be revived, and the
efforts of Henry Jenner in the first years of the twentieth gave impetus to a
revival, though he himself was very dubious about a spoken revival. The
preface to his *Handbook of the Cornish Language* (which makes clear,
incidentally, that conjectures on the language are better made via Breton than
Welsh) counters the views of Arnold, Gilbert and by implication Nicholas
Boson when he denies that a sentimental local patriotism is any threat to a
greater nationalism. Although his argument that "Cornishmen [should] learn
Cornish...because they are Cornishmen" has emotional impact, it does not
bear close scrutiny because it begs too many questions (does being a
Cornishman depend upon birth, domicile, ancestry, interest? is the precept
exclusive?). Indeed, Jenner's ultimate reason for learning Cornish is - his own
word - sentimental, and he denies both practical application and any value to

---

[21]   Gilbert, *Mount Calvary*, p. v; Matthew Arnold, *The Study of Celtic Literature*
(London, 1905), p. 10. Arnold's 1867 lectures aided the establishment of a Chair of Celtic.
There is a more positive biography of Davies Gilbert (1767-1843; originally Giddy, although
he took his wife's name) by A. C. Todd, *Beyond the Blaze* (Truro, 1967), indicating that the
interest in Cornish was a minor part of Gilbert's many activities, a number of which helped
Cornwall in other ways. Gilbert, MP for Bodmin, had controversial views on education
(Todd, p. 179).

the literature (which is "scanty and of no great originality or value," a remark just as damning as Gilbert's in some ways).[22]

And yet there *was* a revival. Nationalism, and particularly linguistic nationalism, is in many ways a matter of fashion, and if the eighteenth century and the antiquarian interest conflicted with the essentially Classical idealism of a supranational culture, a periodically recurring neo-Romanticism seeks identity in a smaller heritages. The revival of Cornish, in which the work of Jenner (from St Columb Major, 1848-1934) was continued by Robert Morton Nance (born in Cardiff, 1873-1959), A. S. D. Smith (from Sussex, 1883-1950) and later E. G. R. Hooper, has nevertheless encouraged a revival in literature just as it has occasioned a *gorsedd* and the taking of bardic names by those writing in Cornish - Jenner was Gwas Myghal. The establishment of a Federation of Old Cornwall Societies and then of a Cornish Language Board further encouraged the writing of literature in revived Cornish. A series of magazines - *Kernow*, "Cornwall," from 1934-1936, for example, *An Lef Kernewek* (originally just *An Lef*) "The Cornish Voice" after the war until 1983, and more recently *An Gannas* "The Ambassador" and *Delyow Derow* "Oak Leaves," - as well as individual books from Cornish presses (such as that of Dyllansow Truran in Redruth) have made material available, albeit to the small numbers able to read it. It is beyond the scope of this work to discuss the various alternatives for revived Cornish, although the absence of an agreed standard probably does little to help the furthering of the literature. Although Jenner had his own system, and at least two systems have been proposed and used since the work of Nance, much modern material has used the so-called Unified Cornish of Nance and Smith.[23]

Assessing the literary products of the revival, however, makes critical demands which are yet again different. The earlier literature may have been by monoglot speakers, the later fragments written at a time when there were

---

[22]   Jenner, *Handbook*, p. xi f. He developed his ideas of Cornwall as a nation (rather than "a mere shire" (which might raise eyebrows in Yorkshire) in a paper to the Pan-Celtic Conference in Caernarvon in 1904: "Cornwall A Celtic Nation," *The Celtic Review* 1 (1904/5), 234-46. In a letter printed in the *Western Morning News* on January 9, 1912 (dated the day before), Jenner saw the revival of spoken Cornish as "fantastic and impossible. See my note on "Henry Jenner in a Scottish Library," *An Baner Kernewek* 68 (May, 1992), 22f. It is beyond the scope of this book to discuss Cornish or other nationalism, although the question of how to define a "Cornishman" continues to be begged. In 1983 a television series called "How to be Celtic" challenged prejudices admirably without venturing any definitions: *How to be Celtic. A Primer* (London, 1983 for Channel 4); see pp. 35-7 on Cornish. The debates continue: Brendan McMahon, "The Uses of the Past: Cornwall on Film," *An Baner Kernewek* 68 (May, 1992), 27f.
[23]   See John J. Parry, "The Revival of Cornish: an Dasserghyans Kernewek," *PMLA* 61 (1946), 258-68. See more recently K. J. George, "The Reforms of Cornish - Revival of a Celtic Language," *Language Reform* 4 (1989), 355-76. Ellis, *Cornish Language*, pp. 147-210 looks at the revivalists, their various societies and organs, and some of the recent literature.

still native speakers, but the situation of revived Cornish is not even as favourable as that of, say, Gaelic, or Yiddish. Questions arise of form and of content; is the literature to be limited to local (or indeed to linguistically introspective) themes? What are the formal models? How self-conscious, plainly artificial is the language? It is, of course, possible for a literary work to be *deliberately* artificial, written in a specific and perhaps limited register for pedagogical purposes. A writer working in a language which by definition has been learned as a second tongue, in the absence of native speakers, and with a paucity of literary models, may well lack the deep structures perceived as part of the process of language. Some questions apply to all writers working in minority languages: why write for a small audience? The answer is always that the poet feels that he can best express what is to be expressed in that particular language. Of course there is a certain circularity in all of these questions: to be capable of sustaining a literature is a criterion for an individual language just as much as the language requires a clear identity if it is to be used for literature. The objective assessment of literary works in the revived language are, however, ill-served by patriotic but insupportable claims about the relative value of the language in contrast with others. A violin, after all, is a wooden box with strings until someone plays it, and they may do so well or badly. The sound will be different from, but no less valid than that of a trumpet or a piano, either of which may appeal more or less to the personal (but only to the personal) taste of any listener.

Various of the scholars interested in Cornish in the nineteenth and early twentieth centuries produced, like their earlier counterparts, material in Cornish. A famous example is Jenner's dedicatory poem in rhymed iambic pentameter couplets to his wife, Kitty, *Dhô'm gwrêg gernûak*, "To my Cornish Wife," in his *Handbook*, a love-poem associating his wife with the Cornish language (*tavas dha dassow*, "the language of my fathers"). Most material in modern Cornish, however, comes from the inter-war years and later. The revival movement edited, adapted and continues to publish versions of the medieval texts, and not only was the tale of *John of Chyannor* adapted and reprinted for pedagogical purposes, but other original prose writings were produced for the same reason. Nance (Mordon) himself, who established Unified Cornish, wrote such stories, and others have done so too. His *Lyver an pymp marthus Seleven* ("Book of the Five Miracles of Seleven, St Levan or Solomon") was written in 1923, though published rather later, and the *Cornish Grammar* of Ralph Allin-Collins (Hal Wyn) which appeared in 1927 included stories of his own. Small collections have appeared since the 1930s, some reprinted, by most of the men involved with the revival: *Nebes whethlow ber* ("A few Short Stories") is by A. S. D. Smith (Caradar), and far more recent collections include the *Whethlow noweth ha coth* ("Tales Old and New") of John Page (Gwas Kenethlow) and the collection by Melville Bennetto, *Whethlow Kernewek* ("Cornish Tales"). The prose competitions of the Cornish gorseth have produced material which has been published, and individual stories have been written for children.[24]

The pedagogical element in recent Cornish is as understandable as the production of translations and imitations of earlier writings. Translations of the Gospels, for example, have been published in recent years, as have versions by Smith of part of the *Mabinogion*, and also of a very well-known folktale, that of the "Seven Sages of Rome," which was printed in English as early as 1493, but which Smith translated, as *Whethlow a seyth den fur a Rom* in 1948 from Welsh in the fifteenth century *Red Book of Hergest*. The style is again simple. Smith translated other Welsh material, and more recently others have done so too. There has even been a translation of *Treasure Island*.[25]

The earlier Cornish material has set the style for imitative pieces. N. J. A. Williams (Golvan), who has also written interesting lyrical verse, imitated the *Ordinalia* in his *Trelyans Sen Pawl* ("Conversion of St Paul") in 1961, and in 1983 Ken George, inspired by the Passion-poem, published his own poem, *Devedhyans Sen Pawl yn Bro Leon* ("St Paul Comes to Leon") about St Paul Aurelian, a saint whose journeys covered Wales, Cornwall and Brittany.[26] The story (in 38 eight-line stanzas imitating those of *Pascon agan Arluth*) uses the ninth-century life by the monk Wrmonoc, including the curious incident when the saint asks for and is refused a bell belonging to King Mark. The style is close to that of the Passion-poem (there is more line-enjambement than in the model), but although the material is again religious, it looks back at early Cornish and Breton history, rather than at biblical times, and the feeling of distancing is somewhat different. Another and rather earlier work is a pastiche of a medieval play rather than an imitation, by Peggy Pollard (Arlodhes Ywerdhon). *Bewnans Alysaryn,* ("Life of Alysaryn"), written for the gorseth in 1940, is a miracle play in eleven scenes, dubbed "days" in the stage directions, which are themselves in pseudo-medieval English and often

---

[24] Nance's *Lyver an pymp marthus Seleven* was republished in 1977 by the CLB; Smith's *Nebes whethlow ber* by Dyllansow Truran (Redruth, n.d.); Page's *Whethlow noweth ha coth* were published by the CLB in 1977 and Bennetto's *Wethlow Kernewek* in 1983. Gorseth stories include those by D. Richards, *Wethlow tus huvel* ("Tales of Ordinary Folk," CLB, 1977). The movement for teaching Cornish to children, *Dalleth*, ("Beginning") has published books of stories and songs, and a magazine.
[25] A. S. D. Smith, *An Mabynogyon yn Kernewek*, ed. E. G. R. Hooper, (CLB, 1975); *Whethlow an seyth den fur a Rom* (Redruth, repr. n.d., [originally 1948]). A variety of other texts are published by the CLB and by Dyllansow Truran in particular.
[26] Williams' play appeared in *An Lef Kernewek* in 1961 and there is an extract in Ellis, *Cornish Language*, p.188. Ken George's poem was published by *Cowethas an Yeth Kernewek*, the Cornish Language Fellowship, in Truro in 1983, but a new edition in the author's revised orthography has since appeared. Note also the parallel English-Cornish prose collection of anecdotes about St Piran, *Kemysk Sen Perran*, by Brian Webb (Redruth, 1992).

very funny - at one point it is suggested that, expense permitting, a
spectacular ending would be provided by setting fire to a house, and one
character "goeth completelie dottie." There are echoes of the early plays in
the characters - even down to the torturers - and verbal reminiscences, often
in the more forceful elements of dialogue (*bram an gath!* "cat's fart!"). There
is also a nice English-Latin macaronic strophe and English words from time
to time. Much of the text is in the familiar heptasyllable form, in six-line
strophes rhyming *aabccb*.[27]

The longest modern poem is on a Cornish theme, a rhymed poem by Smith
adapting Bedier's Tristan-story as *Trystan hag Ysolt*, published for the first
time in incomplete form posthumously in 1951, and completed in 1973 by
David H. Watkins. But shorter poems, too, made considerable impact, and
although many of these appeared in *Kernow* or *An Lef (Kernewek)*, some were
reprinted in the useful collection with the title *Kemysk Kernewek*, published
in 1977 by Hooper and containing poetry and prose.[28] At the other end of the
scale from Smith's Tristan-poem is a self-ironising example by Hooper using
a very specifically English form, the limerick, on writing in Cornish. I cite
from Ellis's *Cornish Language* (p. 183), with my own (free) translation:

> Yth esa den coynt yn Cambron
> a scryfas Kernewek, del won
> ha gul tra yu mar fol
> y teth anedhy dhe goll
> na dhyndylys bythqueth y gon.

> There was an odd chap from Camborne
> who wrote Cornish (it's true as you're born!)
> but a notion so queer
> left him flat broke, I fear.
> and he never could pay for his corn.

Of individual poets in Cornish, it is appropriate to refer to one, namely
Edwin Chirgwin (Map Melyn, 1892-1960), who has been singled out by
critics, quite properly, as a poet of considerable stature. His themes include,

[27]   Peggy Pollard, *Bewnans Alysaryn* (St Ives, 1941). See P. A. Lanyon-Orgill, "The
Cornish Drama," *CR* 1 (1949), 42.
[28]   E. G. R. Hooper, *Kemysk Kernewek* (CLB, 1977) -- a collection of prose, poetry,
letters and sermons from 1930-55, including much that appeared originally in *Kernow*. The
collection contains also Smith's wartime letters in Cornish, translations of nursery rhymes
such as "Twinkle, Twinkle Little Star" and a few lines of Goethe's *Faust* in Cornish and in
Welsh. The Tristan texts are: A. S. D. Smith, *Trystan hag Ysolt* (Redruth, 1951); David H.
Watkins, *Trystan hag Ysolt* (Camborne, 1973).

but go beyond Cornish local topics, although his structural models appear to be those of English verse. A Shakespearean sonnet, *Gorthewer* ("Evening") is a celebrated example, but he does tackle and universalise an important and indeed emblematic Cornish theme in *An jynjy gesys dhe goll* ("The Engine-House in Ruins").[29] In spite of the iambic pentameters, the internal rhymes have Celtic echoes, and the elegiac tone of the whole poem is as impressive as the economy of the images:

> My a gews hep let, my a gan a goll
> War ow fossow los ydhyow gwer a dyf
> Lun a wakter of, ynnof lyes toll
> Genef bryny du powes where a gyf.
>
> My a lever whath a'n bledhynnow pell
> Pan o lun a whel pyth yu gwak yw gwyr;
> Kynth of trygva taw, gwyns ha glaw a dell
> Kepar del o tellys gans tus yn lur.
>
> Aga spyrysyon y'm mysk-vy a vew
> Avel kerens da y a dryk ajy
> Tarosvan of-yn gwel oll yn few
> Nyns us mes nos a guth ow notha-vy.
>
> I talk uninterrupted, sing my fall.
> Upon my stones green creeping ivy grows.
> Emptiness fills me. Each gap in my wall
> provides a rest and roosting for the crows.

---

[29]   George, "Reforms of Cornish," p. 365 brackets Chirgwin (not to be confused with the Edward Chirgwin of the folksong "Pelea era why moaz....") with N. J. A. Williams. Most of Chirgwin's poems appeared in *Kernow*, and his work was singled out by Parry, "Dasserghyans," p. 265-8. The point was endorsed by Ellis, *Cornish Language*, pp. 163-5, though the latter properly disagrees with Parry that the poem of the Engine-House is "flat and trite" in thought. Ellis does, however, call it "The Deserted Engine-Room" (Parry has "House"), and it really means something like "The engine-house left to decay through neglect." Parry translated *Gorthewer* (which appeared in *Kernow* 1 in 1934) and Ellis reprints his translation, which is in loose blank verse and unrhymed, inexplicably changing the last couplet. Ellis translates *An jynjy...*, p. 164f., which appeared in *Kernow* 6, also in 1934, into prose, and provides p. 224, n. 21 a list of other poems. Another famous poem (*An Velyn Goth*, "The Old Mill") is in *Kemysk Kernewek*, as are some of Chirgwin's sermons. The deserted mine becomes a stock image: see Margaret Norris' poem *Poldice*, Ellis, p. 187, and it recurs regularly in journalistic local verse in English, and the ruined engine-houses are often photographed.

> I tell of all the years long left behind,
> when what stands empty now, with work was filled;
> now I'm a silent house, where rain and wind
> drill down, as once the men of old times drilled.
>
> Their spirits still stand by me in my plight
> like loyal friends; around me still they press,
> though I am just a ghost in daylight's sight,
> and naught but night can clothe my nakedness.

The central image is impressive: the silent engine-house is now, paradoxically, permitted uninterrupted speech only when there is no-one to hear it but the crows. Emptiness and silence are the key themes, although the poem *itself* speaks. The mine has become a poetic theme, too, only now that it has ceased to operate. The elegiac irony is almost paradigmatic The theme is Cornish and there are technical words linked with the tin-mines (*jynjy, telly*) but overall the work belongs in the far wider category of *laudatio temporis acti* poems that go back to *The Ruin* in Anglo-Saxon.

It has been noted already that collections like Peter Kennedy's *Folksongs*, or Inglis Gundry's *Canow Kernow* and its predecessors include modern translations of traditional (English) folksongs. Of equal interest are modern Cornish songs, sometimes of protest, sometimes historical, frequently elegiac again, even when ostensibly forceful. A protest song by Brian Webb, the author of the *Kemysk sen Perran*, for example, translated by him into English as well, attacks *estrenyon*, incomers purchasing holiday or second homes within Cornwall, and to an extent driving out those who would like to stay but have to move through economic pressure, a problem not restricted to Cornwall. Webb's poem is called "emmits" in English, the local slang term for such incomers. However, the answer given is to move to England. In a foreign land the Cornish remain Cornish; and even that elegy is a familiar one:[30]

> Y frennons dha dhehen, ny vynnons dha sten
> Y frennons tammow denty yu gwres yn Japan:
> Re bo grassyes Dew na yllons ladha spyrys
> Po y whrussens y gachya ha'y werthe yn can.

---

[30]   Cited from *How to be Celtic*, p. 37 with Webb's English version. There are also new folksongs, some from gorseth competitions, in Inglis Gundry, *Canow an weryn hedhyu* (Padstow, 1979).

They gobble your cream but they don't want your tin,
They go for these knick-knacks made in Japan:
Thank God they're not able to kill off your spirit,
Or they'd have it all packaged and sold by the can.

The first full-length novel in Cornish mixes questions of nationalism, the problems of violence, love and a kind of Arthurian mysticism: *An gurun wosek a Geltya*, by Melville Bennetto ("The Bloody Crown of the Celtic Countries"), a fairly loosely constructed novel ranging over the various Celtic areas. A hoped-for translation has not yet appeared, and one wonders again about the readership in a modern context. Although a further novel has appeared (*Jory*, by Michael Palmer), it is significant, perhaps, to note the appearance of a novel in 1989 English by a Cornish specialist, Myrna Combellack, *The Playing-Place* in English, also published by Dyllansow Truran, the major Cornish publisher, set in Cornwall and thematically Cornish in part (though the emotional conflicts of the characters are at the centre). Whether there is such a thing as "Anglo-Cornish" or "Cornu-English" literature is unclear, although there have, of course, long been Cornish dialect writings on subjects outside the immediate interests of locality, such as the war poems of S. S. Hunt, writing as Bernard Moore in and after the First World War.[31]

In trying to evaluate the literature of revived Cornish, it is difficult to separate the concepts of nationalism (which is itself fluid) and of elegy, the twin themes of the deserted engine house (or the lost language) and the bloody crown. How Cornish literature will develop is an open question, although it is hard not to be pessimistic; languages with a small audience exist and produce literature, it is true, although these are languages with a continuous living tradition, like Icelandic. The most frequently cited analogy is with Hebrew, but it is not a strict one, since Hebrew has a continuous liturgical and study tradition, and has been revived within boundaries sometimes circumscribed by external forces. The development of Cornish literature will depend upon new writers (and a new generation), the possibilities of enlarged readership and an agreed literary standard, as well as on the adoption of themes which are part of a broad cultural perspective, as was the case with the great works of the middle ages in Cornish.

---

[31] On the most recent publications, including the novels, see Ken George, "So Do You Read Cornish?" *The Author* 102 (1991), 144. The Anglo-Cornish writers are Bernard Moore (= S. S. Hunt, sergeant in the Middlesex regiment), *A Cornish Haul* (London, 1917), *A Cornish Chorus* (London, 1919), *Cornish Corners* (London, 1923) and *A Cornish Collection* (London, 1933); and Myrna Combellack, *The Playing-Place* (Redruth, 1989). Donald Rawe has also written plays in English about Cornish saints.

BIBLIOGRAPHY

In this selective bibliography, emphasis is upon literary works, although some material on the language has also been included. It is not always clear what constitutes a published text, as some material exists only in privately printed or even cyclostyled form. Primary materials in other languages are listed only if cited, and secondary literature without direct reference to Cornish has been limited to works felt to be the most useful in helping to place Cornish literature into a broader context. For primary texts in Cornish, only the principal manuscript is noted.

Bibliographies and Details of Manuscripts

David Baker, Isaac Reed, Stephen James, *Biographia Dramatica or, a Companion to the Playhouse II* (London: Longman, 1812)

[James Barker], *The Drama Recorded; or, Barker's List of Plays Alphabetically Arranged* (London: Barker, 1814)

Sidney E. Berger, *Medieval English Drama. An Annotated Bibliography of Recent Criticism* (New York: Garland, 1990)

Rachel Bromwich, *Medieval Celtic Literature. A Select Bibliography* (Toronto: UTP, 1974)

William Llewellyn Davies, *Cornish Manuscripts in the National Library of Wales* (Prepared for the Celtic Congress to be held at Truro, Cornwall, September 12-17, 1939)

G. R. Davis, *Medieval Cartularies of Great Britain* (London: Longmans, 1958)

H. L. Douch, "Thomas Tonkin," *JRIC* NS 4 (1962), 145-80

[Gatley MS], "The Gatley Collection of Cornish Manuscripts," *JRIC* 25 (1937-8), 28f.

Alfred Harbage (revised S. Schoenbaum), *Annals of English Drama, 975-1700* (London: Methuen, 1964, 3. ed. Routledge, 1989

H. Jenner, "Descriptions of Cornish Manuscripts I. The Borlase Manuscript," *JRIC* 19 (1913), 162-76

H. Jenner, "The Cornish Manuscript in the Provincial Library at Bilbao in Spain," *JRIC* 21 (1922-5), 421-37

Ian Lancaster, *Dramatic Texts and Records of Britain: A Chronological Topography to 1558* (Cambridge: CUP, 1984)

Brian Murdoch, *The Medieval Cornish Poem of the Passion* (Redruth: ICS, 1979); see A. Hawke, "The Manuscripts of the Cornish Passion-Poem," *CS* 9 (1981), 23-8

Evelyn S. Newlyn, *Cornish Drama of the Middle Ages. A Bibliography* (Redruth: ICS, 1987)

Oliver Padel, *Catalogue of an Exhibition of Manuscripts and Printed Books on the Cornish Language* ([Redruth: ICS], 1975)

Charles J. Stratman, *Bibliography of Medieval Drama*, 2. ed. (New York: Ungar, 1972), pp. 385-90
[Charles Thomas], *The Cornish Language* (Redruth: ICS, 1972)
[Charles Thomas], *The Medieval Cornish Drama* (Redruth: ICS, 1973)

Printed Texts of Cornish

Donatus-Glosses (BN MS lat. 13029, Paris; MS Bodley 574, for 14 S. C. 2026 (3), Oxford):

H. Arbois de Jubainville, "Mots bretons connus par un auteur français du commencement du IXe siècle," *RC* 27 (1906), 151-4

Tobit-Glosses (Oxoniensis posterior, MS Bodley 572, Oxford):

Joseph Loth, *Vocabulaire Vieux-Breton* (Paris: Vieweg, 1884), pp. 68f., 113, 129. See J. Loth, "Les gloses de l'*Oxoniensis posterior*. Sont-elles Corniques?" *RC* 14 (1893), 70

Bodmin Manumission (Bodmin Gospels, St Petroc's Gospel, BL Add. MS 9381, London):

M. Förster, "Die Freilassungsurkunden des Bodmin-Evangeliars," in: *A Grammatical Miscellany Presented to Otto Jespersen*, ed. N. Bøgholm (Copenhagen: Levin and Munksgaard, 1939), pp. 77- 99. See G. Pawley White, *A Handbook of Cornish Surnames* (2. ed. Redruth: Truran, 1981), p. 71f.

***Vocabularium Cornicum* (Cottonian or Old Cornish Vocabulary, BL MS Cotton Vespasian A XIV, London):**

Norris, *Ancient Cornish Drama* (see below, *Ordinalia*), II, 311-435
Eugene van Tassel Graves, *The Old Cornish Vocabulary* (Diss. PhD, Columbia, 1962: Ann Arbor, Mich: University Microfilms, 1962)

John of Cornwall: *Prophetia Merlini* (Cod. Ottobonianus Lat. 1474, Vatican):

P. Flobert, "La *Prophetia Merlini* de Jean de Cornwall," *EC* 14 (1974f.), 31-41
L. Fleuriot, "Fragments du texte Brittonique de la *Prophetia Merlini*," *EC* 14 (1974f.), 43-56
Michael J. Curley, "A New Edition of John of Cornwall's *Prophetia Merlini*," *Speculum* 57 (1982), 217-49

The Glasney Cartulary (MS Cornwall County Records Office Dd R(S) 59):

J. A. C. Vincent, "The Glasney Cartulary," *JRIC* 6 (1878-81), 213-58
Padel, *Exhibition* (see above, Bibliographies), Nr. 1

Charter Fragment (BL MS Add. Charter 19491, London):

W[hitley] S[tokes], "Cornica IV: The Fragments of a Drama in Add. Ch. 19,491, Mus. Brit.," *RC* 4 (1879-80), 258-62
Henry Jenner, "The Fourteenth-Century Charter Endorsement," *JRIC* 2, (1915-21), 41-48
R. Morton Nance, "The Charter Endorsement in Cornish," *OC* 2 (1932), 34-6
R. Morton Nance, "New Light on Cornish," *OC* 4 (1943-51), 214-16.
Enrico Campanile, "Un frammento scenico medio-cornico," *Studi e saggi linguistici* 3 (1963), 60-80. Text and Italian translation.
Lauran Toorians, *The Middle Cornish Charter Endorsement. The Making of a Marriage in Medieval Cornwall* (Innsbruck: Institut für Sprachwissenschaft, 1991). Text and commentary.

Pascon agan Arluth **(BL MS Harley 1782, London)**:

Davies Gilbert, *Mount Calvary...Interpreted in the English Tongue... by John Keigwin* (London: Nichols, 1826). Text and translation.
Whitley Stokes, "The Passion. A Middle Cornish Poem," *Transactions of the Philological Society* (1860-1), Appendix, 1-100. Text and translation.
R. Morton Nance and A. S. D. Smith, *Passyon agan Arluth*, ed. E. G. R. Hooper (n.p. CLB, 1972). Unified Cornish text with translation.

Ordinalia **(MS Bodl. 791, Oxford)**:

Edwin Norris, *The Ancient Cornish Drama*, 2. vols. (Oxford: OUP, 1859, repr. London and New York: Blom, 1968). Text and translation. Corrections by Whitley Stokes in: *Archiv für celtische Lexikographie* 1 (1898-1900), 161-71 and by J. Loth in *RC* 26 (1905), 218-69
Phyllis Pier Harris, *Origo Mundi. First Play of the Cornish Mystery Cycle, The Ordinalia. A New Edition* (Diss. PhD, University of Washington, 1964; Ann Arbor: University Microfilms, 1964). Text and translation.
Markham Harris, *The Cornish Ordinalia. A Medieval Dramatic Trilogy* (Washington: Catholic University of America Press, 1969). Prose translation. Reviewed by N. Denny, *Medium Aevum* 40 (1971), 305-9
R. Morton Nance and A. S. D. Smith, ed. Graham Sandercock, *The Cornish Ordinalia, Second Play, Christ's Passion* (n.p.: CLB, 1982); *The Cornish Ordinalia, Third Play, Resurrection* (n.p.: CLB, 1984); *The Cornish Ordinalia, First Play, The Creation of the World* (n.p.: CLB, 1989). Unified Cornish with translation. Parts of the Nance and Smith version were

published as *Extracts from the Cornish Texts in Unified Spelling* II, IV, V and VI (originally FOCS, reprinted by the CLB, 1973): *An Tyr Marya* (RD 679-834); *Abram hag Ysak* (OM 1259-1394); *Adam ha Seth* (OM 684-880); *Davyd hag Urry* (OM 2105-2254)

Gwreans an bys (MS Bodley 219, Oxford):

Davies Gilbert, *The Creation of the World with Noah's Flood, written in Cornish in the Year 1611 by Wm. Jordan, with an English Translation by John Keigwin* (London, J. B. Nichols, 1827). Text and translation.

Whitley Stokes, *Gwreans an bys. The Creation of the World* (London and Edinburgh: Williams and Norgate, 1864)

R. Morton Nance and A. S. D. Smith, *Gwryans an bys* (Padstow: FOCS, 1959) Revised ed, by E. G. R. Hooper (Redruth: Truran, 1985); reviewed O. Padel, *OC* 10 (1985), 98f. Unified Cornish text and translation. Extract from the 1959 text (vv. 1053-1390) published as *Cayn hag Abel* (Padstow: Lodenek Press, 1979)

Donald R. Rawe, *The Creation of the World (Gwryans an bys)* (Padstow: Lodenek Press, 1978). English acting text.

Paula Neuss, *The Creacion of the World*. (Diss. PhD, Toronto, 1970), published as: *The Creacion of the World. A Critical Edition and Translation* (New York and London: Garland, 1983); reviewed by T. Tiller, *TLS* 21. 10. 1983, p. 1150

Beunans Meriasek (MS Peniarth 105, NLW, Aberystwyth):

Whitley Stokes, *The Life of St Meriasek, Bishop and Confessor. A Cornish Drama* (London: Trübner, 1872). Text and translation.

Markham Harris, *The Life of Meriasek. A Medieval Cornish Miracle Play* (Washington: Catholic University of America Press, 1977). Prose translation.

Myrna Combellack-Harris, *A Critical Edition of Beunans Meriasek* (Diss. PhD, Exeter, 1985). Edition and translation. To be published in the series: Leeds Texts and Monographs.

Myrna Combellack-Harris, *The Camborne Play. A Verse Translation of Beunans Meriasek* (Redruth: Truran, 1988)

R. Morton Nance and A. S. D. Smith, *Extracts from the Cornish Texts in Unified Spelling* I, III, VIII (FOCS/CLB, 1966-74: *St Meriasek in Cornwall: BM 587-1099; Sylvester ha'n dhragon: BM 3896-4180* and *An venen ha'y map*: BM 3156-3244 and 3444-3802 (from a full but unpublished edition in Unified Cornish with translation)

Tregear Homilies (BL MS Add. 46397, London):

Christopher Bice, *The Tregear Manuscript. Homeliyes XIII in Cornysche* (n.p., n.d., cyclostyled [1969]

Bibliography

R. M. Nance, "The Tregear Manuscript," *OC* 4 (1950), 429-4 (= Unified version of part of sermon X)

E. G. R. Hooper, *Kemysk Kernewek* (see below, modern texts), p. 61 (parts of IX and X)

Andrew Borde: Cornish Phrases:

F. J. Furnivall, *The Fyrst Boke of the Introduction of Knowledge made by Andrew Borde* (London: OUP, 1870, repr. New York: Kraus, 1973 = EETS/ES 10), pp. 122-5

Whitley Stokes, "Cornica," *RC* 4 (1879f.), 262-4

Writings of the Boson Family (BL Add. MS 28 554 = Gwavas Papers plus Gatley MS, Truro, RIC and Tonkin MS B, Truro):

Oliver J. Padel, *The Cornish Writings of the Boson Family* (Redruth: ICS, 1973)

Ludwig Mühlhausen, *Die kornische Geschichte von den drei guten Ratschlägen, nebst Übersetzung und Glossar und zwei irischen Versionen in Übersetzung* (Berlin: printed as manuscript = Schriftenreihe der deutschen Gesellschaft für celtische Studien 2, 1938). John of Chyannor.

R. Morton Nance, *John of Chyannor, or The Three Points of Wisdom, by Nicholas Boson (written c. 1660-70)* (n.p.: CLB, repr. 1969)

John Page, *Jowan Chy an Horth Examined* (Redruth: Truran, 1980).

Other texts and fragments (collected):

Edward Lhuyd, *Archaeologia Britannica*, Vol. I (Oxford, 1707: repr. Menston: Scolar P., 1969), pp. 222-53

William Pryce, *Archaeologia Cornu-Britannica* (Sherborne, 1790: repr. Menston: Scolar Press, 1972)

Gilbert, *Mount Calvary* (see above, *Pascon agan Arluth*), pp. 92-95

Gilbert, *Creation* (see above, *Gwreans an bys*), pp. 189-237

Individual (uncollected) texts and fragments:

A lyttle treatyse called the Image of Idleness, conteynynge certeyne matters moued betwene Walter Wedlocke and Bawdin Bacheler. Traslated out of the Troyane or Cornyshe tounge into Englyshe by Olyuer Oldwanton (London: Wyllyam Seres, n.d. [?1555-65]; "Newly corrected and augmented," 1574). One sentence of Cornish.

Richard Brome, *The Northern Lasse* [1632]: *A Critical Edition of Brome's "The Northern Lasse"*, ed. Harvey Fried (New York and London: Garland, 1980); see pp. 138, 189. One sentence of Cornish.

J. Loth, "Etudes Corniques II," *RC* 23 (1902), 173-200 (biblical extracts from the Gwavas papers) and V, *RC* 24 (1903), 1-10 (Ten Commandments)

J. Loth, "Cornoviana," *RC* 32 (1911), 442-5, 34 (1913), 176-81 and 35 (1914), 215f.

R. M. Nance, "A New Found Traditional Sentence of Cornish," *JRIC* 22 (1926), 281-7

R. M. Nance, "John Keigwin's Cornish Translation of King Charles the First's Letter," *OC* 1 (1925-31) 4, 35-40 and 5, 26f.

R. M. Nance, "John Davey, of Boswednack, and his Cornish Rhyme," *JRIC* 21 (1922-5), 146-53

R. M. Nance, "Kanna Kernuak. By T. [*recte* J] Tonkin of St Just, c. 1693-4," *OC* 1 (1925-31), 41-2 and 2/1 (1931), 24-7.

R. M. Nance, "William Allen's Cornish Rhyme," *OC* 4 (1938), 325f.

R. M. Nance, "William Bodener's Letter," *OC* 3 (1940), 306-8

R. M. Nance, "The Cornish of Wm. Rowe (Wella Kerew)," *OC* 2/11 (1948), 32-4 and 12 (1948), 25-7

Some twentieth-century texts:

(Journals such as *Kernow, An Lef Kernewek, Hedhyu* and others are not included)

Melville Bennetto, *An gurun wosek a Geltya* (Redruth: Truran, 1984)

Melville Bennetto, *Whethlow Kernewek* (Camborne: CLB, 1983)

K. J. George, *Devedhyans Sen Pawl yn Bro Leon* (n.p.: Cowethas an yeth Kernewek, 1983)

E. G. R. Hooper, *Kemysk Kernewek* (Camborne: An Lef, 1964, repr. Camborne: CLB, 1977)

John Page, *Whethlow noweth ha coth* (Camborne: CLB, 1977)

Peggy Pollard, *Bewnans Alysaryn* (St Ives: Lanham, 1941)

G. M. Sandercock, *When an Wedhowes* (n. p.: Cowethas an yeth Kernewek, 1983)

A. S. D. Smith, *Nebes Whethlow Ber* (Camborne, 1947, repr. Redruth: Truran, n.d.)

A. S. D. Smith, *Whethlow an Seyth den fur a Rom* (Camborne, 1948, repr. Redruth: Truran, n.d.)

A. S. D. Smith, *Trystan hag Ysolt* (Redruth: privately printed, 1951. Completed by David H. Watkins, *Trystan hag Ysolt* (Camborne: An Lef Kernewek, 1973)

B. Webb, *Kemysk Sen Perran* (Redruth: Truran, 1982)

Folksongs (all modern, apart from that by Chirgwin):

Inglis Gundry, *Canow Kernow. Songs and Dances from Cornwall* (3rd ed. Redruth: Truran, n.d.)

Peter Kennedy, *Folksongs of Britain and Ireland* (London: Cassell, 1975), pp. 205-43

R. M. Nance, "Edwin Chirgwin's Cornish Song," *OC* 4 (1938), 210-13

Bibliography

Selected Primary Texts Originally in Languages other than Cornish

Breton:

Roparz Hemon, *Christmas Hymns in the Vannes Dialect of Breton* (Dublin: IAS, 1956)
Roparz Hemon, *Trois Poèmes en Moyen-Breton* (Dublin: IAS, 1962)
J. Loth, *Chrestomathie Bretonne I. Breton-Armoricain* (Paris: Bouillon, 1890)
    Middle-Breton Hours, ed. Whitley Stokes (Calcutta, 1876)
Le Grand Mystère de Jésus, ed. Hersart de la Villemarqué, (Paris: Didier, 1865)
"L'ancien *Mystère de Saint Gwénolé*," ed. E. Ernault, *Annales de Bretagne* 40 (1932), 2-35, 104-41 and 318-79
"*Vie de S. Guénolé*. Mystère Breton," ed. P. Le Nestour, *RC* 15 (1894), 245-71 and
"La *Vie de Sainte Nonne*," ed. E. Ernault, *RC* 8 (1887), 230-301 and 406-91 (See Yann-Ber Piriou, "Note de lecture: la *Vie de Sainte Nonne*," *EC* 23 (1986), 215-31)

English:

Aelfric, *Glossary: Aelfrices Grammatik und Glossar*, ed. J. Zupitza (Berlin: 1880, repr. Darmstadt: WBG, 1967)
E. K. Chambers and Frank Sidgwick, *Early English Lyrics* (London: Sidgwick and Jackson, 1947)
The Chester Mystery Cycle, ed. R. M. Lumiansky and David Mills (London: OUP, 1974, 1986 = EETS/SS 3 and 9)
Cursor Mundi, ed. Richard Morris (London: OUP, 1874-93, repr. 1961-6 = EETS/OS 57-68)
Norman Davis, *Non-Cycle Mystery Plays and Fragments* (London: OUP, 1970 = EETS/SS 1)
The Digby Plays, ed. F. J. Furnivall (London: OUP, 1896 = EETS/ES 70)
F. J. Furnivall, *Early English Poems and Lives of Saints* (Berlin: Ascher, 1862)
Betty Hill, "The Fifteenth-Century Prose Legend of the Cross before Christ," *Medium Aevum* 34 (1965), 203-22
William H. Hulme, *The Middle English Harrowing of Hell and the Gospel of Nicodemus* (London: OUP, 1907 = EETS/ES 100)
Joseph Jacobs, *Celtic Fairy Tales* (London: Nutt, 1892, repr. with *More Celtic Fairy Tales*, 1894, London: Studio, 1990)
The Macro Plays, ed. F. J. Furnivall and Alfred W. Pollard (London: OUP, 1904 = EETS/ES 91)
The Metrical Life of Christ from MS BM Add 39996, ed. Walter Sauer (Heidelberg: Winter, 1977)
Mirk's Festial: a Collection of Homilies I, ed. Theodor Erbe (London: OUP, 1905 = EETS/ES 96)
Richard Morris, *Legends of the Holy Rood* (London: OUP, 1871 = EETS/OS 46)

Cornish Literature

N-Town (Hegge) Plays: *Ludus Coventriae or The Plaie Called Corpus Christi*, ed. K. S. Block (London: OUP, 1922 = EETS/ES 20); *The N-Town Play*, ed. Stephen Spector (London: OUP, 1991 = EETS/SS 11f.)

Arthur S. Napier, *History of the Holy Rood-Tree* (London: Kegan Paul, 1894 = EETS/OS 103)

The Northern Passion, ed. Frances A. Foster and Wilhelm Heuser (London: OUP, 1913, 1916, 1930 = EETS/OS 145, 147, 183)

The Southern Passion, ed. Beatrice D. Brown (London: OUP, 1927 = EETS/OS 169)

Stanzaic Life of Christ, ed. Frances A. Foster (London: OUP, 1926 = EETS/OS 166)

Michael Swanton, *Anglo-Saxon Prose* (London: Dent, 1975)

The Towneley Plays, ed. George England and Alfred W. Pollard (London: OUP, 1897 = EETS/ES 71); *The Wakefield Pageants in the Towneley Cycle*, ed. A. C. Cawley (Manchester: MUP, 1958)

The York Plays, ed. Richard Beadle (London: Arnold, 1982)

French and Spanish:

Alfonso IX el Sabio, *Cantígas de Santa Maria*, ed. H. Mettmann (Coimbra: Acta Univers. Coimbrig., 1959)

Arnoul Greban, *Mystère de la Passion*, ed. Gaston Paris and Gaston Reynard (Paris: Vieweg, 1878)

Jean Michel, *Le Mystère de la Passion* (Angers, 1486), ed. Omer Jodogne (Gembloux: Duculot, 1959)

Miracles de Nostre Dame, ed. Gaston Paris and Ulysse Robert (Paris: Didot, 1876-93)

Le Mystère d'Adam, ed. Paul Studer (Manchester: UP, repr. 1949); Trans. Edward N. Stone, *Adam* (Seattle: U Washington P, 1928)

Le Mystère de la Passion de Troyes, ed. Jean-Claude Bibolet (Geneva: Droz, 1987)

Le Mistére du Viel Testament, ed. James de Rothschild (Paris: Didot, 1878-91)

La Passion d'Auvergne, ed. Graham A. Runnalls (Geneva: Droz, 1982)

La Passion du Palatinus, ed. Grace Frank (Paris: Champion, 1922, repr. 1970)

The *Passion de Semur*, ed. P. T. Durbin, Lynette Muir (Leeds: Centre for Medieval Studies, 1981)

[*Passion St Geneviève*]: Edward J., Gallagher, *A Critical Edition of La Passion Nostre Seigneur* (Chapel Hill: UNC/Dept of Romance Langs., 1976); and Graham A.Runnalls, *Le Mystère de la Passion Nostre Seigneur* (Paris: Minard, 1974)

German:

[Hans Folz]: Brian Murdoch, *Hans Folz and the Adam Legends* (Amsterdam:Rodopi, 1977)

Arnold Immessen, *Der Sündenfall*, ed. F. Krage (Heidelberg: Winter, 1912)

158

Bibliography

Rudolf Meier, *Das Innsbrucker Osterspiel und Das Osterspiel von Muri*, Stuttgart: Reclam, 1962)
Das Redentiner Osterspiel, ed. tr. Brigitta Schottmann (Stuttgart: Reclam, 1975)
Jacob Ruf, *Adam und Heva*, ed. H. M. Kottinger (Quedlinburg and Leipzig: Basse, 1848)

Latin and Greek:

Acta Sanctorum (Antwerp, 1643-1770, Brussels, 1780-1940, Tongerlo, 1794; later edd. include microfiches, Zug: Inter Documentation)
Bede, *A History of the English Church and People*, tr. Leo Shirley-Price (Harmondsworth: Penguin, 1955)
Henry Bettenson, *Documents of the Christian Church*, 2. ed., (London: OUP, 1963)
Caesarius of Heisterbach, *Dialogus Miraculorum*, ed. J. Strange (Cologne, 1851, repr. Ridgewood, NJ: Gregg, 1966)
R. H. Charles, *Apocrypha and Pseudigrapha of the Old Testament* (Oxford: Clarendon, 1913, repr. 1963)
[Domesday Book], Cornwall, ed. Caroline and Frank Thorn, draft transl. O. J. Padel (Chichester: Phillimore, 1979)
Geoffrey of Monmouth, *The History of the Kings of Britain*, tr. Lewis Thorpe (Harmondsworth: Penguin, 1966)
Gesta Romanorum, tr. Charles Swan, rev. Wynnard Hooper (London: Bell, 1877)
Gildas, *The Ruin of Britain*, ed. tr. Michael Winterbottom (London: Phillimore, 1978)
Johannes Herolt called Discipulus, *Miracles of the Blessed Virgin Mary*, tr. C. C. Swinton Bland (London: Routledge, 1928)
Ranulph Higden, *Polychronicon Ranulphi Higden...with the English translation of John Trevisa etc.*, ed. Churchill Babington and Joseph R. Lumby (London: Longmans, 1865-1886)
James of Vorazzo (Jacobus a Voragine etc.), *Legenda aurea*, ed. Theodor Graesse, 3. ed. [1890] repr. (Osnabrück: Zeller, 1969); tr. Granger Ryan and Helmut Ripperger, *The Golden Legend* (New York: Arno, 1969)
Montague Rhodes James, *The Apocryphal New Testament* (Oxford: Clarendon, 1924, repr. 1975)
Henry Marsh, *Dark Age Britain* (Newton Abbot: David and Charles, 1970)
Wilhelm Meyer, "Die Geschichte des Kreuzholzes vor Christi," *Abhandlungen der bayerischen Akademie* (München), philos.-philol. Klasse 16/ii (1882), 101-66
J. P. Migne, *Patrologia...Latina* (Paris: Migne, 1844-64)
J. R. Mozley, "A New Text of the Story of the Cross," *Journal of Theological Studies* 31 (1930), 113-27
Nennius, *British History and the Welsh Annals*, ed. tr. John Morris (London: Phillimore, 1980)
Ordinale Exon., ed. J. N. Dalton etc. (London: Henry Bradshaw Society, 1909-1940)
[St Samson, *Vita*]: R. Fawtier, *La Vie de Saint Samson* (Paris: Ecole des Hautes Etudes, 1912); tr. T. Taylor, *The Life of St Samson of Dol* (London: SPCK, 1925, repr. Felinfach: Llanerch 1991)

Cornish Literature

Aurelio de Santo Otero, *Los Evangelios Apocrifos* (Madrid: Biblioteca de autores Cristianos, 1956)

Sarum Manual, ed. A. Jefferies Collins, *Manuale ad usum... Sarisburensis* (London: Henry Bradshaw Society, 1960)

Sarum Missal, ed. J. W. Legg (Oxford: Clarendon, 1916); tr. Frederick E. Warren, *The Sarum Missal in English* (London: Mowbray, 1913)

H. F. D. Sparks, *The Apocryphal Old Testament* (Oxford: Clarendon, 1984)

Vita Ade et Evae, ed. Wilhelm Meyer, *Abhandlungen der bayerischen Akademie* (München), philos.-philol. Kl. 14/iii (1879), 185-250

Alexander Walker, *Apocryphal Gospels, Acts and Revelations* (Edinburgh: Black, 1870)

Doris Werner, *Pylatus* (Düsseldorf: Henn, 1972)

Welsh:

John Jenkins, "Medieval Welsh Scriptures, Religious Legends, and Midrash," *Transactions of the Honourable Society of Cymmrodorion* 1919/20, pp. 95-140

Gwenan Jones, *A Study of Three Welsh Religious Plays* (PhD Diss. Minnesota, 1918, printed Aberystwyth: Bala, 1939)

The Mabinogion, tr. Jeffrey Gantz (Harmondsworth: Penguin, 1976)

Secondary Studies (Cornish and Celtic Literature)

Jane A. Bakere, *The Cornish Ordinalia. A Critical Study* (Cardiff: UWP, 1980); reviewed by A. Hawke, *Studia Celtica* 16/17 (1981-2), 363-72 and L. Fleuriot EC 18 (1981), 360f.

A. le Braz, *Le théâtre Celtique* (Paris: Calmann-Levy,n.d. [1904])

Andrew C. Breeze, "The Number of Christ's Wounds," *BBCS* 32 (1985), 84-91

Andrew C. Breeze. "The Blessed Virgin and the Sunbeam through Glass," *Barcelona English Language and Literature Studies* 1 (1988), 53-64

T. D. Crawford, "The Composition of the Cornish *Ordinalia*," *OC* 9 (1979-85), 145-53

T. D. Crawford, "Stanza Forms and Social Status in *Beunans Meriasek*," *OC* 9 (1979-85), 431-9 and 485-92

Sally Joyce Cross, "Torturers and Tricksters in the Cornish *Ordinalia*," *Neuphilologische Mitteilungen* 84 (1983), 448-53

J. Cuillandre, "Contribution a l'étude des textes Corniques," *RC* 48 (1931), 1-41 and 49 (19332), 109-31

Neville Denny, "Arena Staging and Dramatic Quality in the Cornish Passion Play," in his: *Medieval Drama* (London: Edward Arnold, 1973), pp. 124-533

P. Berresford Ellis, *The Cornish Language and its Literature* (London and Boston: RKP, 1974); reviewed by D. Simon Evans in *Medium Aevum*, 45, 1976, 242f.

160

O. F. Emerson, "Legends of Cain, Especially in Old and Middle English," *PMLA* 21 (1906), 831-924

D. Simon Evans, *Medieval Religious Literature* (Writers of Wales) (Cardiff: UWP, 1986)

David C. Fowler, "John Trevisa and the English Bible," *Modern Philology* 58 (1960-1), 81-98

David C. Fowler, *Piers the Plowman* (Seattle: U Washington Press, 1961)

David C. Fowler, "The Date of the Cornish *Ordinalia*," *Medieval Studies* 23 (1961), 91-125

Crysten Fudge, "Aspects of Form in the Cornish *Ordinalia*," *OC* 8 (1973-9), 457-64, 491-8

Crysten Fudge, *The Life of Cornish* (Redruth: Truran, 1982)

Ken George, "A Comparison of Word-Order in Middle Breton and Middle Cornish," in: *Readings in the Brythonic Languages. Festschrift for T. Arwyn Watkins*, ed. Martin Ball etc.(Amsterdam: Benjamin, 1990), pp. 225-40

Ken George, "So Do You Read Cornish?" *The Author* 102 (1991), 144

F. E. Halliday, *The Legend of the Rood* (London: Duckworth, 1955)

Andrew Hawke, "A Lost Manuscript of the Cornish Ordinalia?" *CS* 7 (1979), 45-6

Mark J. Herniman, "*Pascon agan Arluth*: A Critical Study of the Cornish Passion Poem," (Diss. MA, Exeter University, 1984)

Treve Holman, "Cornish Plays and Playing-Places," *Theatre Notebook* 4 (1949-50), 52-4

Henry Jenner, "The History and Literature of the Ancient Cornish Language," *Journal of the British Archaeological Association* 33 (1877), 137-57

Henry Jenner, "The Cornish Drama I and II," *Celtic Review* 3 (1906-7), 360-75 and 4 (1907-8), 41-68

Henry Jenner, *A Handbook of the Cornish Language* (London: Nutt, 1904)

W. S. Lach-Szyrma, "A Cornish Drama," *Journal of the British Archaeological Association* OS 35 (1879), 413-22

W. S. Lach-Szyrma, "Miracle Plays in Cornwall," *The Antiquary* 1 (1880), 241-1

P. A. Lanyon-Orgill, "The Cornish Drama," *CR* 1 (1949), 38-42

F. R. Long, "New Light on the Mystery Plays of Cornwall," *OC* 7 (1972), 458f.

Robert Longsworth, *The Cornish Ordinalia. Religion and Dramaturgy* (Cambridge, Mass.: Harvard UP, 1967)

J. Loth, "La métrique Cornique," in: *Cours de littérature Celtique*, ed. H. d'Arbois de Jubainville (Paris: Thorin, 1883-1902), II (1902), pp. 204-16

J. Loth, "Etudes Corniques I," *RC* 18 (1897), 401-25 and VI, *RC* 26 (1905), 218-67

C. W. Marx, "The Problems of the Doctrine of the Redemption in the ME Mystery Plays and the Cornish *Ordinalia*," *Medium Aevum* 54 (1985), 20-32

W. J. McCann, "Tristan: the Celtic Material," in: *Gottfried von Strassburg and the Medieval Tristan Legend*, ed. Adrian Stevens and Roy Wisbey (London: Germanic Institute, 1990), pp. 19-28

R. T. Meyer, "The Liturgical Background of Medieval Cornish Drama," *Trivium* 3 (1968), 48-58

R. T. Meyer, "The Middle Cornish Play *Beunans Meriasek*," *Comparative Drama* 3 (1969), 54-64

J. R. Moore, "Miracle Plays, Minstrels and Jigs," *PMLA* 48 (1933), 943-5

Brian Murdoch, *The Recapitulated Fall* (Amsterdam: Rodopi, 1974)

Brian Murdoch, "Devils, Vices and the Fall," *Maske und Kothurn* 23 (1977), 16-30

Brian Murdoch, "The Breton *Creation Ar Bet* and the Medieval Drama of Adam," *Zeitschrift für celtische Philologie* 36 (1977), 157-79

Brian Murdoch, "Thematic Analogues of Paradise Regained," *Etudes Anglaises* 31 (1978), 203-7

Brian Murdoch, "*Pascon agan Arluth*: the Literary Position of the Cornish Poem of the Passion," *Studi Medievali* 22 (1981), 822-36

Brian Murdoch, "Creation, Fall and After in the Cornish *Gwreans an bys*," *Studi Medievali* 29 (1988), 685-705

Brian Murdoch, "The Holy Hostage: *de filio mulieris* in the Middle Cornish Play *Beunans Meriasek*," *Medium Aevum* 58 (1989), 258-73

Brian Murdoch, "Nebbaz Gerriau dro tho Carnoack," *Antiquarian Book Monthly Review* 17 (1990), 58-63

Brian Murdoch, "The Place-Names in the Cornish *Passio Christi*," *BBCS* 37 (1990), 116-8

Brian Murdoch, "Jacob Ruf's *Adam und Heva*," *Modern Language Review* 86 (1991), 111-25

Brian Murdoch, "Henry Jenner in a Scottish Library," *An Baner Kernewek* 68 (May 1992), 22-3

Brian Murdoch, "The Cornish Drama" in: Richard Beadle, *Cambridge Companion to Medieval English Theatre* (Cambridge: CUP, 1993), in press..

R. Morton Nance, "The Plen an Gwary or Cornish Playing-Place," *JRIC* 24 (1935), 190-211

R. Morton Nance, "A Cornish Poem Restored," *OC* 4 (1943-51), 368-70

R. Morton Nance, "More about the Tregear Manuscript," *OC* 5 (1951), 21-27

R. M. Nance, "Painted Windows and Miracle Plays," *OC* 5 (1955), 244-8

Paula Neuss, "Memorial Reconstruction in a Cornish Miracle Play," *Comparative Drama* 5 (1971), 129-37

Paula Neuss, "The Staging of *The Creacion of the World*," *Theatre Notebook* 33 (1979), 116-25

Evelyn S. Newlyn, "Between the Pit and the Pedestal: Images of Eve and Mary in Medieval Cornish Drama," in: Edelgard DuBruck, *New Images of Medieval Women* (Lampeter: Mellen, 1989), pp. 121-64

O. J. Padel, "Miscellanea Cornica," *Studia Celtica* 14/15 (1979f.), 233-45

O. J. Padel, "The Cornish Background of the Tristan Stories," *CMCS* 1 (1981), 53-81

R. W. Parry, "Cyfieithwyr y dramau Cernyweg," *BBCS* 8 (1935-7), 127-34

Thurstan C. Peter, *The Old Cornish Drama* (London: Elliot Stock, 1906)

[Piran Round, Perranporth], *Souvenir Programme, July 1969* (contains articles by Charles Thomas and Neville Denny on medieval Cornish drama and its production, pp. 6-9 and 12f.)

P. A. S. Pool, *The Death of Cornish 1600-1800* (Penzance, 1975, 2. ed. Saltash: CLB, 1982)

Bibliography

Esther Casier Quinn, *The Quest of Seth for the Oil of Life* (Chicago and London: U. Chicago P., 1962)

John Rowe, "Old Cornwall Societies and Federations," *An Baner Kernewek* (August 1990), 25-27

W. Sandys, "On the Cornish Drama," *JRIC* OS 1 (1865), 1-18

A. S. D. Smith, *The Commentary on "Gwryans an Bys"*, ed. E. G. R. Hooper (Camborne: An Lef Kernewek, 1962)

Whitley Stokes, "Cornica," *RC* 3 (1876-8), 85f. and 4 (1879f.), 258-64

Geoffrey H. Sutton, *Konciza Historio pri la Kornvala Linguo kaj gia Literaturo* (Blackburn: Universal Esperanto Association, 1969)

Lauran Toorians, "Passie, lief en leed; de oudste poëzie van het Keltische Cornwall," *Kruispunt* 129 (March, 1990), 3-55

W. Ann Trindade, "The Celtic Connexions of the Tristan Story," *Reading Medieval Studies* 12 (1986), 93-107 and 13 (1987), 71-80

Frank A. Turk and Myrna C. Combellack, "Doctors and Disease in Medieval Cornwall: Exegetical Notes on Some Passages in *Beunans Meriasek*," *CS* 4/5 (1976-7), 56-76

George F. Wellwarth, "Methods of Production in the Medieval Cornish Drama," *Speech Monographs* 24 (1957), 212-28

H. M. Whitley, " Cornish Rounds or Playing Places," *Devon and Cornwall Notes and Queries* 7 (1912-3), 172-4

N. J. A. Williams, "Three Middle Cornish Notes," *BBCS* 23 (1968-70), 320-22

N. J. A. Williams, "Four Textual Notes on the Middle Cornish Drama," *BBCS* 22 (1966-8), 236-8

Medieval Drama

M. D. Anderson, *Drama and Imagery in English Medieval Churches* (Cambridge: CUP, 1963)

Richard Axton, *European Drama of the Early Middle Ages* (London: Hutchinson, 1974)

David Bevington, *From "Mankind" to Marlowe* (Cambridge, Mass.: Harvard UP, 1962)

John K. Bonnell, "The Serpent with a Human Head in Art and in Mystery Play," *American Journal of Archaeology* 21 (1917), 255-91

John K. Bonnell, "Cain's Jaw Bone," *PMLA* 39 (1924), 140-6

David Brett-Evans, *Von Hrotsvit bis Folz und Gengenbach* (Berlin: Schmidt, 1975)

Oscar Cargill, *Drama and Liturgy* (New York: Columbia UP, 193)

A. C. Cawley, "Medieval Drama and Didacticism," in: *The Drama of Medieval Europe* (Leeds: Graduate Centre for Medieval Studies, 1975), pp. 3-21

A. C. Cawley et al., *Medieval Drama* (London: Methuen, 1983)

E. K. Chambers, *The Medieval Stage* (Oxford: Clarendon, 1903)

Carla Dauven-van Knippenberg, *...einer von den Soldaten öffnete seine Seite...Eine Untersuchung der Longinuslegende* (Amsterdam: Rodopi, 1990)

Clifford Davidson et al., *The Drama of the Middle Ages* (New York: AMS, 1982)

Clifford Davidson (ed), *The Saint Play in Medieval Europe* (Kalamazoo: Medieval Institute, 1986)

Inga-Stina Ewbank, "The House of David in Renaissance Drama," *Renaissance Drama* 8 (1965), 3-40

Grace Frank, *The Medieval French Drama* (Oxford: Clarendon, 1954, repr. corr. 1960)

Harold C. Gardiner, *Mysteries' End* (New Haven: Yale UP, 1946)

O.B. Hardison, *Christian Rite and Christian Drama in the Middle Ages* (Baltimore and London: Johns Hopkins, 1965)

Carl Klimke, *Das volkstümliche Paradiesspiel* (Breslau, 1902, repr. Hildesheim: Olms, 1977)

J. V. A. Kolve, *The Play Called Corpus Christi* (London: Arnold, 1966)

J. M. R. Margeson, *The Origin of English Tragedy* (Oxford: Clarendon, 1967)

Lynette Muir, *Liturgy and Drama in the Anglo-Norman "Adam"* (Oxford: Blackwell, 1973)

Paula Neuss (ed), *Aspects of Early English Drama* (Cambridge: Brewer, 1983)

Thomas Pettitt, "English Folk Drama and the Early German Fastnachtspiele," *Renaissance Drama* 13 (1982), 1-34

Eleanor C. Prosser, *Drama and Religion in the English Mystery Plays* (Stanford, Cal.: Stanford UP, 1961)

Edmund Reiss, "The Story of Lamech and its Place in Medieval Drama," *Journal of Medieval and Renaissance Studies* 2 (1972), 35-48

Christine Richardson and Jackie Johnston, *Medieval Drama* (London: Macmillan, 1991)

Leah Sinanoglou, "The Christ-Child as Sacrifice," *Speculum* 48 (1973), 491-509

Richard Southern, *The Medieval Theatre in the Round* (London: Faber, 1957)

Martin Stevens, *Four Middle English Mystery Cycles* (Princeton, NJ: UP, 1987)

Sandro Sticca (ed), *The Medieval Drama* (Albany, NY: SUNY, 1972)

Jerome Taylor and Alan H. Nelson (eds.), *Medieval English Drama* (Chicago and London: U Chicago P, 1972)

Ronald W. Vince, *A Companion to Medieval Theatre* (New York: Greenwood, 1989)

A. W. Ward and A. R. Waller (edd), *The Cambridge History of English Literature V: The Drama to 1643: Part I* (Cambridge: UP, 1910, repr. 1970)

Rainer Warning, *Funktion und Struktur. Die Ambivalenzen des geistlichen Spiels* (Munich: Fink, 1974). See the review article by F. Ohly in *Romanische Forschungen* 91 (1979), 111-42

Glynne Wickham, *Early English Stages 1300-1600* (London: RKP, 1959-81)

Glynne Wickham, *The Medieval Theatre* (London: Weidenfeld and Nicolson, 1974, repr. 1977)

Arnold Williams, *The Characterisation of Pilate in the Towneley Plays* (East Lansing, Mich.: MSU Press, 1950)

Raymond Williams, *Drama in Performance* (Harmondsworth: Penguin, 1972)

Rosemary Woolf, *The English Mystery Plays* (London, RKP, 1972)

Bibliography

Karl Young, *The Drama of the Medieval Church* (Oxford: Clarendon, 1933, repr. 1962-7)

N. H. J. Zwijnenberg, *Die Veronicagestalt in den deutschen Passionspielen des 15. und 16. Jahrhunderts* (Amsterdam: Rodopi, 1988)

Other Secondary Studies

Geoffrey Ashe, *The Virgin* (London: RKP, 1976)

Walter Berschin, *Biographie und Epochenstil im lateinischen Mittelalter* (Stuttgart: Hiersemann, 1986-8)

S. G. F. Brandon, "Pontius Pilate in History and Legend," *History Today* 18 (1968), 523-30

Auguste Brieger, *Kain und Abel in der deutschen Dichtung* (Berlin and Leipzig: de Gruyter, 1934)

Wilhelm Creizenach, "Legenden und Sagen von Pilatus," *Beiträge zur Geschichte der deutschen Sprache und Literatur* 1 (1874), 89-107

Walther Delius, *Geschichte der Marienverehrung* (Munich and Basle: Reinhardt, 1963)

Hans Martin von Erffa, *Ikonologie der Genesis I* (Stuttgart: Deutscher Kunstverlag, 1989)

J. M. Evans, *"Paradise Lost" and the Genesis Tradition* (Oxford: Clarendon, 1968)

D. Simon Evans, *Medieval Religious Literature* (Cardiff: UWP, 1986)

Adrian Fortescue, *The Mass* (London: Longmans, Green, 1912)

Hilda Graef, *Mary. A History of Doctrine and Devotion* (London: Sheed and Ward, 1963)

H. Grauert, "Die konstantinische Schenkung," *Historisches Jahrbuch* 3 (1882), 3-30

Yrjö Hirn, "La verrière symbole de la maternité virginale," *Neuphilologische Mitteilungen* 29 (1928), 33-39

Leopold Kretzenbacher, "Verkauft um dreissig Silberlinge," *Schweizerisches Archiv für Volkskunde* 57 (1961), 1-17

Pierre Kunstmann, *Vierge et merveille* (Paris: Union Générale, 1981)

G. Laehr, *Die konstantinische Schenkung in der abendländischen Literatur des Mittelalters* (Berlin: Ebering, 1926, repr. Vaduz: Kraus, 1965)

Paul L. Maier, "The Fate of Pontius Pilate," *Hermes* 99 (1971), 362-71

Olin H. Moore, "The Infernal Council," *Modern Philology* 16 (1918), 1-25

Rose J. Peebles, *The Legend of Longinus* (Baltimore: Bryn Mawr College Monographs, 1911)

F. P. Pickering, *Essays on Medieval German Literature and Iconography* (Cambridge: CUP, 1980)

V. Propp, *Morphology of the Folktale*, tr. L. Scott, rev. L. A. Wagner (Austin and London: U Texas P, 1968)

Kari Sajavaara, "The Withered Footprints on the Green Street of Paradise," *Neuphilologische Mitteilungen* 76 (1975), 34-8

Marina Warner, *Alone of All Her Sex* (London; Weidenfeld and Nicolson, 1976)

J. E. Caerwyn Williams, *The Poets of the Welsh Princes* (Cardiff: UWP, 1978)
R. M. Wilson, *The Lost Literature of Medieval England* (London: Methuen, 2. ed., 1970, repr. 1972)
Maria-Magdalena Witte, *Elias und Henoch* (Frankfurt/Main: Lang, 1987)

Historical Studies (Cornish and Celtic History)

J. M. Adams, "The Medieval Chapels of Cornwall," *JRIC* NS 3 (1957), 48-65
Denys Val Baker, *The Spirit of Cornwall* (London: Allen, 1980)
S. Baring-Gould and John Fisher, *Lives of the British Saints* (London: Cymmrodorion, 1907-13); selections, ed. Derek Bryce (Felinfach: Llanerch, 1990)
S. T. Bindoff, *Tudor England* (Harmondsworth: Penguin, 1950)
William Borlase, *Antiquities Historical and Monumental of... Cornwall* (London: Bowyer and Nichol, 1754, 2. ed. 1769. (See pp. 415-64 for Cornish vocabulary)
William Borlase, *The Natural History of Cornwall* (Oxford: Clarendon, 1758)
E. G. Bowen, *Saints, Seaways and Settlements in the Celtic Lands* (Cardiff: UWP, 2nd. ed., 1977, repr. 1983)
Andrew Breeze, "Welsh and Cornish at Valladolid, 1591-1600," *BBCS* 37 (1990), 108-11
[William Camden, *Britannia*]: Edmund Gibson, *Camden's Britannia* (London, 1695, repr. Newton Abbot: David and Charles, 1971)
Richard Carew, *The Survey of Cornwall* (Stafford: Jaggard, 1602: Ann Arbor: University Microfilms, reel 1197, nr 4165)
∨ J. Charles Cox, *County Churches: Cornwall* (London: Allen, 1912)
Robin Davidson, Cornwall (London: Batsford, 1978)
Jean Delumeau (ed.), *Histoire de la Bretagne* (Toulouse: Privat, 1969)
Gilbert H. Doble, *St Meriadoc. Bishop and Confessor* (Truro: Netherton and Worth, 1935) (= Cornish Saints, 34)
Gilbert H. Doble, *The Saints of Cornwall* (= his *Cornish Saints* collected), (Truro: Cathedral, 1960ff.)
L. E. Elliot-Binns, *Medieval Cornwall* (London: Methuen, 1955)
Davies Gilbert, *Parochial History of Cornwall* (London: n. pub., 1838)
Michael Gill and Stephen Colwill, *The Saints' Way* (n.p.: n. pub., 1986)
F. E. Halliday, *A History of Cornwall* (London: Duckworth, 1959)
∨ Charles Henderson, *Parochial History of Cornwall* (Truro, 1925, repr. as *The Cornish Church Guide*, Truro: RIC/ T. Bradford Barton, 1964)
Charles Henderson, *Essays in Cornish History*, ed. A. L. Rowse and M. I. Henderson (Oxford: Clarendon, 1935)
Henry Jenner, "Cornwall A Celtic Nation," *Celtic Review* 1 (1905), 234-46
Catherine Rachel John, *The Saints of Cornwall* (Redruth: Truran, 1981, repr. 1986)

Bibliography

Ronald T. Jones, "Penryn and its Contribution to Literature," *An Baner Kernewek* 66 (November 1991), 15f.

David Knowles and R. Neville Hadcock, *Medieval Religious Houses. England and Wales* (London: Longmans, 1953)

J. W. Lambert, *Cornwall* (Harmondsworth: Penguin, rev. ed. 1949)

Diana Leatham, *Celtic Sunrise* (London: Hodder and Stoughton, 1951)

John Le Neve, *Fasti Ecclesiae Anglicanae 1300-1541. IX: Exeter Diocese,* compiled by Joyce M. Horn (London: Athlone, 1964)

Brendan McMahon, "The Uses of the Past: Cornwall on Film," *An Baner Kernewek* 68 (May, 1992), 27f.

John T. McNeil, *The Celtic Churches* (Chicago: UCP, 1974)

Daphne du Maurier, *Vanishing Cornwall* (Harmonndsworth: Penguin, 1972)

Peter S. Noble, "Saints in the Tristan Legend," *Reading Medieval Studies* 16 (1990), 119-25

John Norden, *Speculi Britanniae Pars...Cornwall* (London: Bateman, 1728)

B. Lynette Olson and O. J. Padel, "A Tenth-Century List of Cornish Parochial Saints," *CMCS* 12 (Winter 1986), 33-71

Lynette Ollson, *Early Monasteries in Cornwall* (Woodbridge: Boydell and Brewer, 1989)

Nicholas Orme, *Education in the West of England 1066-1548* (Exeter: UP, 1976)

Nicholas Orme, *The Minor Clergy of Exeter Cathedral, 1300-1548* (Exeter: UP, 1980)

O. J. Padel, "Geoffrey of Monmouth and Cornwall," *CMCS* 8 (Winter, 1984), 1-28

W. H. Pascoe, *Teudar. A King of Cornwall* (Redruth: Truran, 1985)

Thurstan Peter, *The History of Glasney Collegiate Church* (Camborne: Camborne Printing, 1903)

Richard Polwhele, *History of Cornwall* (London, 1803-8), see vol. V (1806) and VI (1808)

J. Polsue, *Parochial History of the County of Cornwall* (Truro: Lake, 1867-73), repr. with intro. by Charles Thomas (Wakefield: E.P. Publishing, 1974)

A. L. Rowse, *Tudor Cornwall* (London: Cape, 1941)

Julia M. Smith, "Oral and Written: Saints, Miracles, and Relics in Brittany, c. 850-1250," *Speculum* 65 (1990), 309-43

C. E. Stevens, "Magnus Maximus in British History," *EC* 3 (1938), 86-94

Bob Stewart, *Where is Saint George? Pagan Imagery in English Folksong* (London: Blandford, 1988)

Charles Thomas, *Christian Antiquities of Camborne* (St Austell: Warne, 1967)

Janet Thomas, *The Wheels Went Around. The Story of Camborne Town* (Redruth: Truran, 1987)

Victoria History of the Counties of England: Cornwall (London: Constable, 1906)

James Whetter, *Cornish Essays 1971-76* (St Austell: CNP, 1977)

James Whetter, *The History of Glasney College* (Padstow: Tabb House, 1988)

Cornish and Celtic Languages

Dictionaries and Reference Works:

Fred. W. P. Jago, *An English-Cornish Dictionary* (London: Simpkin, Marshall, 1887, repr. New York: AMS, 1984)

R. Morton Nance, *An English-Cornish and Cornish-English Dictionary* (CLB, 1978 = one vol. version of 2. ed. See the *Cornish Dictionary Supplement* 1 and 2, by J. Anthony N. Snell and William A. Morris (CLB 1981, 1984)

Oliver J. Padel, *Cornish Place-Name Elements* (Nottingham: English Place-Name Society, 1985)

Oliver J. Padel, *A Popular Dictionary of Cornish Place-Names* (Penzance: Hodge, 1988)

Whitley Stokes, "A Glossary to the Cornish Drama *Beunans Meriasek*," *Archiv für celtische Lexikographie* 1 (1897-1900), 101-42

Christine Truran, *A Short Cornish Dictionary* (Redruth: Truran, 1986)

Robert Williams, *Lexicon Cornu-Britannicum* (Llandovery and London, 1865); expanded and corrected in Whitley Stokes, "A Cornish Glossary," *Transactions of the Philological Society* 1868f., 137-251 and in J. Loth, "Remarques et corrections au Lexicon Cornu-Britannicum de Williams," *RC* 23 (1902), 237-302

Studies:

Daines Barrington, "On The Expiration of the Cornish Language," *Archaeologia* 3 (1777), 278-84

Daines Barrington, "On Some Additional Information Relative to the Continuance of the Cornish Language," *Archaeologia* 5 (1779), 81-6

Wella Brown, *A Grammar of Modern Cornish* (Saltash: CLB, 1984)

Enrico Campanile, *Profilo etimologico del Cornico antico* (Pisa: Bibl...di Studi e Saggi Linguistici, 1974). Rev: P. Y. Lambert, *EC* 14 (1974/5), 655-7

P. Berresford Ellis, *The Story of the Cornish Language* ([1971], 2. ed. Penryn: Tor Mark, 1990)

Basil Cottle, *The Triumph of English, 1350-1400* (London: Blandford, 1969)

D. Simon Evans, "The Story of Cornish," *University of Liverpool Studies* 58 (1969), 293-308

R. M. Gendall, *Kernewek Bew* (Camborne: CLB, 1972)

K. J. George, "The Phonological History of Cornish," unpub. diss. PhD (Univ. de Bretagne, Brest, 1984

K. J. George, "The Reforms of Cornish - Revival of a Celtic Language," *Language Reform* 4 (1989), 355-76

Arthur Grigg, *Place-Names in Devon and Cornwall* (Plymouth: College of St Mark and St John, 1988)

Reg Hindley, *The Death of the Irish Language* (London: Routledge, 1991)

Bibliography

Kenneth Jackson, *Language and History in Early Britain* (Edinburgh: UP, 1953, repr. 1971)

Fred. W. P. Jago, *The Ancient Language and the Dialect of Cornwall* (Truro: Netherton and Worth, 1882)

Henry Jenner, "The Cornish Language," *Transactions of the Phililogical Society* 1873/4, pp. 165-85

Henry Lewis, *Llawlyfr Cernyweg Canol* ([1923], 2. ed. Cardiff: UWP, 1946, repr. 1980). See A. S. D. Smith and R. Morton Nance, *Comments on "Llawlyfr Cernyweg Canol" Henry Lewis*, ed. E. G. R. Hooper (Camborne: An Lef Kernewek, 1968)

Henry Lewis, *Yr elfen Ladin yn yr iaith Gymraeg* (Cardiff: UWP, 1943, repr. 1980)

W. B. Lockwood, *Languages of the British Isles Past and Present* (London: Deutsch, 1975)

R. M. Nance, *Cornish for All. A Guide to Unified Cornish* (St Ives: FOCS, 1949) (contains some texts)

John J. Parry, "The Revival of Cornish: an Dasserghyans Kernewek," *PMLA* 61 (1946), 258-68

A. S. D. Smith, *Cornish Simplified*, 2. ed. by E. G. R. Hooper (Redruth: Truran, 1972)

A. S. D. Smith, *The Story of the Cornish Language*, 2. ed. (Camborne: An Lef Kernewek, 1969)

Martyn F. Wakelin, *Language and History in Cornwall* (Leicester: UP, 1975)

Ifor Williams, "Vocabularium Cornicum," *BBCS* 11 (1940), 1-12 and 92-100

Johann Caspar Zeuss, *Grammatica Celtica*, 2. ed. by H. Ebel (Berlin: Weidmann, 1868-71)

INDEX

Cornish works to which a full chapter has been devoted are not included, and modern critics and editors are listed only as the authors of literary works in their own right.